FREEDOM
IN THIS
VILLAGE

FREEDOM
IN THIS
VILLAGE

TWENTY-FIVE YEARS OF BLACK GAY MEN'S WRITING,
1979 TO THE PRESENT

E. LYNN HARRIS

CARROLL & GRAF PUBLISHERS
NEW YORK

FREEDOM IN THIS VILLAGE
TWENTY-FIVE YEARS OF BLACK GAY MEN'S WRITING,
1979 TO THE PRESENT

Carroll & Graf Publishers
An Imprint of Avalon Publishing Group Inc.
245 West 17th Street
New York, NY 10011

AVALON
publishing group incorporated

First Carroll & Graf edition 2005

Library of Congress Cataloging-in-Publication Data is available.

ISBN: 0-7867-1387-9

Printed in the United States of America
Interior design by Maria Elias
Distributed by Publishers Group West

Mother, do you know
I roam alone at night?
I wear colognes,
tight pants, and
chains of gold,
as I search
for men willing
to come back
to candlelight.

I'm not scared of these men
though some are killers
of sons like me. I learned
there is no tender mercy
for men of color,
for sons who love men
like me.

Do not feel shame for how I live.
I chose this tribe
of warriors and outlaws.
Do not feel you failed
some test of motherhood.
My life has borne fruit
no woman could have given me
anyway.

If one of these thick-lipped,
wet, black nights
while I'm out walking,
I find freedom in this village.
If I can take it with my tribe
I'll bring you here.
And you will never notice
the absence of rice
and bridesmaids.

—Essex Hemphill, "In the Life"

Contents

INTRODUCTION

A lmost twenty years ago, Joseph Beam edited the groundbreaking *In the Life: A Black Gay Anthology.* The first collection of literature by and about black gay men ever published, *In the Life* marked the most radical, most visible showcase of black gay writing since the Harlem Renaissance. Indeed, only a small handful of books with black gay themes were published between the end of the Harlem Renaissance around 1940 and the publication of *In the Life* in 1986. And unlike the closeted literary forbears of the 1920s and 30s—Langston Hughes, Countee Cullen, and Wallace Thurman—the writers published by Joseph were out, proud black men.

Never before had the world seen the likes of Melvin Dixon, Essex Hemphill, and Assotto Saint, to name several of the authors whose unabashedly gay, often sexually explicit writings shaped the course of black gay, African American, and gay literature up to the present day. Here for the first time was a group of writers who had the courage to proclaim, "We are Black men who are proudly gay. What we offer is our lives, our love, our visions. We are risin' to the love we *all* need. We are coming home with our heads held up high." I count myself among those writers whose work has been profoundly influenced by this vanguard of post-Stonewall black gay authors, especially Melvin Dixon, whose fiction inspired my career as a novelist.

Of course, any strides toward openness and sexual candor in the 1980s are directly linked to the political and cultural breakthroughs of the African American civil rights, feminist, and gay liberation movements of the last middle-century. No longer voiceless, oppressed minorities struggling for meager social concessions, women, gays, and people of color discovered personal empowerment in political resistance. Yet none of these movements embraced black gay men; one need only consider the rocky path of civil rights giant Bayard Rustin to witness the extent to which the topic of black homosexuality was either sidelined or silenced outright by civil rights leadership—regardless of one's heroism or tireless commitment to social justice.

Furthermore, black gay writers of the African American civil rights and gay liberation era experienced similar marginalization. Although new works by the ever-prolific James Baldwin along with the innovative science fiction/fantasy stories and novels of Samuel R. Delany appeared in the 1960s and 70s, the majority of gay writing of this period was told from the perspective of pioneering gay white authors such as Andrew Holleran, Larry Kramer, and Edmund White. Black gay writing, on the other hand, was essentially unseen outside of black gay and lesbian journals and newspapers, including *Blacklight* and *Yemonja*.

By the 1980s, black gay men took matters into their own hands. *In the Life* was only one of several literary milestones from this period. Writers groups like Blackheart and, later, Other Countries were formed to foster and promote black gay male literature. More than a mere literary movement, however, these artistic endeavors assumed greater depth of purpose via the AIDS epidemic that had surfaced in 1981. Much of this sudden outpouring of literary activity was organized in response to— indeed, a function of—AIDS. Tragically, Joseph Beam succumbed to AIDS in 1988, leaving behind not only a promising movement of writers, but also an unfinished follow-up anthology, *Brother to Brother*, which poet Essex Hemphill published just four years before his own AIDS-related death in 1995. With the 1990s, some of our most prominent black gay figures—Steven Corbin, Melvin Dixon, David Frechette, Craig G. Harris, Marlon Riggs, Assotto Saint, and Donald W. Woods—were also dead from AIDS.

Today one can't help wonder how much richer our body of contemporary black gay literature—not to mention our daily lives as black gay people—would be had these men not perished. At the same time, many talented writers who were first published by Joseph Beam and in other landmark black gay anthologies (*Sojourner: Black Gay Voices in the Age of AIDS, The Road Before Us: 100 Gay Black Poets, Here to Dare: 10 Gay Black Poets,* and *Milking Black Bull*) have survived the epidemic. Authors as varied as Thomas Glave, Reginald Shepherd, Marvin K. White, and Bil Wright, among others, continue to produce new works that carry on the spirit of their departed brothers. Furthermore, new anthologies have appeared over the past ten years (*Shade: An Anthology of Fiction by Gay Men of African Descent, Fighting Words: Personal Essays by Black Gay Men,* and *Black Like Us: A Century of Lesbian, Gay and Bisexual African American Fiction*) that have showcased, advanced, and honored our body of writing.

For the first time ever, *Freedom in This Village: Twenty-Five Years of Black Gay Men's Writing* chronicles the vital but all-too-often overlooked course of black gay literature from roughly the emergence of AIDS up through the present day. One of the secondary tragedies of AIDS has been the figurative death of works by black gay men who have died. With the exception of reissued editions of books by Essex Hemphill and Melvin Dixon, most contemporary black gay writing has disappeared from public view with each new death. All of the landmark anthologies named above, including *In the Life* and *Brother to Brother,* are out of print, and the majority of pioneering authors included in these books are virtually unknown to new generations of readers. Thus, *Freedom in This Village* highlights our neglected past, while showcasing exciting new work by today's writers.

Although this collection follows its forebears in including only black gay men writing from explicitly black gay perspectives, it breaks with tradition by being historical in both scope and purpose, covering the last twenty-five years of publishing. Beginning with James Baldwin, the spiritual father of contemporary black gay men's literature, followed by men whose works are closely associated with the birth of the AIDS era, then on to the current scene of younger writers such as James Earl Hardy, Brian Keith Jackson, Tim'm West, and Keith Boykin, *Freedom in This Village* features forty-seven poets, novelists, short story writers, and essayists. It includes writings from those earlier collections in addition to stories and essays from more recent but unavailable black gay anthologies. Lastly, I've included a handful of unpublished short stories, as well as excerpts from books that will be released soon. All told, *Freedom in This Village* offers one of the most diverse arrays of black gay literature I've ever seen.

Preserving and documenting our literary heritage is of crucial importance to black gay men. Indeed, it is our mandate. No one made the point better than Melvin Dixon, who, shortly before his death in 1993, said in a speech to a gay literary gathering, "I may not be well enough or alive next year to attend the lesbian and gay writers conference, but I'll be somewhere listening for my name. I may not be around to celebrate with you the publication of gay literary history. But I'll be somewhere listening for my name. . . . You, then, are in charge by the possibility of your good health, by the broadness of your vision, to remember us." *Freedom in This Village* remembers Melvin, Essex, Marlon, Assotto, Joseph, and so many more. This book is dedicated to their memory, as well as to the promise of a bold, new black gay literary future to come.

E. Lynn Harris
September 2004

FROM JUST ABOVE MY HEAD (1979)

James Baldwin

I haven't known Jimmy all of my life, but I've known him all of his—a curious difference, as time goes on. I hardly ever noticed him, until I started going with Julia. Until then, he'd just been Julia's snot-nosed, noisy little brother, an absolute drag, and, every once in a while, I'd have to step over him, politely, or push him aside, politely, or indicate, politely, that he go fuck himself. I had nothing against him. I just didn't need him.

While I was going with Julia, I remember him, mainly, coming in the door, or going out of it: he no longer lived at home. But then, just the same, he became more real to me: I knew how much he meant to Julia.

Julia and I were going together in 1957, the year that Arthur went solo. Julia and I, for reasons that I will have to go into later, didn't last too long; but Arthur, solo, did. So in 1960 or thereabouts, Arthur was doing a Civil Rights benefit in a church in the back-woods of Florida; and his regular pianist was in jail, in Alabama. I went with Arthur on this trip because I had become a little frightened for him—perhaps also because, without quite admitting it, I was becoming more involved myself. I had a whole lot of reservations about nonviolent protest, and praying for your enemies, and freedom songs, and all that. But those white crackers were far from nonviolent. You could hear the blows and the screams and the prayers from Mississippi to Harlem. You could catch it on your TV set when you came home. There was no way—for some people—to act like you didn't know. I say, "some people," and I say it with great bitterness, and even hatred in my heart for, God knows, "some people" were not most people. Most Americans did not give a shit about those black boys and girls and men and women—and some white boys and girls and white men and women—being beaten and murdered, in their name. Most Americans proved themselves to be absolute cowards—that's the truth, and the record bears me out. But I'm running ahead of myself. Some of the kids drove us to the church, because Arthur was determined, and we found Jimmy there, Jimmy had been working in the South for about two years.

Now Julia had told me this, and I also knew that Jimmy played piano: but none of this registered until that moment Arthur and I walked into the church, and found Jimmy sitting there. He was sitting in the kitchen, which was in the church basement. This basement had already been bombed twice. There were sandbags in one corner, and in the hole where one of the windows had been.

Jimmy was sitting on the kitchen table, chewing on a bacon sandwich, wearing a torn green sweater, blue jeans, and sneakers. He was very thin. I didn't recognize him right away, but Arthur did.

Jimmy grinned, and said, "Welcome to the slaughter, children. And don't go nowhere without your comb, your washrag, and your toothbrush—some of these jails have running water." Then he said to Arthur, "I hear your main man's been detained, in the cradle of the Confederacy. I'll play for you, if you want."

"Beautiful," Arthur said. "You want to run through a couple with me, right quick? Just so we'll get a sense of each other."

Jimmy stood up, and finished his sandwich. "At your service," he said, and we walked upstairs, into the church. Jimmy sat down at the piano. A couple of kids gathered around. Two black men stood at the doors, watching the street. It was about two hours before the church service—which was really a protest rally—would begin. Arthur's name hung in banners outside the church. The air was heavy with a tension I was eventually to come to know as well as I know my name.

Jimmy began to play. Arthur waited a little, then he began to sing; he and Jimmy grinned at each other, briefly, as each began to enter the other's beat. A few more kids gathered around the altar. A couple of women, arms folded, stood in the aisle. A telephone rang in the church office; someone immediately picked it up, closing the office door. I joined the two men as the music began to come alive, and stood at the door with them, staring out at the pastoral, apocalyptic streets.

More than a year later, one rainy night in Harlem, we let the rain sort of float us from one bar to another, and we walked and talked, alone on the black-and-silver streets, surrounded by the rain, water dropping from our hair and our eyelashes, from the tips of our noses, and down our backs. Arthur had just come in from London.

No one knows very much about the life of another. This ignorance becomes vivid, if you love another. Love sets the imagination on fire, and, also, eventually, chars the imagination into a harder element: imagination cannot match love, cannot plunge so deep, or range so wide.

Ruth was in the hospital with Tony then, and Arthur and I had had dinner alone. It was raining as we walked out of the restaurant, which was near the Renaissance Theatre, on Seventh Avenue. My apartment, in one of those damn, disastrous housing projects, was behind us, slightly to the east.

Arthur had been very silent during dinner. I watched his face. It was a face I knew and didn't know. He had something on his mind.

We walked out, silently, and found the rain, but we did not start back toward my apartment. We started slowly down the long, loud avenue, long with silence, loud with rain. Cars rocked, proudly amphibious, throwing up buckets of water. People stood in vestibules, in little circles of light, hugged the walls of buildings, splashed furiously through puddles: we walked very slowly. I was wearing a cap, but Arthur was bareheaded, holding a folded newspaper on top of his head. Arthur stopped before Dickie Wells. We looked briefly at each other, and walked in, and sat down at the bar. It was early, that is, it was not yet midnight, and the place was quiet.

The bartender served us, and Arthur looked down into his glass, and then he looked up at me, and he said, "So. We're finally going to work together."

We had decided that, just before he'd gone to London. It was Arthur who insisted. I worked in the advertising department of a black magazine—at least, it said it was black; and the job wasn't bad, but Arthur said that it was turning me into a schizo: and I could see that that might be true.

Arthur was around twenty-six, which means that we had edged into the sixties. Without having yet, as the proverb goes, "made it," Arthur was a tremendous drawing card, absolutely individual, and had reached that curious point through which all memorable careers seem to pass: when you must either go up and over, or down and out.

We were due to sign for his first record album in a matter of days, and this, too, was very much on his mind.

"Are you having second thoughts about us working together?"

He grinned. "You can't get out of it *that* way, baby."

Then again he was silent, and I watched his face.

"When you sing," he said, suddenly, "you can't sing *outside* the song. You've got to *be* the song you sing. You've got to make a confession."

He turned his drink around, and said, in another tone, "Every time I pass that corner, next to the Renaissance, I remember this man who was standing on the corner one day when I came by, and he asked me to go to the store for him. I was about thirteen. He was about thirty or forty, a very rough-looking dude, tall and thin, he wore a hat. He said we had to go to his house to get the money."

Arthur looked at me sideways, with a little grin, a shrug. "He looked like he might give me a nickel, or a dime."

I watched Arthur, and held my breath.

"The house he said he lived in was very close to the corner, and we walked in the hall and started up the stairs. It was funny, I'll never forget it, but the minute we started up those stairs, I knew that man did not live in this house. I knew it. I got scared like I'd never been scared before, but I didn't turn and run, it was like I was hypnotized. I just followed him up those stairs, till we got to the third landing."

I try to see the scene as a minor, adolescent misadventure, as common as dirt. But this is not what Arthur's eyes are saying, nor his voice.

"He said I was a cute boy—something like that—and he touched me on the face, and I just stood there, looking at him. And, while I was looking at him, his eyes got darker, like the sky, you know? and he didn't seem to be looking at me, just like the sky. And it was silent on those stairs, like you could hear silence just growing, like it was going to explode!"

Arthur looked at me and looked away, and took another swallow of his drink.

"He took out *his* cock, and I just stared at the thing pointing at me, and man, you know how we were raised, I did not know who to scream for, and then he put his hand on *my* cock and my cock jumped and then I couldn't move at all. I just stood there, waiting, paralyzed, and he opened my pants and took it out, and it got big and I had never seen it that way, it was the first time and so it meant that I must be just like this man, and then he knelt down and took it in his mouth. I thought he was going to bite it off. But, all the time, it kept getting bigger, and I started to cry.

"A door slammed somewhere over our heads, and he stood up,

and he put some money in my hand, and he hurried down the steps. I got my pants closed best as I could and I ran home. I mean, I ran all the way. I locked myself in the bathroom, and I looked at the money; it was a quarter and two dimes. I threw them out the window."

He finished his drink. "And I had just started singing."

A shyness I might not have felt with a friend, or a stranger, refused to release my tongue. Nothing so terrible had happened, after all; much worse might have happened. This thought made me ashamed of myself: how do *I* know that? It was not *my* initiation. I am ashamed of myself for another reason; that Arthur never thought to tell his older brother of this violation: he could certainly have told no one else.

But I had been twenty when Arthur was thirteen, far above the childlike concerns of my little brother. It would probably never have occurred to him to look for me, to talk to me. He would have been too frightened, and too ashamed.

"I never forgot that man," Arthur said, slowly, "not so much because of the physical thing—but—"

Arthur stopped, and looked at me, and it was as though I had never before looked into his eyes, or had never before realized how enormous they were, and how deep.

"—it was the way he made me feel about myself. That man made it impossible for me to touch anybody, man or woman, for a long time, and still, he filled me with a terrible curiosity. And, all that time, I was singing, man, I was singing up a storm." Then he stopped laughing. "I've got to live the life I sing about in my song," he said.

He put some money on the bar, and picked up his wet newspaper. "Come on," he said, "let's pub crawl. *I* don't mind getting wet," and he grinned, and propelled me to the door.

We walked out into the rain again, and started down the avenue.

We walked slowly, in silence, head down, the only people on the street. Had there been anyone to see us, we would have been a strange sight.

Arthur put his newspaper on his head again, where it began its final disintegration. "If you knew me better, I'm sure you'd say I was a fool, and, if I wasn't your brother, you might laugh at me—but I've had very little experience, and I've always been afraid. And I've stayed busy. And, if you notice, I've kind of stayed away from you. Because I've always looked up to you, and I love you, and I wouldn't be able to live, man, if I thought you were ashamed of me."

I made a sound like a laugh, a thin, demented sound against the torrent. "Why should I be ashamed of you?"

"Look. You're going to be hanging out with me more and more." We were now beginning to be soaked, we started walking faster, staying close to the walls of buildings; Arthur dropped the sodden newspaper, and we headed for the next bar. "You're going to see my life. I don't want to hide anything from you, brother."

"Why should you hide anything from me?" But my voice sounded hollow, and, yes, I was afraid.

We walked into the bar. This was a bar we no longer knew very well, a poor bar. It can be said that all bars in Harlem are poor, but there are degrees, degrees of visibility; and this bar was poor.

We were very visible, too, as we walked through the bar, and sat down in a booth in the back. The jukebox was going very loud, and so were the people.

Arthur went into the bathroom, to wipe his streaming face, and hair. The barmaid, an elderly woman with a pleasant face, came over to me.

"That the one who sings?"

"Yes." Then, "That's my brother."

"What's his name?"

"Arthur Montana."

"I knew it. That's him. My sister keep talking about him. He got a beautiful voice. You *really* his brother?"

"Why would I say I was, if I wasn't?"

"I don't know why people say a lot of things. You tell him he got a beautiful voice. I heard him at Reverend Larrabee's, me and my sister."

She took the order, and went away. Presently, I heard "—a *gospel* singer? He ain't going save no souls in *here*." Laughter. "He can get wet, just like everybody else," someone said. "And thirsty, too," said another. "Man, didn't nobody say he was no *preacher*." "Let's get him to sing 'Didn't It Rain.' " "You no good sinners," said the barmaid, calmly, "you don't know He's everywhere." More laughter. "Preach it, Minnie!" Dinah and Brook Benton were singing "A Rocking Good Way." "Dinah started out in gospel," somebody said.

Arthur came back, not very much drier—our hair holds the rain—and took off his jacket, and sat down. The barmaid set her tray down on the table. "Give me them wet things," she said, and she took my cap, and coat, and Arthur's jacket, and placed them on a nearby table. "That's better," she said, and poured us our drinks.

"Thank you," Arthur said.

"Don't you let the whiskey ruin that pretty voice," she said, and went back behind the bar.

Arthur stared in her direction, and then stared at me. "You been talking about me?"

"Baby, she heard you sing at Reverend Larrabee's, and she's already told everybody here. She told *me*."

Arthur looked astounded, then—unwillingly—delighted, then thoughtful. He lit a cigarette.

"Don't let them cigarettes wreck that pretty voice," I said.

Arthur grinned, suddenly looking about ten years old, and he said, "Now, don't you do me like that, brother." I remembered teaching him to tie his shoes—his sneakers—years ago, they were brown and white, and I have no idea why I remember that.

"*I'm* not doing it," I said. "It's fame."

"You think I'm going to be famous?"

"Yes," I said, "I do!" and, for the first time, I felt that it was as though a cold wind blew, for an instant, between Arthur and myself: into this void rushed the sound of the jukebox and the voices of the people at the bar.

And Arthur raised his eyes and looked out over the bar, as though he were seeing something for the first time, as though he were hearing a new sound.

I was facing Arthur, my back was to the bar, and so I could not see what he was seeing. Well: there was the gray-haired man, with the yellow teeth, and the foolish grin, who had been standing at the end of the bar as we entered, both hands wrapped around his glass, leaning inward, wearing a torn, black raincoat. Seated on the stool next to him was a heavy black lady, with long, curling, bright red hair, and deep purple lipstick, which made her lips look bruised. She seemed to be more than acquainted with, and to be hoping to escape from, the gray-haired man; his patience, though, was probably as ruthless as his grin. Next to this discontent stood a high yellow dude, in a brown suit, staring into his drink, and ignoring, equally (with an equal effort) the lady of the bruised lips and the tall man standing next to him; who wore a bright mustard jacket, suggesting tweed, and had an unlit pipe, eyeglasses brighter than the wrath of God, a long chin, and heavy rings flashing from compulsive fingers: he tapped his feet in the same way, to no particular music. Two girls and two boys stood next to him, as high as they were weary, playing the jukebox, while waiting for a change in the weather. A fat man stood all alone, nursing a beer. A silent girl sat next to him, wearing a yellow blouse and a long, blue skirt. Two schoolteacher types stood against the wall, chattering and grinning, and very aware of the tall boy in the corduroy pants, who stood alone at the bar, and who seemed to be a friend of the bartender's—

the bartender was short, round, and cheerful, with a mustache, and he and the tall boy talked together, whenever the bartender was free. A woman and a man sat silently together, near the window, the rain falling endlessly behind them. The barmaid talked to everyone and saw everything, moved placidly behind the bar, rinsing glasses, checking stock, sometimes sending the bartender into the basement, for this or that. The music played, endlessly, as endlessly as the rain fell. The voices rose and fell like a river, a swollen river, searching the dam. The bottles glittered like malice against the crowded mirror. The cash register clanged, at intervals, like a bell alerting prisoners to judgment, or release. The door kept opening and closing, people entered and people left, but mainly, people entered. The clock on the wall said quarter past two. There was a pencil portrait of Malcolm X beneath it.

Arthur looked back at me.

"Well," he said, "whatever it is—you'll see me through it, won't you? I got nobody but you."

"Oh, come on," I said.

He grinned. I felt that the grin hurt him, and it hurt me. "It's true. You, you've got Ruth, and, now, you've got little Tony, lying up there in his name tag and his diapers—but me, I've only got you." He grinned again, a brighter grin this time. "Don't be upset. My demands are very modest."

"Baby, do you know that you are full of shit?"

"That is no way to talk to a gospel singer."

We both started laughing. "Buy me another drink, you stupid motherfucker; hanging out with you, man, I better get drunk."

"Right. And you—we—have a new life to celebrate." He looked toward the bar, and, as though she had been waiting for this light from the lighthouse, the barmaid immediately appeared.

"Now I warned you," she said, picking up the glasses, "to be careful about that voice."

"It's all right. I'm with my brother."

She did not exactly smile, but she looked at me again, and then looked back at Arthur. "He the only brother you got?"

"That's right."

Then she looked at me. "Don't you worry about it, then."

We went, eventually, from the poor bar—and the rain kept pouring down—into the after-hours joint, in a cellar, somewhere way west on 118th Street, where everyone knew Arthur. Or, so it seemed to me. This was one of the very last times I was ever to be confused as to who knew Arthur, and who didn't. It was one of the very last times I was ever to allow myself to get drunk when I was out with Arthur. It was the first time I ever watched my brother in a world which was his, not mine. I was drunk that night, and I knew that Arthur was trying to show me something, something which I might not have been able to see if I had not been drunk.

Or, if Tony had not been born two nights before. That joy and wonder and terror and pride surged and danced in me that night, making my life new, making my brother new. It was incredible to me that the first time I had seen him, he had been as helpless and tiny and furious as Tony was now, his eyes as tightly closed, his fists and legs as futile, every inch of him resisting the violence of his meeting with the air.

PASSION (1981)

Sidney Brinkley

I remember the first time I saw him. I was in a record store, browsing through the stacks of discounted albums, when he came walking down the aisle. A sexual . . . rush surged through my body then centered itself in my groin and I felt the first stirrings of an erection. It must have been all over my face, because he smiled, and I, embarrassed, quickly looked away. When I looked back, he was still smiling and all I could do was shrug.

That was the beginning.

Love came later. Much later. It seemed to sneak up on us both, but it caught me first. When we were apart images of him would crowd my brain, leaving room for little else: his smile, the way he looked when he wanted to make love, the feel of his body on mine. At day's end I collapsed into bed mentally exhausted, emotionally spent, and physically drained.

Yes, I was in love.

Now, we share the same bed. Arms and legs entwine, bodies glistening with sweat in the low light, we move across each other with an intimacy that has been years in the making. Five long years during which we've fought, made up, separated, and come back together, surviving infidelity and boredom. Going through all the changes that two people, *two men*, can face. And after all that, sometimes I look at him and still get weak, just like that first time. Nobody moves me the way he does when we lie together like this deep in the night.

The same mouth that will speak ordinary words now says things only meant for me as it roams my face and neck. Hands that will casually grip a stranger's neck now travel lovingly down the curve of my back, pulling me closer. Though two thin layers of skin keep us apart, spirit knows no such boundaries and indeed we are one.

I thrust my tongue into his ear. He gasps and tries to escape. He loves it and hates it. I hold on, licking and pushing it deeper. Biting small patches of skin tart with the taste of salt and sweat, I move down to work the erect knob of his nipple. Going down: damp hairs brush my face; his earthy scent fills my nostrils.

I run my tongue up and down the inside of his thigh while I fondle the most private part of him. It throbs and jumps in spastic movement. I take him in. His hands clutch the sides of my head and his thighs draw up. Soon he'll moan, real low.

"Ummmmmmmm."

Yes, I know him well.

In one move I reverse myself and we are head to toe. His mouth finds me and I sink into his warmth. I shiver, snort, and make other strange sounds. Sensing my own flood, I pull out, falling on my back, breathing deeply. He reaches for the lubricant on the night table and rubs it up and down the length of him then lies on his back holding himself as I lower myself onto his body. Eyes closed, he smiles when, like a hand sliding into a comfortable glove, he slowly slides into me.

When I come to rest, he sits up, propping his arms behind him. We are face to face, chest to chest, and I, impaled, am sitting in his lap, my legs wrapped around his waist. Pleasure is joined by just a touch of pain as he throbs deep inside of me.

"Okay, cowboy," he says as he begins to move.

Cowboy. That's what he calls me when we are like this. It's as if I'm sitting in a saddle and he is my horse. And when he starts to buck, I ride. He finds his spot inside of me and he strokes it—again, and again, and again. He says he can feel each tremor that rolls through my body.

We roll onto our sides and he begins to pump in smooth fluid movements, like a well-oiled machine. He's in me; he's on me; he's all around me. I feel totally possessed. My toes curl and my hands claw at his back as he grows larger and harder. Not caught up in his own pleasure, he reaches between us and begins to fondle me. I'm feeling things I've yet to learn to put into words. Perhaps there are no words, but it's for this that we risk the wrath of God and man.

But it's all too much and soon I feel my river rising, rising till it spills over, flooding the hairy landscape where our bodies join. This sends him over his own edge: his mouth puckers, his body becomes rigid, unintelligible sounds fall from his mouth. I swear I can feel him come inside of me, filling me with the very essence of his life.

*　*　*

Now all is still. Sounds that had been pushed aside now creep back into the room: the tick of the clock on the dresser; the hum of traffic from the street below; the muffled music from the apartment above. The air is hot, humid, and heavy with the smell of sex. My legs relax around his waist. All soft now, he slowly begins to pull out. One last tug and he is free. I grab the towel from the bedpost and clean him, then myself. Few words are exchanged; none are needed.

Our bed is a mess of disheveled sheets and pillows but we are too tired to do much about it. He pulls me to him for one last kiss. I pull the crumpled sheets around us and move closer to his soft, warm body. Quickly, he falls into a deep sleep, lightly snoring. Soon, I'll follow. But for now I lie awake and savor the moment, for I want to remember this—all of this—when there was no space but this space, no time but this time, no man but this man.

Assumption about the Harlem Brown Baby (1983)

Salih Michael Fisher

Do not assume I came out on Christopher Street
as the piers and tracks began to heat and dance in the
night

I came out at fifteen in the streets of Harlem and South
Bronx
On rooftop jungles . . . pulling tigers and leopards to my
rhythmic past
Spurting . . . spurting fountains . . . and baking bread
never laid . . . upon the table
Never laid upon the table before any human's hands . . .
mouths . . . dragon unasleep
It was natural . . . a raw kind of primitive dance . . . it
was my ritualistic dance
into manhood . . . into the passage of blood sung in
Benin linguistic breathing patterns

Breathing . . . breathing down my neck . . . breathing in
my face
Between the cries of baby this and that . . . and feelings
of being good . . . of ooh I feel good!

And back then I was Eschu . . . the trickster . . . a
chameleon
in my identity . . . I played the butch-queen games well
For the period of blood can be a time of confusion . . .
Of direct lines between straight and narrow paths not
taken

But the lullabies of nights remembered on roofs . . .
Was knocking at my door . . . and the black and latin men
made love to those nights so long ago were calling

I came . . . and came again to the hallways . . . and Mt.
Morris Park
To sing the song of the bushes in black heat . . . black
heat rising
rising in my eyes . . . rising in your eyes . . . your eyes
piercing my eyes
in unison . . . the stars now fall and shoot themselves. . . .
from our scepters held to the morning sun . . . rising . . .
rising . . . rising

And do not assume . . . you . . . my friend
that the first bars I went to were gay
and had men posing as wax barbie dolls
and twisted g. i. joes

The first bars that I went to find a man
was mixed and three-fourth straight
And the first man I walked out with . . .
had a thirty-eight between his belt

And a road called "sudden paradise"
He was a dope dealer . . . he was a saint
a devil in disguise . . . and he taught me to bleed
at sixteen . . . with the first heart broken

I did go to gay bars later . . . back then . . . the bars
that spoke the words from the outside "Black Only"
Whites who come in . . . come in at your own risk

And in those places . . . the queens and drags were
respected
and sometime feared . . . they were the ones that kept the
place together
And if someone wanted to play the macho butch and read
they would make sure . . . they could not sow future seeds

They were no slouch these queens
They carried blades and guns filled with lead
Go off wrong with them . . . you were dead!

And when I came out . . . there were no definite gay code
of dress
What got you from A to Z with a man was whether you
had nice labels
or looked street cool . . . not whether you were a cowboy
or leatherman
or even showing half of your can . . . if you did the
queens would look
and read you as being a desperate man

So do not assume that I was some Harlem brown baby
that came out in your world . . . your ghetto . . . your
constructs
of your reality . . . I came out in my own

Knowing the even flow to life . . . knowing which cards
had been marked and played . . . the sea . . . the sea
is now at rest . . . fill your bowels of passion with my
wisdom

Brother to Brother: Words from the Heart (1984)

Joseph Beam

> . . . *what is most important to me must be spoken, made verbal and shared, even at the risk of having it bruised or misunderstood.*[1]

> *I know the anger that lies inside me like I know the beat of my heart and the taste of my spit. It is easier to be angry than to hurt. Anger is what I do best. It is easier to be furious than to be yearning. Easier to crucify myself in you than to take on the threatening universe of whiteness by admitting that we are worth wanting each other.*[2]

I, too, know anger. My body contains as much anger as water. It is the material from which I have built my house: blood red bricks that cry in the rain. It is what pulls my tie and gold chains taut around my neck; fills my penny loafers and my Nikes; molds my Calvins and gray flannels to my torso. It is the face and posture I show the world. It is the way, sometimes the only way, I am granted an audience. It is sometimes the way I show affection. I am angry because of the treatment I am afforded as a Black man. That fiery anger is stoked additionally with the fuels of contempt and despisal shown me by my community because I am gay. *I cannot go home as who I am.*

When I speak of home, I mean not only the familial constellation from which I grew, but the entire Black community: the Black press, the Black church, Black academicians, the Black literati, and the Black left. Where is my reflection? I am most often rendered invisible, perceived as a threat to the family, or am tolerated if I am silent and inconspicuous. I cannot go home as who I am and that hurts me deeply.

Almost every morning I have coffee at the same donut shop. Almost every morning I encounter the same Black man who used to acknowledge me from across the counter. I can only surmise that it is my earrings and earcuffs that have tipped him off that I am gay. He no longer speaks, instead looks disdainfully through me as if I were glass. But glass reflects, so I am not even that. He sees no part of himself in me—not my Blackness nor my maleness. "There's nothing in me that is not in everyone else, and nothing in everyone else that is not in me."[3] Should our glances meet, he is quick to use his *Wall Street Journal* as a shield while I wince and admire the brown of my coffee in my cup.

I do not expect his approval—only his acknowledgement. The struggles of Black people are too perilous and too pervasive for us to dismiss one another, in such cursory fashion, because of perceived differences. Gil Scott-Heron called it "dealing in externals," that is, giving great importance to visual information and ignoring real aspects of commonality. Aren't all hearts and fists and minds needed in this struggle or will this faggot be tossed into the fire? In this very critical time everyone from the corner to the corporation is desparately needed.

> . . . [Brother] the war goes on
> respecting no white flags
> taking no prisoners
> giving no time out for women and children
> to leave the area

whether we return their fire
or not
whether we're busy attacking each other
or not . . .[4]

If you could put your newspaper aside for a moment, I think you, too, would remember that it has not always been this way between us. I remember. I remember the times before different meant separate, before different meant outsider. I remember Sunday school and backyard barbeques and picnics in the Park and the Avenue and parties in dimly lit basements and skateboards fashioned from two-by-fours and b-ball and . . . I remember. I also recall secretly playing jacks and jumping rope on the back porch, and the dreams I had when I spent the night at your house.

But that was before different meant anything at all, certainly anything substantial. That was prior to considerations such as too light/too dark; or good/bad hair; before college/army/jail; before working/middle class; before gay/straight. But I am no longer content on the back porch; I want to play with my jacks on the front porch. There is no reason for me to hide. Our differences should promote dialogue rather than erect new obstacles in our paths.

On another day: I am walking down Spruce/Castro/Christopher Street on my way to work. A half block away, walking towards me, is another Black gay man. We have seen each other in the clubs. Side by side, and at the precise moment that our eyes should meet, he studies the intricate detail of a building. I check my white sneakers for scuff marks. What is it that we see in each other that makes us avert our eyes so quickly? Does he see the same thing in me that the brother in the donut shop sees? Do we turn away from each other in order not to see our collective anger and sadness?

It is my pain I see reflected in your eyes. Our angers ricochet between us like the bullets we fire in battles which are not our own nor with each other.

The same angry face, donned for safety in the white world, is the same expression I bring to you. I am cool and unemotive, distant from what I need most. "It is easier to be furious than to be yearning. Easier to crucify myself in you . . ." And perhaps easiest to ingest that anger until it threatens to consume me, or apply a salve of substitutes to the wound.

But real anger accepts few substitutes and sneers at sublimation. The anger-hurt I feel cannot be washed down with a Coke (old or new) or a Colt 45; cannot be danced away; cannot be mollified by a white lover, nor lost in the mirror reflections of a Black lover; cannot evaporate like sweat after a Nautilus workout; nor drift away in a cloud of reefer smoke. I cannot leave it in Atlantic City, or Rio, or even Berlin when I vacation. I cannot hope it will be gobbled up by the alligators on my clothing; nor can I lose it in therapeutic catharsis. I cannot offer it to Jesus/Allah/Jah. So, I must mold and direct that fiery cool mass of angry energy—use it before it uses me! *Anger unvented becomes pain, pain unspoken becomes rage, rage released becomes violence.*

Use it to create a Black gay community in which I can build my home surrounded by institutions that reflect and sustain me. Concurrent with that vision is the necessity to repave the road home, widening it, so I can return with all I have created to the home which is my birthright.

II

Silence is what I hear after the handshake and the slap of five; after the salutations: what's happenin'/what's up/how you feel; after our terms of endearment: homeboy, cuzz, "girlfriend," blood, running buddy, and Miss Thing. I can hear the silence. When talking with a "girlfriend," I am more likely to muse about my latest piece or so-and-so's party at Club She-She than about the anger and hurt I felt that morning when a jeweler refused me entrance to his store because I am Black and male, and we are all perceived as thieves. I will swallow that hurt and should I speak of it, will vocalize only the anger, saying: I have bust out his fuckin' windows! Some of the anger will be exorcised, but the hurt, which has not been given voice, prevails and accumulates.

Silence is a way to grin and bear it. A way not to acknowledge how much my life is discounted each day—100% OFF ALL BLACK MEN TODAY—EVERY DAY! I strive to appear strong and silent. I learn to ingest hatred at a geometric rate and to count (silently) to 10 . . . 10 thousand . . . 10 million. But as I have learned to mute my cries of anguish, so have I learned to squelch my exclamations of joy. What remains is the rap.

My father is a warm brown man of seventy, who was born in Barbados. He is kind and gentle, and has worked hard for me so that I am able to write these words. We are not friends: he is my father, I am his son. We are silent when alone together. I do not ask him about his island childhood or his twelve years as a janitor or about the restaurant he once owned where he met my mother. He does not ask me about being gay or why I wish to write about it. Yet we are connected: his past is my present, our present a foundation for the future. I have never said to him that his thick calloused hands have led me this far and given me options he never dreamed of. How difficult it is to speak of my appreciation, saying: Dad, I love you. *I am here because of you, much deeper than sperm meeting egg, much deeper than sighs in the night, I am here because of you.* Our love for each other, though great, may never be spoken. It is the often unspoken love that Black men give to other Black men in a world where we are forced to cup our hands over our mouths or suffer under the lash of imprisonment, unemployment, or even death. But these words, which fail, are precisely the words that are life-giving and continuing. They must be given voice. What legacy is to be found in our silence?

Because of the silence among us, each one of us, as Black boys and men maturing, must all begin the struggle to survive anew. With the incomplete knowledge of what has gone before, our struggles to endure and maintain, at best, save us only as individuals. Collectively we falter and stumble, covering up our experiences in limp aphorisms: Times are hard! Watch out for the Man! This is the depth of the sage advice we offer each other—at arm's length. We must begin to speak of our love and concern for each other as vigorously as we argue party politics or the particular merits of an athletic team.

Daydream: 29 April 1984
Today was the first beautiful day that I have not had to spend at work. Precisely the kind of day I want to share with a lover: gazing at the blue sky; making love in the western sunlight on the brown-sheeted bed; massaging each other with the musk oil that warms on the window sill. We'd shower together, and return to the bed to dry in the sunlight as we had sweated when we made love.

Today, I think also of Bryan, and of myself as the hopeless romantic that I sometimes am. How can I be so taken with you, boy-man, who I met only two weeks ago? Why is it that I want to share all my waking moments with you? Share my world with you? Protect you? Tell you things no one told me when I was 22. You are like the little brother I never had; the playmates I was not supposed to touch. You are the lover who is considerate; the son I will not issue, eyes bright and inquisitive. I want to hold you the way my father never held me. I want to know your face, the oily brownness of your skin: its shadows, the darkness around the elbows and under the buttocks. I daydream of brown-on-brown-on-brown.

I am at a poetry reading. The brother at the podium is reading a poem about his running buddy who was killed in Vietnam. At the gravesite of his dead friend, the poet reminisces about the big fun they'd had, sharing bottles of wine and hanging on the corner. Only when everyone has gone and he stares at the mound of dirt that covers his homeboy, can he utter: "Man, I really loved you. I really, really loved you."

Why does it take us so long?

I, too, have been there. Two good high school buddies died within a year of our graduation: Chris in a charter plane crash on his way back to college, Steve of a heart attack while playing basketball. We were all nineteen and assumed life would go on. There seemed to be no rush to speak of how we cherished one another's friendship. I was away at college when they were both buried; I will always regret that silence.

We have few traditions like those of Black women. No kitchen tables around which to assemble. No intimate spaces in which to explore our feelings of love and friendship. No books like *The Color Purple*. We gather in public places: barber shops, bars, lodges, fraternities, and street corners, places where bravado rather than intimacy are the rule. We assemble to *do* something rather than *be* with each other. We can talk about the Man, but not about how we must constantly vie with one another for the scant crumbs thrown our way. We can talk about dick and ass and pussy, but not of the fierce competition for too few jobs and scholarships. We can talk about sporting events in amazing detail, but not about how we are pitted, one against the other, as permanent adversaries.

Dream: 15 February 1984

We have all gathered in the largest classroom I have ever been in. Black men of all kinds and colors. We sit and talk and listen, telling the stories of our lives. All of the things we have ever wanted to say to each other but did not. There is much laughter but also many tears. Why has it taken us so long? Our silence has hurt us so much.

III

Dreams are what propel us through life, and allow us to focus above and beyond the hurdles that dot our passage. Medger, Martin, and Malcolm were dreamers. And they were killed. I dare myself to dream. If I cannot vocalize a dream, which is the first step towards its realization, then I have no dream. It remains a thought, a vision without form. I dare myself to dream that our blood is thicker than difference.

In the fall of 1980, I did not know that one of every four Black men would experience prison in his lifetime. Nor did I know that my motivation for writing to prisoners arose from a deep sense of my captivity as a closeted gay man and an oppressed Black man, rather than as an act of righteousness. Finally, I had no idea that such a correspondence would become an integral part of my life and a place for dreaming.

Ombaka and I began writing to each other under unusual circumstances. I had been writing to another prisoner named Morris, who had been transferred or released, but, in any case, had vacated the particular cell, which was to be Ombaka's new home. Ombaka found my last letter to Morris, read it and responded. He apologized profusely in that first letter about how contrary it was to prison etiquette to read someone else's mail and even ruder to respond to it. Almost four years, and forty letters later, it seems ironic that this friendship, one of the most important in my life, is the result of such a chance occurrence. More ironic and sadder is that we probably would not have met any other way; we are that different.

I am gay and from the north; he is straight and from the south. I'm an agnostic; he's a Muslim. When I was attending prep school, Ombaka was busily acquiring his street smarts. While I studied in college, he was finishing his stint in the Army. When I was beginning graduate school, he had just begun his prison sentence. Under other circumstances these differences might have separated us. What could have been used as weapons of castigation became tools of sharing.

Our initial letters were filled with the tentative gestures one employs with new friends, the shyness, the formality, and the small talk. We searched for common ground for dialogue and the soft spots to be avoided. We spoke of the advantages and disadvantages of street smarts versus formal education. We talked at length about sexuality and how we became the sexual beings that we are. We discussed our use of language: I greatly admired his rural tongue with its graceful turn of phrase, which seemed more natural than my stilted style, which he respected. He told me of his experiences as a Muslim and as a father; I related tales from college and gay life in the big city. We talked and talked about our differences, but we also gave each other permission to dream and to speak of those dreams. What an exciting yet fearful prospect, dreaming in the open.

Black dreams are dashed as assuredly as Black dreamers are killed. We are allowed to dream of being athletes, entertainers, and lotto winners. These are the dreams which have been dreamt for us to maintain us just where we are. How little support there is, from one another or from society, for dreams borne of personal conviction and desire. I dare myself to dream.

Astronaut Guy Bluford and I grew up on the same block. It was no secret that he dreamed of being an astronaut, but in the early sixties it was difficult for little Black boys to imagine being anything other than what we had seen. And we had seen no Black astronauts nor Black mayors of major U.S. cities. We all thought Bluford was crazy, but his dreams became a reality. We can dream the dark, the seemingly impossible.

Ombaka and I dreamt of being writers. During the course of our correspondence we *became* writers. Several months ago he sent me a 260-page manuscript of his first novel, and I am beginning to work on a major writing project (*In the Life*). I am extremely happy that our friendship was not lost to anger, or silence, or perceived differences. I dare myself to dream.

I dare myself to dream of us moving from survival to potential, from merely getting by to a positive getting over. I dream of Black men loving and supporting other Black men, and relieving Black women from the role of primary nurturers in our community. I dream, too, that as we receive more of what we want from each other that our special anger reserved for Black women will disappear. For too long have we expected from Black women that which we could only obtain from other men. I dare myself to dream.

I dream of a time when it is not Black men who fill the nation's prisons; when we will not seek solace in a bottle and Top papers; and when the service is not the only viable alternative to high civilian unemployment.

I dare myself to dream of a time when I will pass a group of brothers on the corner, and the words "fuckin' faggot" will not move the air around my ears; and when my gay brother approaches me on the street that we can embrace if we choose.

I dare *us* to dream that we are worth wanting each other.

IV

Black men loving Black men is the revolutionary act of the eighties.

At eighteen, David could have been a dancer: legs grown strong from daily walks from his remote neighborhood to downtown in search of employment that would free him from his abusive family situation. David, soft-spoken and articulate, could have been a waiter gliding gracefully among the tables of a three-star restaurant. David could have performed numerous jobs, but lacking the connections that come with age and race, the Army seemed a reasonable choice. His grace and demeanor will be of little importance in Nicaragua.

Earl is always a good time. His appearance at parties, whether it's a smart cocktail sip or basement gig, is mandatory. He wakes with coffee and speed, enjoys three-joint lunches, and chases his bedtime Valium with Johnny Walker Red. None of his friends, of which he has many, suggest that he needs help. His substance abuse is ignored by all.

Stacy is a delirious queen, a concoction of current pop stars, bound eclectically in thrift store threads. His sharp and witty tongue can transform the most boring, listless evenings. In private, minus the dangles and bangles, he appears solemn and pensive, and speaks of the paucity of role models, mentors, and possibilities.

Maurice has a propensity for white people, which is more than preference—it's policy. He dismisses potential Black friendships as quickly as he switches off rap music and discredits progressive movements. He consistently votes Republican. At night he dreams of razors cutting away thin slivers of his Black skin.

Bubba and Ray had been lovers for so long that the neighbors presumed them to be brothers or widowers. For decades their socializing had been done among an intimate circle of gay couples, so when Ray died Bubba felt too old to venture the new gay scene. Occassionally he has visitors, an equally old friend or a much younger cousin or nephew. But mostly he sits, weather permitting, on the front porch where with a can of beer over ice, he silently weaves marvelous tales of "the life" in the thirties and forties. Yet there isn't anyone who listens.

Bobbi, a former drag queen, has plenty of time to write poetry. Gone are his makeup and high heels since he began serving his two-to-five year sentence. He had not wanted to kick that bouncer's ass, however, he, not unlike the more macho sissies clad in leather and denim, rightfully deserved admittance to that bar. Although he has had no visitors and just a couple of letters, he maintains a sense of humor typified by the title of a recent set of poems: *Where can a decent drag queen get a decent drink?*

Paul is hospitalized with AIDS. The severity of his illness is not known to his family or friends. They cannot know that he is gay; it is his secret and he will expire with it. Living a lie is one thing, but it is quite another to die within its confines.

Charles is a ventman with beautiful dreads. On days when he is not drinking and is lucid, he will tell you how he winters on the south side of the square and sleeps facing the east so that he wakes with the sun in his eyes. He is only an obstacle to passersby.

Ty and Reggie have been lovers since they met in the service seven years ago. They both perform dull and menial jobs for spiteful employers, but plan to help each other through college. Ty will attend first. Their two-room apartment, which is neither fashionably appointed nor in a fashionable neighborhood, is clearly a respite from the madness that awaits outside their door. They would never imagine themselves as revolutionaries.

Black men loving Black men is the revolutionary act of the eighties, not only because sixties' revolutionaries like Bobby Seale, Huey Newton, and Eldridge Cleaver dare speak our name; but because as Black men we were never meant to be together—not as father and son, brother and brother—and certainly not as lovers.

Black men loving Black men is an autonomous agenda for the eighties, which is not rooted in any particular sexual, political, or class affiliation, but in our mutual survival. The ways in which we manifest that love are as myriad as the issues we must address. Unemployment, substance abuse, self-hatred, and the lack of positive images are but some of the barriers to our loving.

Black men loving Black men is a call to action, an acknowledgement of responsibility. We take care of our own kind when the night grows cold and silent. These days the nights are cold-blooded and the silence echoes with complicity.

NOTES

[1] Lorde, Audre. The Cancer Journals. Argyle, NY: Spinster's Ink, 1980.

[2] Lorde, Audre. Sister Outsider. Ithaca, NY: Crossing Press, 1984.

[3] Baldwin, James. Village Voice, Vol. 29, No. 26, p. 14.

[4] Blackwomon, Julie. *Revolutionary Blues and Other Fevers.* Philadelphia: self-published, 1984. (Distributed by Kitchen Table: Women of Color Press, PO Box 908, Latham, New York.)

FROM FLIGHT FROM NEVÈRŸON (1985)

Samuel R. Delany

In Nevèrÿon there is, of course, a model for the outbreak of the disease: some years before, an epidemic struck the outlying Ulvayn Islands, during which the empress, whose reign has been, on occasion, both caring and compassionate, sent ships and physicians to help evacuate those who were still healthy and who wished to come to the mainland.

The leaders of Nevèrÿon's capital and port, Kolhari—most modern, most sophisticated, most progressive of primitive cities— have some sense of the conservative nature of the Artaudian plague, even if, without Artaud's text, they carry that sense on a more primitive level than we do. Thanks to reports from the islands, they know that *that* is what their city must never come to look like.

Once, that night, Pheron, who was twenty-four (a fact that, several times in the midst of all this, had astonished him), woke in darkness, feeling better. Well, that had happened before; he did not consider miraculous cures.

Lying on soft straw and under a cover he had given its luminous oranges and ceruleans, he turned to his side (his lower back throbbed, distracting him from the queasiness pulsing in his throat), thought about his father, and smiled.

He had been seventeen, working out at the tanning troughs.

His father had been laboring at the construction site of the New Market.

One day in every twelve his father had off, coming home late that night and sleeping far into the next morning.

Pheron had two days off in every ten.

His third off-time coincided with one of his father's, to both their surprise; the evening before, they sat in the dark room with the lamp on the table Pheron had lit from the cook-fire coals.

His father leaned his arm in front of his bowl. Lamplight doubled the number of hairs over the blocky forearm strung with high veins, putting a shadow hair beside each real one on the brown skin.

The lamp flame wavered.

Half the hairs moved.

With a wooden paddle in his other hand, his father ate noisily from the grain, peppers, and fat Pheron had stewed together. 'Maybe then, tomorrow,' his father said, 'we'll go someplace. You and me.' He gestured with the paddle. 'Together.'

'Sure,' Pheron said, unsure what he meant.

Then both went to bed, Pheron sleeping with his heel wedged back between the big toe and the toe over of his other foot, fists curled in straw by his face, fingers smelling of garlic and the new barbaric spice, cinnamon (one of his recent enthusiasms his father put up with), and the acid from the bark that soaked in the stone troughs, their tides and ripplings littoral to his day.

Lingering at the mouth of the Bridge of Lost Desire, his father pulled at his earlobe, where gray hairs grew, with heavy workman's fingers and said in flat tones that signed a kind of nervousness (as a boy, Pheron had feared those tones because often they presaged punishment): 'You ever come here before . . . ?'

Certainly Pheron had crossed the bridge to the Old Market. As certainly, he knew that that was not what his father meant. But 'No' would be easy and appeasing.

Perhaps because the tanning work meant he was grown, or because being grown meant you stayed tired enough that the appeasements you'd once indulged you didn't have the energy for now, he said, anyway: 'No . . . ' Then, louder 'I mean, yes. I've been here. Yes. Before.'

His father smiled a little. 'I thought it was about time I took you to get yourself a woman. After your mother died, I came here enough—more than I should have. I don't too much now. But we may still meet some lady who remembers me.' His father rubbed his ear again. 'Only now you tell me you've already beat me. That means, I guess, I do neglect you—more than a father should. Well, then, you know how it's done.'

With the veil of exhaustion that lay, these days, over both working and nonworking time, blatant confession seemed as out of keeping as blatant denial. 'Why don't you find yourself a woman,' Pheron said, 'and I'll meet you back here in a few hours?'

'No, ' his father said. 'Come on. We'll go together, you and me. Besides, if we both use the same room, it'll be cheaper.'

They began to walk across.

'Go on,' his father said. 'Tell me which ones you like the most.'

A strangeness in it all—it *was* his father—made him want to smile. And, very deeply, dark discomfort streamed through. The strangest thing, however, was how ordinary it all—humor and discomfort—seemed. Father and son? he thought. Two workmen, an older and a younger, come to the bridge for sex? It was a pattern someone must have fit in the very stones of the bridge itself. 'I guess . . . ' Pheron shrugged. 'Well, that one's cute—'

'Ah, you like them young!' His father chuckled. 'Not me! Even when I was your age. I always thought the older ones would give me a better time. And I'm right, too. Your mother was four years older than I was—and if she'd been fourteen years older, it wouldn't have been so bad.'

'Father,' Pheron said, suddenly, recklessly: 'I don't want a woman.' Then: 'If I was going to buy anyone here, it would be a man. And besides: when I come here, men pay me!' And added: 'Sometimes.' Because he'd only done that three times anyway, and that at the instigation of an outrageous friend he didn't see much of now.

He walked with his father half a dozen more steps. He felt light-headed, silly, brave. (He imagined some tangle of shuttle and warp quickly, aggressively, finally unknotted.) Yes, his heart was beating faster. But the tiredness was gone. The soles of his feet tingled in his sandals; so did his palms.

His father stopped.

The sky was clear. Under Pheron's jaw and on the back of his arm, where sun did not touch, were cool. Across the walkway, a red-headed boy herded ahead half a dozen goats. They lifted bearded muzzles to glance about, yellow eyes slit with black, bleating and bleating. One raised a short tail, spilling black pellets from a puckered sphincter, only to get pushed on by three others. Two older women at the far wall laughed—though whether at the goats or the goatherd, Pheron couldn't tell. A donkey cart passed in the opposite direction.

'Then your mother was right,' his father said, finally.

Pheron thought, *He must be furious*, and waited for the loud words, for the recriminations, for the distance glimmering between them to be struck away by anger.

'I suppose I knew she was. But I always said it was something you'd grow out of. Now, there! See, maybe you *will* grow out of it.'

'I'm seventeen, father. It's just the way I am. I don't . . . ' He shrugged. 'I don't *want* to grow out of it!'

His father started walking again; so Pheron walked too.

His father said: 'You should try a woman. You might be surprised. You can find nice ones, here. I don't mean just pretty. I mean ones who're fun, even kind. Someone like you, you see: you need one who's kind, patient—that's because you're sensitive, young, unsure of yourself. I should have brought you here before. I know that, now.'

'I've tried it,' Pheron said. 'Before. With a few women.' Well, one, he thought. And there'd been another boy with them. 'I didn't like it that much. Not like with men. That's better. For me, I mean . . . '

His father was getting ahead, so Pheron hurried. 'You like women. Suppose someone told you to grow out of that?'

'Ha!' his father said. 'No. No, I guess there's not much chance of that!'

Pheron laughed. 'Then what do you want to do? You get a woman, I'll get a man?' (For some reason, that morning there were no male hustlers in sight, though there were many girls and women about.) 'And we'll *both* share a room? Maybe *you* should try a man!' He laughed again, feeling nervous. Not his father's nervousness, either. It was all his. 'Men are cheaper than women, here. Did you know that? It's true. Some people go with either. If you were one of those who could do that, you could save yourself some money—'

'Oh, no!' his father said, still a step ahead. He waved his hand behind. 'No—'

Then he stopped again.

The sound he made was not a shout:

'*Ahhhii—!*'

A grown man might make it at sudden pain: a sigh with much too much voice to it, perhaps a quarter of the sound a full shout might carry.

Pheron stopped too.

His father looked back. 'You don't want this? With me? Go on then!'

'Maybe—'

'Go on home,' his father said. 'You don't need to be here with me, for this. Go on, I say!' He looked back. 'What do I want you here with me for? Get out of here—now!'

Ahead, goats bleated.

Their arms around each other's shoulders, two prostitutes walked by with a third chattering after them.

Pheron turned back toward the bridge mouth. By the time he came off, he was trembling and angry. Halfway home, wrestling the anger silently, he felt the tiredness again. He walked half a dozen streets he wouldn't have ordinarily taken—a long route home. When he reached the door to their dark rooms, set back in the shoulder-wide alley between the stable and the brickyard, he was mumbling: 'I'm too tired to be angry. I'm too tired . . . ' It was something his mother had occasionally said. Usually she hadn't meant it either.

Under his bed frame was a handloom. When he got inside he pulled it out and sat in front of it cross-legged on the earthen floor. The strip he'd been weaving was wide as the length of his forearm laid across it. The finished material was rolled in a bundle on the loom's back bar. Currently he was in the midst of a ten shuttle pattern, at least for this part, for he'd varied his design along the three meters he'd done so far, now using yarns of different thicknesses, now of different colors, now varying the pattern itself, sometimes using a knotted weave, sometimes a plain one, the whole an endless experiment.

He wove furiously till the window dimmed.

Then he got out the jar of good oil and filled and lit three lamps from the banked coals under the ashes in the fireplace. He set two lamps on the corners of the table and one down on the floor at his side—waiting for the moon.

A running argument with his father went: 'If you're going to work after dark, Pheron, don't waste expensive oil. Take it up on the roof and work by moonlight!' which Pheron always said he would do, only—'I'm just using the lamps till the moon comes out, anyway, father.' But often, once started, he would weave by lamplight half the night, while the full moon came, went away again, and he, refilling the lamps half a dozen times, never even looked out the window to see. 'Pheron, I *told* you—'

He wove again.

He got up and went to look out the window; for the moon should be full or near so. But it wasn't out yet. So he sat back down on the floor.

He wove some more.

The hanging across the door whispered. He heard his father push through and didn't look up.

His father moved around the room and, after a while, said:

'Here. You like this stuff.'

So he glanced over.

'I got you something.'

The yarn bundles dropped on the table. One rolled between the lamps and fell to the floor, spinning in the air on dark string.

By the lamplight, he could only make out the brighter hues.

'Oh.' He put the shuttles down. 'Hey . . . !' He pushed himself up to his knees.

'In the Old Market,' his father said. He stood by the table, beard all under-lit, his arms still bent with the ghost of their gift. 'I don't know whether they're colors you want. But I figured, you could use them. For something.' He reached up to pull his ear. 'Some of that stuff is expensive, you know?' Now he picked up one and another of the skeins, frowning. 'I just thought . . . '

Pheron stood, his back stiff, his thighs aching from crouching so long on the floor. 'Thanks . . . ' He tried to think of something else to say. 'You want something to eat? I'll stop and fix some—'

'No,' his father said. 'No, I ate. You fix for yourself if you want. Not me. I got something while I was out.'

His father, Pheron realized, was slightly drunk.

'Is this stuff something you can use? You like it?'

'Yeah,' Pheron said. 'Yes. Thanks. Thanks a lot.'

'You go on,' his father said. 'You go on working. I just thought you might like, might use . . . some of these.'

'No,' Pheron said. 'I'll stop for a little.' Then he asked, because there just didn't seem any way not to: 'Did you find a woman?'

His father pretended not to have heard.

The two of them sat at the table together awhile.

Some of the skeins had come undone.

Several times his father buried the fingers of one hand in the yarns to lift a tangle from the table in the lamplight, blinking through the strands as if to determine the color in the inadequate glow.

His father said, finally: 'I didn't get a woman. I didn't want one. I got you this. See? Instead.'

Pheron thought: This isn't the kind of apology I wanted. I wanted him to have his woman and I wanted him to say, too, 'I thought about it, Pheron, and I was wrong. I'm sorry. You're my son. And I want you to be my son any way you are. Any way. You have your way. I have mine. But whoever you are, it's fine with me. Do you forgive me?' (How many times while he'd woven had he rehearsed what his father should tell him?) But, as he leaned his elbows on the table, he thought: That's just not who he is. That's just not what he can give. And I'm too tired to ask for it, or even—he realized after a while—to want it that much.

Through raised strands, his father blinked. 'What's the matter with you?' He put his tangled hand down.

Sitting back on the bench, Pheron rubbed his wet eyes with two forefingers which were growing rougher with each day at the troughs. 'Nothing.'

'The moon's out,' his father said. 'You want to work, I know. Take it up to the roof. So you don't waste good oil.'

'No,' he said. 'I . . . Well—yeah. Maybe. All right.' He stood up, looking at the dark yarn piled on the table. 'Thanks for all this stuff. Thanks.' He picked one of the skeins to take with him, though he wasn't sure *what* color it was.

His father grunted.

Pheron turned and picked up his handloom. Shuttles swung and clicked. 'You all right?' he asked.

His father nodded. 'Don't stay up too long, though.'

'I won't,' Pheron said.

Behind him, his father blew out first one, then the other lamp, so that the only light came from the one still on the floor, below the table.

Pheron lay in the dark (seven years later), not thinking of his father's death three years before, but of this; and of squatting before his handloom on the roof, moonlight bleaching the colors from his design's intricacies, while he wove on into night.

Michael Stewart Is Dead (1985)

Isaac Jackson

*(Michael Stewart was brutally murdered by New York City transit police in the
fall of 1983. His eyes were removed and destroyed illegally by the coroner's office
to prevent justice from being brought to bear on the guilty transit policemen. Michael
Stewart worked as a busboy in the Pyramid Club, a gay-owned and operated club
on Manhattan's Lower East Side.)*

on the number one/going downtown to the
garage/two white cops/standin' in front of me/
description of crimes and suspects/blare out/
of his box/offending my sense/if it was my radio/
i'd get a ticket.

one sez to the other: wouldn't it be funny if/
when a call went out/the guy was sitting right in
front of you/wouldn't it be funny/and easy to do/
two against one/two hands against a gun/
it could have been me.

i waz living on the lower east side/a few blocks
from the pyramid/when i first noticed him/
picking up empty beer glasses/pushing thru
the mixed crowd/gays/lesbians/straights/

bridge & tunnel crowd/shoulder to shoulder w/
east village artists/thin dreads hanging into his
eyes/i often commented to friends i might
consider trimming my dreads like his/
long in front/short on the sides/like the black guy
in/The Thompson Twins/'Hush my baby . . .
don't you cry . . . we have one weapon in our
defense/silence'/

at the fourteen street stop/on the II line/
doing my art in the subways/drawing sketches/
influenced by graffiti art/left no marks on the
walls/anywhere/working hard/sketching the
Statue of Liberty/leading the people/to some
billboard Liberia/i'm doing this sketch for the
anti-gentrification show/and this transit worker
gets irate/and rips my painting/to shreads/
Miz Liberty to shreads/screams/yells/tears/
i walk away/and live to complain.

i never knew his name before/i learned it by
reading in the paper/of the death of a young
man/ a young dread-locked graffiti artist/
in the custody of transit police/following an arrest.

Michael Stewart is dead/and wouldn't it be
funny/if the suspect/waz already standing in
front of you/and easy to do two against one/
two hands against a gun/it could have been me/
this time i got away.

ON NOT BEING WHITE (1986)

Reginald Shepherd

I wrote this essay in the mid nineteen-eighties; a lot has changed since then, including me. I was in my very early twenties, living in Boston doing various menial office jobs after having dropped out of college. It was the first thing I ever published, except for a poem in the now defunct Boston gay journal Fag Rag, *and I feel very ambivalent about it. On the one hand, I think it's quite well written and insightful; on the other hand, it reminds me of a very unhappy period in my life. I oscillate between thinking "Wow, this is very well written" and thinking "Wow, this guy is very fucked up." Though I wrote it with no thought of an audience (if I had imagined a possible audience's response, I might not have written it at all), it has proven to be rather controversial. In my extreme isolation and naïveté (the one entailed the other), I had no idea that there was a "discourse" to which I was contributing, let alone that my piece would play a formative role in that (at the time) still-emergent discourse. I thought that I was simply writing down my experience, my observations, and my thoughts about what I had experienced and seen. But the essay has been taken as some kind of manifesto. Some have read it as an anti-black statement, some have read it as an anti-interracialist statement. All have reified the speaker and the essay to stand in for some position, usually one with which they disagree rather vehemently.* The Gay and Lesbian Literary Heritage *calls it "an exquisitely painful statement on colonial desire," which I suppose is some kind of compliment, though I think that in global terms I'm much more metropolitan than colonial.*

So, much to my surprise, it's become not just part of my personal history, but part of the discourse of black gay identity. I still believe that many of the things I say in the piece are true of many black gay men (or is it gay black men?), and that much of the negative response it has received is in the nature of anger at airing dirty laundry or of making people confront things they would rather ignore or deny. I stand by the envoi that the editor excised from the original publication: "I think that there is a difference between accepting oneself as a black person and identifying with black people as a group. I hope that my piece doesn't lend itself to interpretation as some sort of 'apology for being an oreo.' What I deplore in myself is my racism, not my lack of a 'black identity.' Frankly, I find the concept of 'black identity' a bit absurd. Then again, I find the notion of 'white identity' insane, and it has certainly proven the more dangerous. So."

The version of the essay presented here is somewhat revised from its original publication in In the Life, mostly by way of reincorporating material originally excised by me or Joseph Beam, the book's editor. I wouldn't attempt to recapture the state of mind in which I wrote the piece, and probably couldn't if I tried, which is doubtless a blessing, as it wasn't a very pleasant place to be.

I 'd like to speak of a young man of my acquaintance. All his friends call him Little Wing, but he flies rings around them all. That's not my line, of course. I'm just groping for the words to make him real to you, an objective correlative to give these aimless feelings some sense of shape. They have an object but no reason for existing; he's beautiful but I don't know him. His name is Pablo, he looks younger than he is. He lives in my neighborhood. All of this means nothing to you; it's everything to me. I want you to know how this comes about. His name could be anything, David or Ross or anyone. I could list his names but they're only words. Hugh. Shane. Arthur. Eric. I write down my desires to make them real, tokens or talismans. Today his name is Pablo. Little Wing, don't fly away. I set you down in words and keep you there. The way I keep you in desire, whatever your name this time.

Actually, Pablo's not really white; he's Hispanic. So it's okay; I'm making progress after all. (This is called irony.) That's a joke I tell myself, but no one laughs, especially me: I hated Puerto Ricans as a kid, they were the ones who beat me up most often. But Pablo has the cutest accent, and a wonderful little butt; he's no threat to me. I see him in clubs, I pass him on the street; he says hi. I saw him on the train and we had a nice little conversation. I make so much of these things. This boy's in love again. Somehow I never learn. That's a bad joke: another song about love. Its chorus: color me.

Call this a definition by example of the difficulty I find in expressing myself directly on a topic so fraught with dangers. The fears and the dangers are part of the topic. Quoting another obscure song, the soundtrack of my days, "My love wears forbidden colors." That's the burden of this essay, though only one among the burdens of my life. Words often fail me in my moments of greatest need, my accustomed glibness turns to stammering when confronted with the necessity of such intimate speech. It's easier this way, speaking on paper to an hypothesis of you, *hypocrite lecteur*. The danger is not to speak at all, to keep silence and thus deny my own existence. As Audre Lorde has written, my silence will not protect me. The things I have to say in this essay are not all things I would wish to say; they are certainly not things many would wish to hear, or if they do, they wish to hear them for the wrong reasons. But I want to be honest this once, if only for my own sake. Someone said the truth will set you free and I'd like to find out. But this is only an essay, an attempt at a self-definition with which I can live.

So here I am thinking about myself on paper, in the hope that some of my obsessions might fruitfully provoke a response (more than simple anger or disgust: nothing is ever simple) in a possible reader. "Myself" being in this context a twenty-two year old black gay man (how odd to think of myself as a "man": isn't it always the others who are *men*?) with a nearly exclusive attraction to white men. A black man who fears and sometimes loathes most other black men. A black man, also, afraid of white men and deeply resentful of their power over me, both sexual and social. A gay man afraid of men. Naturally concomitant is that I'm afraid of myself. Every fear is a desire. Every desire is a fear. That's a quote, but I won't tell you from whom.

The burden of my identity has always been the burden of not being white. Growing up, I was always, in my mind and in many of my social surrounds, the one who wasn't white; even now it is difficult to think of myself as "a black man," an identity not determined by lack. I live between worlds, to employ a cliché, more drawn to one than to the other but belonging to neither. Call me an individual by necessity. Too often my identity has been an absence, a list of the things I was not or a list of the things I should not be. I was the wrong one: wrong lips, wrong nose, wrong self. As a child I would go to sleep wishing that when I awoke I would be white. I am no longer a child, but that child has not died. And so I write. Writing makes things real but it also makes things not me; in that double gesture I become less imprisoned by the self I have written down. I can exorcise my ruling ghosts for as long as the words continue. In the silence, that is when the shades come crowding around, asking for love, asking for blood, asking to keep me in Hades surrounded by shadows of loss and desire, denial and self-hatred. So consider this essay my Sibyl, my psychopomp through Hades who keeps clear the path to the upper air.

Writing these words in this context, "Hades," "Sibyl," words which mean beauty to me, truth and nobility and achieved grace, I am reminded that in the opinions of many, black and white, these words should be alien to me, a language oppression has imposed upon me or withheld from me, representing the values of those who would see me disappear. Far from being my oppressors, these words have been my saviors. Nor are they any less mine than someone's whose ancestors, say, sacked Rome, or more likely slept through it all: more, in fact, because I understand and cherish them. There are those who would see this claim as a betrayal. There are those who would see this claim as a presumption. White racism says that all black people are the same, with no right to or understanding of these words. Too much of what I have seen of black society simply assumes the reverse, that these words are irrelevant to or destructive of "black culture", as if Western culture (to which black people have contributed mightily in this most Western of hemispheres) belonged exclusively to the melanin-deficient. The two attitudes mirror one another quite precisely.

The very language with which I write this, then, embodies a quandary. In order to choose or refuse to "be black," one must first have a concept of what it is to be black. None of those on offer have seemed to fit. This is a crux of the matter of this essay: to be a white person in this country is to be a person; to be black is to be another sort of thing. If one is lucky, it is to be another sort of person. But one can never take oneself for granted. Approached as an opportunity, this situation encourages one to construct an identity of one's own; but few such difficulties can be so approached in childhood, when one wants to know above all the answer to the question "Who am I?" If one is black, there is no dearth of chthonic voices to answer that question all too well. I've had since childhood notions, negative each one, of what it is to *seem* black: to look black, to talk black, to walk black, to dress black. Need I list the stigmata any further? For me, as a child, to be black came to mean to be those things, to do those things, to *suffer* those things. Contrary images seemed very far away: Martin Luther King was certainly no one *I* knew, and he was dead. The language of culture and education was not among those all-too-available semblances of blackness. I have shaped for myself a manner of appearing quite other than, but hardly free of, those baleful images.

If one didn't say those things, wear those things, if one didn't do things *that way*, then one would never be branded with that awful word: though of course one was. That word does not appear in this essay. Susan Sontag has noted that our manner of being *is* our manner of appearing; the acceptance I sought and seek still is by no means wholly external. The process of "acculturation" was not one of changing myself but one of claiming what I saw was mine; certainly what I saw around me in the various tenements and housing projects of my youth didn't belong to me. Nothing forced me to acquire culture, though much militated against that acquisition. I didn't realize until much later just how much an act of defiance and rebellion that simple claim was; I didn't realize that culture was a privilege to which I had no right. That willful ignorance was a species of salvation.

I sought to shed the baggage of history, to shed even the baggage I didn't know I carried. How eager I was to declare at the customs gate that separated the ghetto from the "larger" world that I had nothing to declare. I wanted to erase the past, erase the present, and live only in the future. It wasn't my past, after all: all those dead people. Things are different today. Yesterday don't matter if it's gone. The Rolling Stones sang that, but they were white. (To the best of my knowledge, they still are, and wealthy to boot.) The operative word, of course, is "if." William Faulkner, that closet Confederate apologist, wrote that "The past is never gone. It is not even past." I have always been an adherent of the philosophy of "as if," even more so of "if only." But black people don't read Hans Vaihinger, do they? They probably don't even read Faulkner. Black people are poor and uneducated and shiftless and poor (again) and *are never going to get anywhere.* I don't know where I have gone, but I don't live in the projects any more. So I couldn't be one of *them.* So I will behave *as if* I were not. Not that it ever mattered: everyone at my various private schools knew I was different, black and poor and weird on top of it (you would be too, if it happened to you). Everyone knew what I couldn't admit to myself. Don't talk about it and it will go away. "Don't look, it's ugly. It's a monster." The monster in my mind was always me.

Perhaps I have been too abstract. If so, it is only in self-defense: I'm remembering things I would prefer never to have known. Let me begin again, provide this time a context for my ramblings. What contextualizes more than history? What traps more irredeemably? I've learned something since I was a child.

I was born and raised in New York City, afraid of everything. ("It was a dark and stormy night . . ."). Specifically (yes, let us be as specific as possible), I was raised in the Bronx, not the South Bronx but close enough to be a "bad neighborhood." Whatever the neighborhood we found, it always turned out to be bad, full of the wrong sort of people, niggers and spics. (That's called segregation, I later found out.) I was raised by my mother, my father was an occasional negative mention and a "weekly" child support check every few months. Psychologists would have a field day. I identified with the Supremes' "Love Child" when it played on the radio, but my life didn't have a catchy chorus. Illegitimacy was the least of my problems: I longed for a father for years, and when I got one found that Cinderella had nothing on me in the matter of demented step-parents.

The overriding fact of our lives, that determined everything we did or did not do or longed to do, was poverty. Though we did our best to deny or transcend it (it is only those with no power who must rise above their circumstances), though my mother wrangled credit card shopping sprees and never-paid-for trips to Jamaica and Walt Disney World, weekends in Montreal and scholarships for me to the best private schools (at which I was asked to play Little Black Sambo in a third grade performance: I played Robinson Crusoe, shipwrecked as always), though she managed to spoil me to the point where I would throw tantrums when I had to wait until tomorrow to buy the record I wanted *today* (how little some things change), we were poor and we were black and all our efforts could not change those conditions, conditions which came to seem synonymous: as they statistically too often are.

My mother considered her life a failure and a disappointment and herself to be better than the circumstances into which she had been forced. She *was* better, and I was to redeem her failure, the prodigy who was both instrument and beneficiary of all her machinations. It is ironic that it was only her death when I was fourteen, a loss I am still learning properly how to mourn, which freed me from our entrapment. It is worse that I spent my life with her blaming her for that entrapment. For two years after her death I inhabited another trap: Macon, Georgia, site of one of the largest malls in the Southeast (or so they said), a hell of an altogether other sort. But this particular hell I didn't know didn't know me either: that is how Odysseus escaped the Cyclops. In Macon I was an anomaly, an unknowable quantity. No one among my Georgia relatives had ever been to college. They laughed at me because I read books and "talked funny"; I despised them because they were ignorant and insular. Reading, to them, was a "bad habit": you weren't having fun and you weren't making money. "Them books ever gonna make you any money?" Those books have, actually. Macon could not imprison me the way the Bronx might have; it wasn't my hell. For that much I am grateful. There is little else.

When I went to college I chose the most expensive school in the country, a tiny elite artistic colony nestled in the woods of a state whose black population may well have reached .05 percent now. I was one of six black students at Bennington College (admittedly, Bennington only *had* six hundred students). I was the brightest and most "promising" literature student in the college, the school poet, and everyone's friend (that is, I was friends with everyone at least briefly: it's that sort of place). After three years, the suffocating isolation and lack of sexual outlets began to drive me insane. (Life is unfortunately often made up of ironic juxtapositions.) Like most liberal institutions, Bennington College is enamored of talk and terrified of action. I was everyone's gay friend (and everyone had to have at least one) and yet could *do* nothing (or should I write, no *one*). Race was not an issue, or so minor an issue that one could feel it not to be; for that I loved the make-believe of a place I called home for three years. There was a certain merit to everyone's pretence that they didn't notice I was black. (I did mention something about appearing and being. . . .)

Growing up, I knew what black people were like (doesn't everyone, black and white, whatever they're willing to admit?), and I knew I wasn't one of them, I wouldn't let myself be. Black people were ignorant and they were criminals and they couldn't even stick together, not like those white people, sure not like those Puerto Ricans. There was one next door (a Puerto Rican, that is) who beat me up almost daily, whose family always lied for him: he was always at home watching TV at the exact moment he was bruising me. "Look at his face," they said when my mother confronted them, "it isn't even red." My mother once chased that boy around the block with a belt, a fat woman out of breath who'd never catch up with a laughing teenage spic. I was more humiliated than when he'd slapped me and torn up my book club package.

Black people were dirty and didn't comb their hair and had street fights and died young: the statistics proved it (and they still do). Worst of all, they were poor and they always would be. Too many people seemed to mistake me for one: the black kids who knocked my school books out of my hand when I got off the bus, the Italian kids up the street who threw vegetable crates on my head and called out "Hey chocolate milk!" because I was walking on their turf. Those kids were too young to be left at home alone.

Though I can recognize and righteously abhor the attitudes I took for granted as a child even while consoling myself that the kids at the Riverdale Country Day School hid my bookbag and tripped me on the athletic field (one of three) just because I was black and smarter than they were (a fact), those attitudes are still part of me, and part, I suspect, of many black people. I cannot ignore or deny them, though many people, white and black, tell me I must. There seems a consensus in this realm called "race" that if one simply ignores or denies things they will go away, or will never have existed at all, but in fact they simply fester. There was that little something about the truth, and some possibility of freedom, however remote.

II

I have spoken of myself of a black man, now let me speak of myself as a gay man; let me explore the connections between the two selves. I have spent years proudly and often militantly defining myself as a gay man; I am still tentatively moving toward equally proudly defining myself as a black man. The process of reconciling myself to each of my social identities has and has had much to do with how and to what extent those around me bring the two together and keep them separate. My feelings about men are too entangled with my feelings about white men, and my feelings about white men too entangled with my feelings about white people, and about black people, especially black men, for me to be very clear about their genealogies or their boundaries. How to determine how much is racial and how much is sexual when the two are so entwined that they are in practice identical? I cannot, either, separate any of the above feelings from my feelings about myself, about myself as a black person, or about myself as a black man: all three of them quite distinct to me. I was black before I was consciously sexual, but I was sexual long before I had the words for sex or race; and when did I become "I"? I read my childhood by the markings I have made on the map of the self I have become and am able to identify sunken mountain ranges I took for islands or random jutting rocks, but there are wilds of the interior I've not explored in years, vast wastes of which I can only affirm, "Here be monsters," as on medieval maps of Africa. There is so much I have conveniently forgotten. Freud called it repression, or so I've heard.

Is my desire for a beautiful man a desire to possess that ultimately validating prize, the white man; or is my desire for white men a desire to possess that ultimate validating prize, the beautiful man? How can I separate them when whiteness and beauty are equated in my society and in my mind, when my definition of one inevitably encompasses that of the other? We all absorb in different ways and differing intensities the images, of self and of other, and the distances between the two, on which our society so virulently insists. So I write about men, and most of them are white, and I write about white men, and most of them are beautiful. So I write about beautiful white men.

That my confusion mirrors and is mirrored by a confusion of American society in general and the gay male "community" in particular and with particular intensity makes it no less of a quagmire, exactly the reverse, for my confusion is thus assured of being both total and inescapable. In the gay "community" especially, being, having, and seeming (that is, appearing, and we are obsessed with appearances, of ourselves, of other men, of things, of ourselves and of other men as things) are the holy trinity, three essences with one substance, or perhaps, frighteningly, three substances with one essence. How much of wanting another man is the desire to be that man? So many gay men love not men but the idea of masculinity: their desire is not for any individual man but for maleness as an ideal, exactly that which defines them as other and lesser. This perhaps contributes to the promiscuity so many gay men pursue, because no particular individual can embody an ideal, or not for long, whereas that one (the one across the bar, the one you don't know yet) may well be everything you ever wanted, everything you ever needed, manhood itself. If one cannot be a real man, which by definition no homosexual is, then at least one can have a real man, though that's always problematic, since real men don't have sex with other men, certainly not with other real men. I think many gay men worship the power that oppresses them. I think, too, all sexual relations in our society are about power over another or the submission to the power of another. For a gay man, both roles are simultaneously available.

How much of wanting to be with another man is the desire to be seen with him? If I am seen with a beautiful man, not only am I thus one who can acquire a valuable prize, but I am by the same operation (as a man with a man having it both ways) transformed into such a prize myself, sought after and acquired by the man I am with. And of course if I in particular am seen with a beautiful man, a white man, then in my own mind and the minds of those around me, around us, I am thereby one worthy of beauty, of whiteness. By being seen with him, I am made an honorary white man so long as I am with him. Suddenly I am part of the community. Suddenly bouncers stop carding me. (I am not making this up.) So by being with him I have him and by being seen with him I manage almost to be him. Almost and not at all.

It's strange how much more willing white men become to approach me or be approached by me once they have seen me with another white man: if I like one I must of course like them all. The reverse is true as well. Often when I have once seen a white man with a black man, that white man becomes more attractive to me, simply because he has thus entered the realm of the possibly available: if he likes one he must of course like them all. Unfortunately, I am not black enough for some; nothing cools the ardor of some white men "attracted" to black men more quickly than a large vocabulary. Then again, this is Boston; I have eyes. The great majority of the black men I see in the

clubs are with white men, and far too many of the white men in the
clubs look at me as if to say, "I couldn't sleep with you. You're black."
Or they desire me merely because I am black (surely I have a large
penis, don't we all?), reject me because I'm not black enough. The
circle is vicious indeed, and the stereotypes are not all on one side. To
the same degree that I am seen as a "black man" and certain assumptions are made thereby, I see those men as "white men" and make a
number of similar if opposing assumptions.

And for myself, I sometimes wonder where my experience as an
individual and my experience as a black man, a black person in a
country the underside of whose consciousness I am, a country that
wishes me similarly to vanish from sight, from thought, begin and
end: where are the boundaries between my personal history and my
racial history? To what degree am I a person at all to the white people
with whom I deal (that is, to the vast majority of the people with
whom I interact) and to what degree am I "a black"? (The transformation of adjective into noun speaks volumes in itself.) How accu-
rately can I separate the two in my own mind?

There are the comments about how my dancing must come naturally to me because of my "tan," about how it really is true that
black people dance better than white. I used to be insulted; now I
take them, cautiously, as the compliments (I presume) they are
intended to be, whatever the subconscious assumptions underlying
them. One takes one's sustenance where one can. And how much of
my desire to emulate the hip club boys, to have just the right shoes
and just the right jeans, is a desire to be like those boys in a more
unattainable way? Only then, after all, will my bangs fall just so, and
blond, over my forehead. I want to be just like those boys, but exercise can't give my stomach muscles that particular tone. Perhaps
that's why I can never be satisfied with my clothes, my records, my
haircut: no matter how numerous and cool my shirts, they will never
change my image quite enough. By now I can't tell the difference

between what I want to own and what I want to become by means of it.

I have written that many gay men are in love with the image and idea of manhood; too often I have been in love with the image and idea of white manhood, which is everything I am not and want to be, and if I cannot be that, I can at least have that, if only for the night, if only for the week or the month: just as, for many gay men, if they cannot be men they can at least have one, one who is looking for exactly the same thing. But my dream never seeks me out; that is also a prerequisite. Like Morrissey, I want the one that I can't have. Those beautiful men are inaccessible, and if they are not then I make them so by assuming them so. I want them but I fear their touch. "Only the very young and the very beautiful can afford to be so aloof," as Tom Robinson sings: nothing to do with any actual man, white or black.

It still comes as a surprise that one of my blond ideals might not be simply cruel or shallow (though many are those things, assuredly) but unintelligent, even that he might not dance well. As Linda Gregg writes in her poem "Growing Silent," "I thought beauty lived in people like a dream/you could keep. But the dreams were fancies or cheats/smart for seduction. That lying I understood/but not the slightness. It was nothing. . . ." I recall some time ago the epiphany of realizing that I am almost invariably more intelligent and interesting than whatever obscure object of desire I am currently longing to pursue. One had so automatically endowed beauty with all possible virtues, one had so easily assumed that beauty implied virtue, that beauty was a virtue, when all it meant was that this boy had clear skin and a good hairdresser. Imagine: all my efforts to impress the beau ideal with my wit and intelligence fail not due to my inadequacies but because he doesn't understand what I'm talking about. That my idol has feet of clay is little consolation: like most revelations. The pain remains quite real, the pang of loss for what I have never had; I am addicted to it. Out of that pain comes my best poetry. My one great subject is my suffering for unrequited desire, "the chivalrous service of love to the appearance," which can never be consummated. Someone else's words again, another pop song: "Instead of finding out that you and I are friends, just keep on dancing, dancing till this music ends. I need another fantasy." I make my approaches, helplessly hoping but never sure for what. Usually I just stand and stare. I'd like just once to be the one to say "No."

Out of that pain also comes intense rage. I recall waiting for the subway one night and seeing one of the beautiful men I dote upon. I'd danced with him, we'd spoken, "polite meaningless words." That night he chose not to recognize me. I recall hating him for being so handsome and so white, so financially and socially comfortable, so confident in his knowledge that he matters in this world. How dare he be so self-assured, so secure in his attractiveness and his ability to provoke and deny desire, taking for granted that he belongs here and the world is his? What did he have that could place him above me: except his beauty and white skin? I'd seen him; he'd seen me. But he was free to ignore my existence, while I could never ignore his. How dare he have such power over me? I recall wanting to see him die slowly and painfully, wanting to see that beautiful face ruined, those expensive clothes in rags. The rage passed but it has not gone away.

Can that rage be liberating, that I should hate him for being white instead of hating myself for not being so pure? That beautiful white boy may not personally own the world, but his kind does, after all, and he reaps the rewards. It's not his fault it's my ruined life. My desire was always also a desire to violate.

Too often the rage is turned against myself, not only for not being what I want but for wanting what I want at all. The curse of self-consciousness: that I should hate myself for hating myself, that I should want to cease to be the person who wants to cease to be me.

I have the clothes now, and the shoes, the attitude and the right way to dance. But I will never have that honey-gold skin nor those green eyes, my hair will never fall into my eyes with such insouciance.

I don't mean to imply that I have no black friends (my best friend all through high school was black, we were alike in every way but sexuality), or even that I don't find individual black men attractive. It happens more and more; I have crushes on black men now. I met a man at the Twelve Seventy; I almost went home with him. But something stopped me. . . .

Among the black men, it's the different ones I notice (why is it that, to me, black people are always them?): the ones who remind me of myself. There's one boy who's always at Buddies; he works at Benetton. He's like me, proving himself white enough to be okay, vying for some white man's attention, for all the white men's attention. He's better at it than I, more poised and self-assured. He probably comes from money. He's comfortable with his role; he gets the attention he seeks (I've seen some of his boyfriends . . .). The trendy black boys always seem to do it just a bit better than the pretty white boys. They should; they've been practicing. Practicing and watching. I know. Of course, the boy I'm writing about is the most aloof of all. Don't blow my cool. Don't blow my cover. Would I sleep with him if I could? He's so pretty. . . .

I say to myself that if I had a lover, some handsome literate blond named Troy or some beautiful Italian painter named Gaetan with whom I'd have everything in common, everything but that, I could be happy. Happy and someone else, free from the burden of being myself, black but no longer having to suffer for it, never having had to suffer for it. I could step up and claim my prize, or rather he'd step up and claim me, choose me and make me real at last, like the hand of God picking out the chosen who live in grace. When the Jews were in Egypt the saving mark was drawn in blood.

I've dreamed of finally being "myself," relieved of the baggage of my history as a member of an oppressed caste, relieved of my too-frequent self-despisal by the beloved's blond approbation. "It has often been my dream to live with one who wasn't there": so Neil Young sings. I've dreamed of stepping out of history: the myth of romantic love is one name for that. But without my history I wouldn't need my blond knight, and how could I live without him? "This is not America," David Bowie sings, but how would he know? He's just a foreigner, like me. The "me" I'd like to be is a product of history (my history and the history that owns me) in all particulars. So I can't live in that other realm of freedom. Freedom's just another word for being nothing, and too often I'm already that.

I read a very moving response to a question in The Hite Report on Male Sexuality, of all places, a response in the section on gay men: "I used to call it 'love' when I was feeling pathologically afraid of and inferior to another person. Now I call it love when I feel free and comfortable to be myself with another person, and the emotion is joy instead of fear." I have yet to reach that point, though I hardly spend my days in sackcloth and ashes. It is still difficult for me to enter the sexual arena with a sense of myself as equal to those I desire (though in many other arenas I feel, if anything, superior: compensation comes in many forms). It's still hard to imagine that someone of whom I want and need something might want, might need, something of me: hard to realize that all he might have to offer is his body.

The Special AKA sing, "If you have a racist friend, now is the time for your friendship to end." I have a friend like that, a friend I call desire. Sometimes I don't know where he ends and I begin. Sometimes I wish I could forget his name, but it sounds too much like mine.

19 A POEM ABOUT KENNY/PORTRAIT OF A HARD ROCK (1986)

Jerry Thompson

he was 19 thousand
miles away from
human decency

teenaged motherfucker
wit no wallet
no pocket to sock it to
the chick across the street

five dollars was 'nuff
to get him through the night
I sat 'n cried/figured
that was alright

cuz anything other
than a fuck from
this monster would not
satisfy my drive for heat!

only 19 years older than
the president of this
trigger tween my legs

street niggah/hard rockin roller
from an era of fools
destined for
early deaths
of sexual confusion

'n I sat up waitin for his return
wit my 5 bucks

waitin for the party starter
the friday night flight
through his load
'n my eclipse

waitin for the next
mornin to see
if he'll always be a fantasy
for those who dream to kill

waitin for his burnin touch
'gainst this moon and
this fire
tween my altered disgust
for three legged criminals

THE TROUBLE I'VE SEEN (1987)

Gil Gerald

Although Bayard Rustin, a black gay man, had been the principal organizer of the 1963 March on Washington for Jobs and Freedom, there was considerable controversy surrounding an open gay or lesbian speaker at the twentieth anniversary march celebrating that historic event.

I t all began quite innocently, on April 16, 1983, when I asked the board of directors of the National Coalition of Black Gays, as NCBLG was then called, to endorse, among other things, the March being planned to celebrate the 20th anniversary of the famous 1963 civil rights march to the nation's capital. NCBG was more preoccupied with survival, as it, unfortunately, has always been, and the issue of endorsing a demonstration in Washington was secondary to some of the other issues being considered—such as how the leadership of NCBG might he restructured. The motion for endorsement was unanimously accepted without controversy.

This development was in itself a small victory, because it provided me, as the new acting executive director, an agenda item to carry out that should not have required a great deal of effort. Our hope was to simply get our name on a list of endorsing organizations on the literature promoting the March. We had no illusions that we were an organization capable of delivering great hordes of Black, openly Gay and Lesbian people on the day of the March.

On April 29, Chris Cothran, then cochair of NCBG, sent a press release announcing the actions of the board, which included the endorsement of the March. This action prompted other individuals and organizations in the Lesbian and Gay community to contact us about their concerns. At the time no other national Lesbian or Gay organization had yet endorsed the event. To say the least, we were proud to be the first, and felt that it was appropriate because we were a Black organization.

A QUESTION OF GAY AND LESBIAN PARTICIPATION

In early May, Frank C. Branchini, a staffer at the now defunct Gay Rights National Lobby (GRNL), and a member of the Society of Friends, informed me that there were problems associated with Lesbian and Gay participation in the planning and program for the March—that we were simply not wanted. For the first time, he informed me of the charge that our "pre-eminent" D.C. Congressional Delegate, Walter Fauntroy, had compared Lesbian and Gay rights to "penguin" rights. According to Branchiniand future press accounts, Michelle Guimarin, a member of the Mobilization for Survival, had suggested at a march organizing meeting that the National Gay Task Force (NGTF) be placed on the national steering committee of the March organization. Fauntroy, who was the chair of the administrative committee of the March, is said to have replied to her suggestion by stating, off-handedly, that Gay rights were as extraneous to the theme of "Jobs Peace and Freedom" as were "penguin rights." If true, this would not have been the first time that he had exhibited his homophobia. I found the statement certainly inappropriate to come from persons who were organizers of this march and who had dubbed themselves the "Coalition of Conscience."

Branchini was adamant about the charges against Fauntroy and mailed me copies of his correspondence to the Congressman; his correspondence to Reverend Ernest Gibson, head of the local D.C.

Coalition of Conscience; and his correspondence to Asia Bennett, executive director of the American Friends Service Committee (AFSC) and a member of the national steering committee of the March. I decided to check things out for myself.

Without hesitation I called the March office and got in contact with Donna Brazile, March coordinator. This was the beginning of a working—and often warring—relationship I would develop with this hardworking and complex woman who, in the future would be the Rainbow Coordinator of the Jackson presidential campaign, and who would also be a key coordinator of the Hands Across America effort.

Brazile assured me that the Gay community was welcome and that we should address our endorsement to Congressman Fauntroy. She promised that the name of NCBG would appear on the next edition of the March promotional literature. She could not understand why other national Gay or Lesbian organizations had not endorsed the March, including NGTF. Sure enough, on May 16, Brazile sent an acknowledgement of our endorsement, and, while not doubting the possibility of Fauntroy having made the alleged remarks, I felt that the issue of NGTF's obtaining a seat on the Steering Committee would have to be resolved by the Task Force. Certainly, to my thinking, NGTF would have to begin by first indicating their endorsement of the March.

The issue remained relatively dormant until sometime in June when we began to make inquiries about where the Lesbian and Gay contingent would be placed in the March and who would speak on behalf of the Lesbian and Gay community. An understanding had developed between NGTF, which by then had communicated its endorsement, that NCBG should take the leadership in working with the Coalition of Conscience on the issue of a Lesbian or Gay speaker. I asked Ray Melrose, who I had deputized to represent the organization when I was not available, and Jeff Levi, Washington representative of NGTF, to accompany me to see Donna Brazile, and present our requests and suggestions for a place on the program.

Melrose and I arrived before Levi, and we both reacted in the same way to Brazile. She was the embodiment of a woman you wouldn't want to mess with. She had an authoritative manner besides being physically large and having a deep voice. I liked this aspect of her style, but I would not remain enamored during the weeks and months to come. Brazile, in her assuring way, told us not to worry and to simply produce a list of possible speakers, and she would be more effective than we could ever be in getting the Coalition of Conscience to go along with the proposal for a speaker. Among some of the suggestions for speakers we discussed that day were Audre Lorde, James Baldwin, Barbara Smith, and Gwen Rogers. It was agreed that I would contact the prospective speakers and produce the suggested list for Brazile in a week's time.

We produced the list even though some of the names on it were just impossible to contact. I recall the effort to contact James Baldwin as being one of the more frustrating. Baldwin's name was high on the list, because he seemed to be perhaps the one spokesperson the Coalition of Conscience would most recognize, and because they would remember that he had been at the first march in 1963. Numerous conversations with his brother in New York, and telegrams to him in France, produced not even the slightest acknowledgement from Baldwin. Audre Lorde was ultimately our best choice for many reasons.

Having complied with our end of the bargain, I began to call Brazile regularly to inquire about the progress she was making towards convincing the March leadership to include a Gay or Lesbian speaker. It became obvious that she was beginning to ignore and avoid my calls. I began to communicate to her by leaving messages with others in the March office. By this time, others in the

D.C. community were becoming extremely concerned about the turn of events and began to take action themselves.

THE COUNTDOWN: AUGUST 12

Around August 12, D.C. activist Phil Pannell and D.C Coalition of Black Gay Men and Women members George Gellinger, Jr. and Lawrence Washington went to the final meeting of the D.C. Coalition of Conscience held at the Mt. Zion Baptist Church, which has Rev. Gibson as its pastor. Phil Pannell, speaking for the delegation representing D.C. s Black Gay community, informed the Coalition of the activities of the Gay community in support of the March and introduced a motion calling on the local chapter of the organization to request that the national organization reverse its decision to not include Lesbian and Gay speakers at the March rally. The crowd in the room remained silent for a long ten seconds that caused Washington to wonder about confronting them verbally about their homophobia. But suddenly, surprising the three, the group broke out into spontaneous, approving applause. Gibson promised to personally advocate the issue before the national group. To this date it is not clear whether or not he did in fact follow through with this promise.

Nationally, Ginny Apuzzo executive director of NGTF, and myself were beginning to apply pressure directly to presumably progressive members of the national steering committee of the Coalition of Conscience. She contacted Judy Goldsmith, President of the National Organization for Women (NOW), and I worked on Asia Bennett, executive director of AFSC. Apuzzo had an interesting confrontation with Goldsmith that she shared with me. Apuzzo, who has a well-known temper, made it clear to Goldsmith that she, as head of the NGTF, deserved to be treated with more deference than she was getting and that it was appropriate for NOW to champion the issue of Gay and Lesbian participation in the program for the March and rally. It was not until Apuzzo and I pressured this organization that it really expressed any concern with this matter. The result of this and other exchanges was that NOW and AFSC were actually considering pulling out of the Coalition of Conscience and withdrawing their support if an agreement was not reached with the Lesbian and Gay community.

AUGUST 15: A DECLARATION OF WAR

With a little more than a week left, around the August 15, I called the March office, for the last time, to inquire about whether a decision to schedule a Lesbian or Gay speaker had been made. Unable to speak to Brazille, I requested that she be informed that I had "declared war" on the Coalition of Conscience. The voice at the other end of the phone simply replied, "fine."

At that time, in 1983, I was working as an architect at the Georgetown firm of Arthur Cotton Moore. We were on a deadline to complete a design submission for the huge Washington Harbour project. Oblivious to the pressure and time constraints created by this project, I began to simply "work" the phone like a maniac on the issue of the March. There was hardly anyone who could potentially wield influence with the March organization that I did not attempt to contact. Oddly enough, my fellow workers did not express any annoyance with me. They seemed somewhat amused and impressed when the likes of Congressman Julian Dixon, then Chairman of the Congressional Black Caucus, personally returned my phone calls. They were even more intrigued when TV crews began calling at the office to interview me. Stacy, a female colleague, remarked that she felt as if she "was on a movie set." I don't think in this period I ever considered the issue of losing the battle.

AUGUST 19: BATTLING IN THE OPEN

I sent mailgrams to every national Lesbian and Gay organization, urging them to get their members to flood the Congressman's office with mail. I sent carefully drafted mailgrams to Coretta Scott King, widow of the slain civil rights leader; to Joseph Lowery, president of the Southern Christian Leadership Conference (SCLC); to Benjamin Hooks, executive director of the National Association for the Advancement of Colored People (NAACP); and Congressman Fauntroy. By Friday, August 19, the fight was out in the open. *The Washington Blade*, D.C.'s Gay weekly, reported on that day that at least six national Lesbian and Gay organizations had become involved in urging the Coalition of Conscience to reverse itself.

As is typical in Washington, work was also going on behind the scenes. Cliff Roberson, a member of the D.C. Coalition of Black Gay Men and Women and a Ward 5 coordinator in the Mayor's Office of Community Services, even provided the staff of Congressman Fauntroy with ominous warning to "move, because a Mack truck is coming your way." D.C. School Board President and pastor of All Souls Unitarian Church, Rev. David Eaton, and Bill Lucy of the Coalition of Black Trade Unionists, were contacted and lobbied by Vic Basile of the Human Rights Campaign Fund (HRCF)and Bill Bogan of the Gertrude Stein Democratic Club.

AUGUST 22 AND 23: THE CONTROVERSY CONTINUES

By Monday August 22 and Tuesday August 23, the two major D.C. papers, *The Washington Post* and *The Washington Times* both carried stories about the controversy. They reported that over the weekend, Congressman Fauntroy had characterized abortion and Gay rights as too "divisive" to be included in the March program. Of interest to historians should be the role played here by a Black Gay reporter in getting the word out in print. Isaiah Poole, a member of Faith Temple, the D.C.-based church with a special ministry to the Third World Lesbian Gay community, was the first to report the controversy in a major newspaper—*The Washington Times*. Needless to say, when Channel 9 News and Cable News Network came to interview me that week, I was incensed enough to characterize Fauntroy over the air as a typical Black preacher who insists that we, Black Lesbians and Gays, "sit in the pews, sing in the choir, but not dare speak our name."

By Tuesday night, August 23, I was desperate. There was no reason for me to be, since I had assurances from people I deeply cared about and respected that, by just raising the issue, we had accomplished a great deal. Most reassuring of all were Audre Lorde and Barbara Smith whom I had been consulting on a daily basis, giving them a blow-by-blow description of the progress we were making. Lorde's voice is always as soothing to me as the voice of my mother. On more than one occasion, she assured me that simply getting the name of NCBG on the March literature was a sign of significant progress.

Late that Tuesday night I called Ray Melrose, my closest confidant in D.C., and discussed with him and Gary Walker what might be done. Members of the D.C. Black Gay community began calling me to indicate their impatience over the lack of progress I was making. On the other side, Brazile alleged she was getting threats from individuals in the Black Gay community who viewed her as an obstacle to a Gay speaker at the March rally as much as Congessman Fauntroy. Walker, a veteran of the civil rights marches and demonstrations of the 60s, along with Melrose, decided that a sit-in at the offices of Congressman Fauntroy would be appropriate. Melrose began to recruit individuals for the demonstration before retiring that evening. Phil Pannell volunteered to contact the media.

August 24: The Sit-in

On Wednesday morning cracks began to appear in the walls of the Coalition of Conscience. *The Washington Times* reported that Congressman Fauntroy "angrily" denied ever making the anti-Gay, "penguin" remark. Brazile called me for the first time since my "declaration of war" to see if I would be available for a telephone conference call with the March leaders. I immediately called Melrose and told him to go ahead with the sit-in, but I had to tell him that the conference call would take precedence over any understanding the sit-in group might reach with Fauntroy because I was ultimately responsible for NCBG's decisions in the matter and could not be available both at the sit-in and for the conference call.

After formulating a list of demands for the conference call and discussing them with Ginny Apuzzo, I went home from work to wait for the call and keep up with the progress of the sit-in. Calls to attorneys Jim Mercer and Susan Silber assured me that they would be available to take care of any legal assistance Melrose and the rest of the demonstrators might require. Although I was very worried about the outcome of the sit-in, I had to discourage any incoming calls so as to keep the lines free for the conference call.

The sit-in had begun at about 4:30 p.m. when the four, Melvin Boozer, Ray Melrose, Phil Pannell, and Gary Walker, walked in, with Melrose as the spokesperson, and asked to see the Congressman. Julius Hobson, Jr., Fauntroy's assistant, indicated that the Congressman was across town and would not be available. Melrose suggested that the Congressman be contacted because the four of them would not leave until they got to see him. Hobson called the police, who, upon arrival, asked the four to leave or face arrest on charges of illegal entry. All four were arrested after the police threatened the news reporters present with arrest if they did not also vacate the premises. Lark McCarthy of Channel 7 News, inquired of the Capitol Police, before leaving the scene as ordered, whether the police intended for the press to not view the brutality they might be going to mete out.

THE CONFERENCE CALL

After what seemed like an interminable period, at 12:30 a.m., the conference call was initiated by Donna Brazile who asked me to remain on the line until the rest of the parties were connected. By this time the demonstration in Congressman Fauntroy's Capitol Hill office had ended, but no one, including Lou Chibaro, a reporter for the *The Washington Blade,* had an exact fix as to where the police had taken the demonstrators. One by one, the participants of the conference call acknowledged their presence on the line. The roll call determined that Walter Fauntroy, Coretta Scott King, Joseph Lowery, Benjamin Hooks, Donna Brazile, Barbara Williams-Skinner, Judy Goldsmith and Virginia Apuzzo, among others were on the line. I remember wondering where Jesse Jackson might be! I had clearly expected him to be on the line as well. The conversation began with a lot of small talk which clearly established the warmth and affection that was shared among these people. Hooks, Lowery, and King joked about past incidents in their lives as activists—events I was not privy to. When it came time for me to speak, I tried very carefully to convey my indignation without being disrespectful. It felt ironic that I, a beneficiary of their struggles with racism in the 50s and 60s, should now be attempting to teach them something about oppression and civil rights. My voice cracked when I tried to convey my feelings about the devastation that AIDS was already having on the Black Gay community. Someone would comment later that Apuzzo and I had crammed ten years of the Gay movement into that two hour conference call. I was left with the clear impression that King was concerned mostly about the threatened pull-outs from the March and with keeping the Coalition of Conscience together. She spoke openly about the conservatism among the Black clergy and expressed concerns about whether the time was right to deal with the Lesbian and Gay issue. Ginny Apuzzo countered with quotations from Dr. Martin Luther King, Jr.'s *Letter From A Birmingham Jail.*

The person who seemed to be most comfortable with the discussion was Dr. Joseph Lowery. But they all agreed that at this late date it would be impossible logisticaly for the Coalition of Conscience to endorse the Gay Rights Bill or to allow time for another major address as had been promised by individuals such as Harry Belafonte or Jesse Jackson. They did agree, however, to schedule a Lesbian and Gay speaker in the portion of the program called a "Litany of Commitment" and to not place the Lesbian and Gay delegation at the end of the March as had been rumored that they planned to do. In response to our demand for an endorsement of the National Gay Rights Bill, they offered to call a press conference on Friday at 11:00 a.m. to announce their individual support for the Bill. Apuzzo and I were left with the distinct impression that we had moved them forward on the Lesbian and Gay issue over the course of the two hour conference call.

A DIFFICULT DECISION

It was solely left up to me as the head of NCBG, to decide whether the Gay community would accept these terms. Apuzzo assured me that NGTF would respect and abide by my decision. The pressure I felt for the next nine hours to make this decision was intense. In order to put a major press conference together, the March organization claimed to need 24 hours, and I would have to render my decision by 11:00 a.m., Thursday morning. Audre Lorde would also have to be notified so she could begin her trek down from Maine. I decided to skip work and stay at home. Patricia Moore, a business partner, insisted that I not worry about the tasks at the office until Monday when the weekend events would have ended.

I began to place calls all over the nation, and D.C. Gay community reactions were mixed. I consulted Melvin Boozer, Ray Melrose, Dr. James Tinney, Billy Jones, Louis Hughes, Audre Lorde, and many others. Some felt we could pressure the Coalition of Conscience for more, while others felt we had extracted as much as were likely to get. The long distance telephone bill I accumulated that morning would go unpaid for years, and I would never get reimbursed for the calls.

During a conversation with Vic Basile, executive director of the Human Rights Campaign Fund, still trying to come to a decision, I broke down in tears from exhaustion and overwrought emotions and did so again during a call from George Bellinger, Jr., who came right over to comfort me. I tried to get Basile, who had worked in the labor movement, to give me some clue as to how in a conference call such as the one that had just taken place one could determine if more concessions could have been made without the benefit of being able to study the facial reactions on the other side of the "bargaining table." At about 11:00 a.m., I decided to communicate our acceptance of the terms of the agreement as worked out during the conference call. It had become evident to me that I would have to make the decision myself and face the music.

And face the music I did, almost instantaneously. That evening, by phone, I was bombarded by charges of having sold out. Phil Pannell felt that the agreement was not worth the bruises from the handcuffs he had worn the night before. Pannell's biggest objection was the implication that we needed to have our cause validated by civil rights leaders at a press conference. He communicated his disgust in no uncertain terms and threatened to disrupt the press conference by both denouncing me and King before the cameras. At one point I came pretty close to cancelling the whole thing when the

Mayor's office could not assure me that they could prevent such a disruption. When I finally got in touch with Audre Lorde and told her of the concerns the March organizing committee had regarding the need to have her remarks edited by a "poet" who was supposedly coordinating all the statements for the Litany of Commitment, she quite appropriately rebuked, "I don't read, do you understand?" It was clear to me then that my battles with the Coalition of Conscience were not over, and I certainly did not know how my phone bills or Lorde's honorarium would be paid. These concerns, however, were neither embraced by those who disagreed with my decision nor by those who hailed the outcome of the events.

THE PRESS CONFERENCE

NGTF and NOW decided to take responsibility for finding a space for the press conference during which the civil rights leaders would announce their support of the Gay Rights Bill and for issuing the press release and contacting the press by phone. Thanks to that effort I did not have to concern myself about those details.

For some people still unresolved was the issue of who should speak for the Lesbian and Gay community at the press conference. Those who felt I had sold out were not comfortable with me, and there were others who objected to Apuzzo. One dynamic which did not play itself out gracefully was the interest of the Gay Rights National Lobby (GRNL) in being at the podium since it was the Gay Rights Bill that was being endorsed and they were the organization responsible for moving it forward in the Congress. But at that time GRNL and NGTF were at the height of their turf battles.

Carlene Cheatam, with the D.C. Coalition of Black Gay Men and Women, finally called me with some good advice. "Disconnect the phone and get a good night's rest," she said. I did this, even though

I was concerned about what I would say at the press conference in the morning.

I got up early, wrote my speech, got dressed, and accepted Jeff Levi's offer to take my handwritten press statement and prepare a typed final draft using the word processor at NGTF. This arrangement would also provide me with a quiet space away from the phones at home. After Apuzzo arrived we went downtown to the Mayor's Conference Room for the press conference.

We were led to a room adjoining the Mayor's office to wait until all the press conference participants arrived. Slowly, one by one, the stalwarts of the civil rights movement (and the participants of the conference call of the two nights earlier) began to walk in. I recognized them and felt a little more discomfort than they possibly could have felt, since this was the first press conference I had ever addressed. When all but Coretta Scott King had arrived, we were led to the conference room where 11 TV cameras pointed at us as we stood behind a lectern with what appeared to be a billion, snake-like microphones.

Joseph Lowery introduced the panel of speakers and then quite matter-of-factly stated that they were all there—major civil rights leaders—to indicate their personal support for the Gay Rights Bill. One of his phrases is particularly memorable. He said, "Twenty years ago we marched, and one year later, the 1964 Civil Rights Act was passed. It is now time to amend that act to extend its protections to Lesbians and Gay men."

Lowery was followed by Judy Goldsmith, Ginny Apuzzo, and myself. After remarks from Rev. Cecil Williams of Glide Memorial in San Francisco indicating his support as a pastor of a Black church with a large Gay membership, a hush descended on the room with anticipation that King was about to arrive. Sure enough, she walked in and received spontaneous applause. With hesitation, though looking very tired, King proceeded to explain her position of support for amending the 1964 Civil Rights Act to guarantee civil rights protections for Lesbians and Gays. Unfortunately, her tired state became obvious when in response to a reporter's question, she asserted the rights that even the Klu Klux Klan enjoy under the constitution. Fortunately, no one pursued this line of her thinking.

After the press conference a number of us went over to have lunch at the Washington Hotel, and Ray Melrose walked me home where I immediately collapsed in from of the TV. A phone conversation with Pannell, who called shortly after I arrived home, seemed to iron out some of the differences we had the previous evening. Everything I could do was now accomplished. My only remaining responsibility would be to show up at the March—to walk behind the 16 foot banner NCBG had specially commissioned for the event.

TOWARD A LIVABLE FUTURE

Saturday, August 27, was a hot day and I truly felt relieved of the burden I had carried the previous three days. *The Washington Post* printed the program for the day's events, and Audre Lorde was on the program as the representative of the Lesbian and Gay community. Audre Lorde, after some difficulty with March officials who, because of her lack of credentials, would not believe her claim that she should be allowed into the stage area, made her now famous speech late in the afternoon. An article in *The Washington Post* on that day would also point out that in 1963, it was women who were almost left out, and that today, 20 years later, it was the Gay and Lesbian community who March organizers were trying to "placate."

Culminating five months of efforts, from the steps of the Lincoln Memorial where Martin Luther King. Jr., twenty years earlier, had announced his "Dream," Audre Lorde spoke these words of challenge: *"I am Audre Lorde, speaking for the National Coalition of Black Gays. Today's march openly joins the Black civil rights movement and the Gay civil rights movement in the struggles we have always shared, the struggles for jobs, for health, for peace, and for freedom. We marched in 1963 with Dr. Martin Luther King, and dared to dream that freedom would include us, because not one of us is free to choose the terms of our living until all of us are free to choose the terms of our living. Today the Black civil rights movement has pledged its support for Gay civil rights legislation. Today we march, Lesbians and Gay men and our children, standing in our own names together with all our struggling sisters and brothers here and around the world—in the Middle East, in Central America, in the Caribbean and South Africa, sharing our commitment to work for a joint livable future. We know we do not have to become copies of each other in order to be able to work together. We know that when we join hands across the table of our difference, our diversity gives us great power. When we can arm ourselves with the strength and vision from all of our diverse communities then we will in truth all be free at last."*

OTHER COUNTRIES: THE IMPORTANCE OF DIFFERENCE (1987)

Daniel Garrett

A s I sit down to write this, I know already that it will not be the work I had initially imagined, for that work would be much more ambitious, scholarly, and projective; this, instead, will be the simple statement of concerns and questions I have as a Black Gay writer. As a writer, I must examine constantly facts which as a citizen I am not supposed to see or acknowledge having seen. I must ask: Why is it necessary to malign a man because his skin or culture is different? What is terrible and terrifying about one man touching another? As a writer, I must ask: What are the myths and rituals which strengthen and weaken individuals, communities?

I am emboldened to write this by the memory of the writers and work that have gone before me. They strengthen *this* individual. I remember reading W.E.B. DuBois, the most important Black intellectual in African-American history, a man who recognized the importance of the movement of both mind and matter in the quest for liberation. I remember reading DuBois briefly discuss a colleague who had been homosexual, and how exposure of this fact proved scandalous, costing the man his employment.* DuBois said that, at the time, he had not recognized the significance, the tragedy of this event, and he regretted it later.† I remember reading Alain Locke's essay on values, his discussion of how all philosophies are

---

* Augustus Dill, Business Editor of *The Crisis*.
† *The Autobiography of W.E.B. DuBois*, ed. Herbert Aptheker (NY: International Publishers, 1982), 282.

products of time and place, how emotion and thought influence values.‡ I remember Locke being one of the principal sources of the famed Harlem Renaissance, as he was a philosopher, editor, professor, writer who knew and supported various Black talents, many of whom, like him, were homosexual, though none but for Bruce Nugent expressed this in his work. I remember all the books by James Baldwin, who writes about interracial, heterosexual and homosexual relationships as if they really occur in the world as natural facts, and they do. Since Mr. Baldwin, there have been others; Samuel Delany, the well-respected science fiction writer; the Blackheart Collective; Joseph Beam, writer and editor; Essex Hemphill, poet and performance artist; and others, men who have written about what it's like to be Black and Gay.

For years the Black Gay male community en masse seemed to lag behind the feminist community, which has raised questions about gender and how it affects relationships, identity, and social roles. In New York, there seemed to be a number of closeted groups but not many public groups. In the early eighties, the writers' group Blackheart was begun, and managed to produce three journal issues. Its demise was decided by Isaac Jackson, the managing editor, who no longer wanted to be publicly involved in Black Gay literature and politics. He had maintained the books, supervised the editing and production process. The finality of his decision had as its context/precedence the fact that his authority was seldom called into question during the time he acted as leader. The spectre of Isaac Jackson would haunt subsequent organizing efforts, with questions of autonomy of leadership and accountability.

There was discussion among the remaining editors (including me) about starting a new publication, but nothing happened. There

‡ Alain Locke, "Values and Imperatives" [1935], in Leonard Harris, ed., *Philosophy Born of Struggle: Anthology of Afro-American Philosophy from 1917* (Dubuque: Kendall/Hunt Pub. Co., 1983), 21-38.

were differences in philosophy and personality which did not facilitate the process.

Inspired by the kind of critical, creative dialogue which exists in the feminist community, and by the words of James Baldwin, I decided to begin a writing workshop I called Other Countries. I sent flyers around which stated:

In *Just Above My Head*, James Baldwin said, "Our history is each other. That is our only guide. One thing is absolutely certain: one can repudiate or despise no one's history without repudiating and despising one's own. Perhaps that is what the gospel singer is singing."[1] Well, in both song and literature there are many questions which have not been asked or answered about black men who want to be friends, lovers, or comrades in struggle. There are many questions about art, love, and politics that have not been addressed. What of ethics and honesty between such men? Is there anything besides oppression that we have in common, any qualities which are personally or socially valuable that have not been celebrated in poetry, prose, or theatre? How does one remain individual and imaginative and still possess a vision which is contemporary, realistic, and politically conscious? How does one avoid the political rhetoric which often mars artistic impulses, creating second and third rate work? Can various traditions such as surrealism, deconstruction, eastern philosophy, so-called foreign traditions, be used without one's mind becoming colonized—if so, where are the examples? Doesn't the flourishing of community require the richness of diversity? How can we support each other's differing visions? Who are some of the writers who have given us pleasure, wisdom, and models for future work? How can my own work be improved?

It would be dishonest to pretend that my interest in beginning Other Countries was merely intellectual, as it was not. In a relatively short period of time (two years), I had been disappointed by Black people (individuals) in significant ways: disappointed by what I perceived as my parents' inability to grow with me past my childhood years; disappointed by two close male friends who refused to accept my sexuality (before this, I had begun to see friends as family, as life); disappointed by my failure to find a lover among men I was meeting, men committed to the pleasure of anonymous, promiscuous sex; disappointed as well by less personal things: a young Black male landlord's exploitive dishonesty and incompetence; the homophobia encountered during a brief stay in Harlem; being mugged twice by groups of young Black men, once at gunpoint; and, importantly, the poverty of vision and power of Black organizations. This disappointment had produced anger, pain, contempt, and fear. Fear. The workshop would be a way of re-connecting with something I thought might still be a vital force.

I thought Other Countries would be a way to heal some of these wounds, and possibly, probably, this is much too much to ask, but as Adrienne Rich has written:

> Can you remember?   when we thought
> the poets taught   how to live?
> That is not the voice of a critic
> nor a common reader
> it is someone young   in anger
> hardly knowing what to ask
> who finds our lines   our glosses
> wanting   in this world.[2]

So I came to the workshop an *outsider* who had created this inside, this workshop. I handed out work I'd copied from various books, writers: Foucault, Lucius Outlaw (on African-American philosophy and deconstruction), Derek Walcott, Audre Lorde, Isaac Jackson, Shulamith Firestone, et al. I copied work by the best, most illuminating, most radical and relevant writers I knew. I was giving what I knew, in a way I knew: thought, books. There weren't very many persons interested. Partly, the distance people felt towards the work was due to its often academic tone. (How does one entice people to read something which might be useful when the form of presentation is alienating? This led to discussion about the importance of accessibility.) The workshop continued, and we spoke about our own work, beginning to raise questions about our relationships to family, society. In the work discussed, there was willingness to embrace pleasure and pain, and the openness of the work inspired a dialog not merely of thought or rage, but of heart, sadness, laughter.

At one of the sessions, I handed out questions toward developing a critique of Black Gay literature: (What of) Craft, the handling of language and form? Metaphor? How is the particular subject handled/transformed by the writer's imagination and made to seem newly illuminated? How is the Black man situated in the work as subject (seer) and object (seen)? Is he a standard of value? Central? How is sensuality and sex presented? What is revealed about the relationships between Black Gay men re pleasure, bonding, rituals, life-giving forces, ethics and philosophy? Is the subversion of common language and sex roles replicated in the work? What is life-giving in Black Gay life that compares to the nurturing of children (creation of culture?)? Is this comparison necessary? How is history—personal and social—dealt with? Is this history used to enlarge the meaning of a current fact? Is the literature at all cognizant of the fact that it's part of world literature? Does it refer to other works (dialogically? critically? imitatively? negatingly?)? Is the literature conscious of itself as a potentially humanizing/dehumanizing tool? Does it encourage the reader to go back to his reality and re-experience it, or does it encourage the acceptance of an idea, emotion, dream (the work) as reality?

Later, we experimented with Black Gay criticism, by having everyone take home a poem which had been presented to us in class, but not read, about which we each had to write. The poem was called "Summerdreams," by Charles Pouncy, and here it is, as it was then:

One of those D.C. nights in the summertime.
Either damp or soggy
at 2:00 a.m.
but always hot
mist cloaks the street lights
no animals on the street
because it's too hot outside
but the men are out.

The air is limp
a membrane of dust, moisture and pollen
incubating anger and violence
witness, the sirens through the night
communicating lust and passion and immediacy
as i walk into Malcolm X Park
and smell the heat
strong like ripe fruit brewing in a trashcan
do you risk a taste?
still the smell compels
drawing you closer and deeper
into the rhythm of the heat
the shadows and instinctive movements.

I walk up the stairs bounding the downward watercourse
my eyes lingering on the forms

positioned along the path
I touch my face
fingers slowly tracing the sweat on my brow
my eyes
searching their black wet faces
for their eyes
(it shows in the eyes)
and I'm hot and keep walking.

Ahead someone walks toward me
an outline
an image with long black limbs
stuffed into tight white shorts
and a shirt open to the waist
set against the thick darkness of the night
but the darkness recedes before him
there is no doubt that I am staring
our eyes touch
a spark flies between us
leaving the smell of lust
lingering in the moist air
I inhale
and it settles in the pit of my stomach.

He stops before me
too close to ask for the time
or a light
he stops
just one hot, damp breath away
sweat drips down the side of his nose
and disappears in the corner
of his mouth

he embraces his lips with his tongue
there are words
hard and provocative and we know the deal.

We turn and climb the stairs
leading to the park's upper level
we stop on the landing
there are words
a joint is produced
we smoke
inhaling each other's breath
he leans back into the shadows of a corner

I lean forward following
he is thin and firm but pliant
he welcomes my arms
and I am lost in his ahs and his sweat
our torsos disengage
but we remain locked below the waist
grinding, groping
I put my hand inside his shirt
the hairs on his chest
sizzle
another spark flies
and I feel his dick pressing into my stomach
I think about assault with a blunt weapon
he widens his stance
he smiles
it's time to go home
I wake up.

This is a survey of what struck me as being the most interesting comments from those who did the assignment:

> Daniel Garrett, "The poem begins like a story being told, a ballad being sung, part of an oral tradition. . . . Describing the night as 'one of those' and 'always' hot suggest how ordinary the scene is. . . . Lust defies reason . . . 'there are words' lets us know that *nothing is being said* that hasn't been said before, *nothing is being said* that *we* haven't heard (or said?). . . . More than a dream of sleep, this poem seems a waking dream of sex, a dream of satisfaction that is somewhat nightmarish; the heat is sexual, geological, and hellish."

> Len Richardson, " 'Summerdreams,' the poetic journey of an unknown and unnamed traveller. . . . 'Summerdreams' raises the issue of underlying violence and possibly death, for the sake of sex—an idea that is not unusual in a world of oppressed and distressed people, with frustrated desires—in any such encounter as this."

> James P., "I view this critique as essentially my personal reaction to this work of art. I refrain from attempting to present an objective universal observation. . . . The general description of the actual physical meeting of the two men could be fuller and more flush.
>
> I believe the work is generally successful in stimulating the senses, and conveying the rush of lust in such a setting."

> Wayne Chambers, "I was deeply touched by 'Summerdreams.' In fact, I began to dismiss the idea of a dry critical evaluation after I finished writing 'I Remember D.C.,'

which was my initial response to 'Summerdreams.' In fact,
a very noted critic was supposed to have said the best criticism of a work is another work. . . ."

Those are just a few lines of the criticism of each writer. Some of
their comments touched on the flow of lines, metre, others on
described action, suggestions for changes, at least one mentioned
AIDS. There were a few overlapping and contradictory comments.

During the life of the workshop, between June '86 when it began
and now (April '87), there have been other sessions on workshop
criticism: one led by Colin Robinson in which he had different
poets read their work, then asked the workshop members to try and
locate common elements. A number of persons mentioned the element of pain; others thought that the fact few of the readers supplied copies made it difficult to assess and answer this question.
Shawn Brown led a discussion aimed at a collaborative definition of
poetry in which he discussed the mechanics of poetry and its purpose. Ali Wadud had a session on the importance of structure in
short story and play-writing. Other workshop sessions have centered on various topics: eroticism, our imaging of West Indians
(both led by Cary Johnson), for instance. The moderator system
allows each workshop member to lead a session, and this system was
proposed by Gary and myself at an historic Other Countries picnic.

II. THE PICNIC. THE JOURNAL. THE TESTING OF THEORY
THROUGH PRACTICE.

Other Countries members have supper together after workshop; it
is a ritual of food, talk, humor, and sharing. The picnic was Ali's
idea, and occurred in early fall of '86. People cooked and baked
food, brought blankets, music, sport equipment; it was a celebration
of the workshop, and it was the day Gary and I decided to make

known our interest in maximizing the efficiency of the workshop and pursuing plans for the journal some of us (Assotto Saint, Mark Foster, Cary and myself) had discussed at the first workshop session. I had composed and typed out the proposal for the first month's moderating system, and the proposal for a journal and journal board structure. Everyone was got in a circle. Cary spoke, then I. Someone—how could I forget? as we seldom got along—Colin asked if decision-making wasn't becoming centralized, to which I answered No, pointing out that this discussion was an example of openness. The discussion was heated, some people fearing the emergence of an elite of "serious writers," some people wanting to intensify the seriousness of the workshop. Tempers flared, mine certainly did. The group did decide to accept the moderator system as an experiment for a month, agreeing to discuss the proposal for a journal. Before we reached this consensus, Assotto asked for a few moments of silent thought. People were to write down their thoughts, feelings. After the silence, these were spoken; and here are some of them:

> "What I want is an outlet for writers (people who have formal experience/exposure as writers)—an outlet for non-writers (people who have no experience)—an outlet for expression of opinions by people other than those who have had formal exposure—arrogance. Moderation on specific topics. The second half of the sessions should consist of people reading freely with random discussions."

> "Other Countries is fulfilling a spiritual gap in my life. I come every Saturday expecting to hear, read and share *literary* experiences about being Black and Gay. I prefer that the work treated in the workshop deal specifically with that subject. I am not satisfied with this workshop just

dealing with work written by Black Gay writers, but work that deals with our lives; this workshop makes us face our fears, our apprehensions and in the long run gives us the *support* we do not find anywhere else, yet are in such need of. Peace, strength, and love."

"I am not a 'serious writer,' though I am someone very interested in expressing myself creatively through writing. I hope this workshop has a place for me."

The picnic, the discussion of a journal were both aspects of community-building, aspects which expanded and tested the theory that a community of Black Gay men, of Black Gay men as writers, could be successful. The group was made up of men of various emotional and intellectual temperaments, creative ambitions, class and cultural backgrounds. Difference personified.

This picnic took place the last weekend in August; and two weeks after we met to discuss my proposal and other proposals which had since been written around the workshop and journal. The question had become one of vision, influence and power in the group. Shawn Brown submitted a workshop/journal proposal. Kent Grey submitted a workshop proposal. Charles Pouncy wrote a letter, as did Cary, who would not be at the discussion because of work in Washington. The proposals and letters did not differ very much; we all were concerned with the autonomy of the workshop, the sharing of responsibility, the encouragement of diversity, and the possible production of a journal. Yet, there was a sense that the writer of whichever proposal was accepted would seem to have a disproportionate influence. Though it sounds too simple, partly, this was a fear of the unknown. What would happen? Could this plan for workshop structure and a publication divide the group? What was growing between us was too precious to be threatened or lost, most people felt.

At the September 20th meeting at which we discussed our future as a group, the group decided not to pursue the idea of a journal. It was a discussion which was briliant, exhilarating and painful. After the discussion, we hugged, and went to dinner.

It seemed to me that these men had decided against the building of institutions, which as an individual, writer, and politicized mind I knew were necessary. (Now, I see even more clearly how the workshop, which is leaderless, is an admirable institution, despite the fact it produces no material product.) The next day, I drafted a letter of resignation, which I mailed. The letter was both noble and bitchy and I cannot quote from it because I still find it painful and embarrassing. I sent the letter and wondered, with a poet's sense of drama: Will this grief, this dying, finish my youth. If family fail, and friends fail, and I cannot count on Black Gay men, what then?

The workshop wrote me requesting I return to discuss my resignation. They were disappointed in me, I was angry. They asked me to return to the workshop. Cary proposed that we develop a committee to investigate how the workshop might be connected to the production of a journal. I waited until the workshop agreed to this before agreeing to return.

There were several intense meetings around the structure of the journal and its relationship to the workshop. We—Assotto, Mark, Cary, Colin, Allen Wright, Len, Redvers Jeanmarie, Kent, Shawn, and myself—decided the journal would be related to the workshop in name only. No formal commitment would be made to publish members' work. There was an election. It seems notable that Colin ran for Coordinating Editor and Essays Editor, as I did, and Kent ran for Graphics Editor as did Donald Woods, who had not come to any of the planning sessions. Ali ran for Drama Editor, and he was not present at the election, nor any planning sessions that I recall, not that this was a criterion, though it seems important, in retrospect. I was elected Coordinating Editor, Cary Managing

Editor, Assotto Poetry Editor, Mark Fiction Editor, Redvers Essays
Editor, Kent Graphics Editor, Ali Drama Editor. This was October,
and the board began meeting in November, approving associate editors, soliciting submissions, discussing events. These are the various
committees as of January 1st, 1987:

Poetry
Assotto Saint
Melvin Dixon
Donald Woods

Fiction
Mark Foster
Allen Wright
Len Richardson

Drama
Ali Wadud
Allan Williams
Wayne Chambers

Essays
Redvers Jeanmarie
Colin Robinson
Dave Frechette

Graphics
Kent Grey
Robert Bell
Ike Paris

Events
Shawn Brown (Chairperson)

Since then, Kent resigned; he had been busy with other projects, and did not have time for this one. Mark resigned as well. There was, as is our habit, more passionate discussion about the replacement of these editors. Terry Taylor became the Graphics Editor, Lea the Fiction Editor.

Terry had designed our flyers for our various fundraising events. We have had different events: on January 19,1987, a Martin King birthday celebration/journal fundraiser at the danceclub Tracks. Very successful. Donald Woods commented on how fitting it was that we read our work in a bar/danceclub, a common meeting place for Black Gay men. In February, there were four evenings of staged readings at Eleo Pomare's Foundation for the Vital Arts, directed by Allan B. Williams. This association with a Black Gay elder was significant. In March Colin Robinson and James Keenan organized a reading for Keenan's organization Men of All Colors Together. After the reading there was a question and answer session between readers and audience, a first for our group. In April, there was a private party/fundraiser at Shawn's apartment, and a reading and dance at Tracks, organized by Donald Woods, utilizing Allan Williams' staging.

In all the months since the beginning of this organization, there has been a tremendous marshalling of group forces. There has been conflict arising out of our differences, but respect for those differences as well. Community.

III. Toward a Black Gay Aesthetic

As I think the body of this essay suggests, literature is in no way separated from life. Literature is writing which is assumed to be infused with an intended special meaning; in most discourses, it is differentiated from journalism, letters, shopping lists. Literature takes a "special form" such as poetry, fiction (short stories and novels), and essays. It is something conceived in private but prepared for a public. Very often it is assumed that this privacy is a kind of purity, but it is not. Values are involved. The language and form one decides to use are often influenced by the values placed on these by what we refer to as society. I really think that the division between art and life, with art being idealized, privileged, says a lot about what we have allowed our lives to become. The privileging of literature, which is a certain kind of discourse, is the institution of certain kinds of values. Literature embodies the myths and rituals which strengthen and weaken individuals, communities. Western literature has often posited the heterosexual white male as hero, with Gays, Blacks and women as Other.

Our marginality in their minds, and our marginality in relation to power are reflected in literature. As Redvers Jeanmarie has said, "Our literature is our history. It validates our lives and values as individuals in society." Redvers was revising Baldwin's line about our history being each other; both are true, though literature as history seems very Western, and people as history seems Eastern and African. Difference and mutuality again. The development of Black literature, women's literature, Gay literature, and now Black Gay literature is not so much a rewriting of history as an additional writing of it; together these various literatures, like our various selves, produce history.

Our histories, our identities are defined by what we value and how we act on our values. Our past as Black Gay men is only now being examined. Our pasts consist of more than slavery, of more than mockery and pain. There is among us a knowledge of the relativity of roles, of languages. We have each struggled to find our own values and identities, and often this makes us sensitive, sometimes insensitive. Because we have struggled so hard *individually*, we do not always listen to the wisdom our brother has found.

We are beginning to listen more carefully. The workshop and journal are part of this, are part of a movement of Black Gay men to take control of their own history. In New York, there are other groups such as the National Coalition of Black Lesbians and Gays, Gay Men of Afrikan Descent, Adodi New York. Our literature must speak of our successes and failures, our self-love and self-hatred, our knowledge and ignorance. I look forward to many Black Gay aesthetics. The one I look forward to *most* is one which will speak of pleasure between men who care deeply for one another. Men who see, hear, and reach each other unafraid, with pride.

ENDNOTES

[1] James Baldwin, *Just Above My Head* (New York: Dell, 1979).

[2] Adrienne Rich, *Your Native Land, Your Life* (New York: Norton, 1986).

Authors Note: The author acknowledges the helpful suggestions of Redvers Jean-marie, Cary Alan Johnson, and Colin Robinson in revising this essay. Special mention: Assotto Saint, Charles Pouncy and Shawn Brown—models, peers.

Dedication: For Cary, Guy-Mark and Kent who were there (in different ways) and for Sheilla and Desiree, who were not, but who know all I say and cannot say.

COUCH POEM (1989)

Donald W. Woods

wake in yesterday's clothing
roll the T
to a damp ball
your fingers tweezers
separate cotton briefs
from sleeping member

futon rolled and
neatly sheathed
lonely by choice

poor bed
no stories to tell
no dreams to soak up
shame

sigh for the new day
fall into the morning on
the rattle of your own breathing
alarm clock tweets like
birds above a tent on a lake in Burkina Faso

stretch
unfix the benevolent smile
of Good Morning America
plod on tiptoes to privacy
your reflection
of questions symbols signs
poses reminiscent of poses
when someone else is backdrop
their eyes cameras
recording you
climbing into the shower
all manly and such

wash yourself quickly
soap your privates
rinse them   towel them dry   powder them   blame them
even as you swallow vitamins
too numerous to mention and shit
all the time pleased at the effortless disposal
the regularity of your movement

iron a shirt to wear
dress them
your limbs
are softer now
fashionable in your mind

leave the crib
walk the row of brownstones
speak to the single man and Tiffany his poodle

smile at children
their lucky mothers
busy fathers and
walk this way to work

like a dog
work like a fiend
work like this is your first day
work like this is your last day
and folks will remember you

so respectable
so responsible
he worked like a dog or cat or a kite
in a balmy breeze

blowing the way fortune blew
and sitting up nights on the
couch watching people make their millions
unlock the cubicle happy
at the something to do
day-long escapade
a transparent fascination with decay

(at night when the others make love
laugh at dinner in Soho
sit and write down your writing
you can memorize your fingers at a keyboard
you can leave micro bytes of your living
to be deciphered by

people who loved to love you
who hated to hate you and
loved to hate you and hated to love you all
out of fear and no damn choice)

when nothing else will come you may
search for significance in the farewell
of the security guard who never inquires your life
beyond the walls you share

the waitresses all by name
who love the lord and hate crack
and call you baby
they don't question
they bring the plate
liver and onions or chicken smothered
call you darling and ask if you tired
call you baby and listen
for your answer at the Apollo restaurant

where you eat
with conviction
the meals of mighty men and women
as if you belonged to them
eat quickly solemnly chew
swallow in all seriousness
your nourishment and you

tip her tonight the usual tip

move into the street a new man
walking in an instant like a freed slave
and wait on the subway like a warrior
stand on the subway and leap the stairs
and glow with your own strength
walk past the brownstones
humming a spiritual
and up the stairs
and up the stairs again and
with three more flights to go
it has left you

and you reach the door
defeated in your head and retreat to the couch
that has waited all day
expectant

BROTHERS LOVING BROTHERS (1989)

Vega

Respect yourself, my brother,
for we are so many wondrous things.

Like a black rose,
you are a rarity to be found.
Our leaves intertwine as I reach out to you
after the release of a gentle rain.

You precious gem,
black pearl that warms the heart,
symbol of ageless wisdom,
I derive strength
from the touch of your hand.

Our lives blend together
like rays of light;
we are men of color,
adorned in shades of tan, red,
beige, black, and brown.

Brothers born from the same earth womb.
Brothers reaching for the same star.

Love me as your equal.
Love me, brother to brother.

"NON, JE NE REGRETTE RIEN" (1989)

David Frechette

for Keith Barrow and Larry McKeithan

I had big fun if I don't get well no more.
    —"Going Down Slow"
as sung by Bobby "Blue" Bland

Sister Chitlin', Brother Neck Bone and
Several of their oxymoron minions
Circle round my sick room,
Swathed in paper surgical gowns.

Brandishing crosses, clutching bibles,
(God, *please* don't let them sing hymns!)
Pestering me to recant the
Wicked ways that brought me here.

"Renounce your sins and return to Jesus!"
Shouts one of the zealous flock.
"The truth is I never left Him,"
I reply with a fingersnap.
"Don't you wish you'd chosen a *normal* lifestyle?"
"Sister, for *me*, I'm *sure* I did."

Let the congregation work overtime
For my eleventh-hour conversion.

Their futile efforts fortify
My unrepentant resolve.

Though my body be racked by
Capricious pains and fevers,
I'm not even *about* to yield to
Fashionable gay Black temptation.

Mother Piaf's second greatest hit title
Is taped to the inside of my brain
And silently repeated like a mantra:
"Non, Je Ne Regrette Rien."

I don't regret the hot Latino boxer
I made love to on Riverside Drive
Prior to the Washington match.
I don't regret wild Jersey nights
Spent in the arms of conflicted satyrs;
I don't regret late night and early a.m.
Encounters with world-class insatiables.

My only regrets are being ill,
Bed-ridden and having no boyfriend
To pray over me.
And that now I'll never see Europe
Or my African homeland except
In photos in a book or magazine.

Engrave on my tombstone:
"Here sleeps a *happy* Black faggot

Who lived to love and died
With no guilt."

No, I regret nothing
Of the gay life I've led and
There's no way in Heaven or Hell
I'll let anyone make me.

THE TOMB OF SORROW (1989)

Essex Hemphill

for Mahomet

I cannot say
that I have gone to hell
for your love
but often
found myself there
in your pursuit.
                    —William Carlos Williams
              "Asphodel, That Greeny Flower"

I

Gunshots ring out above our heads
as we sit beneath your favorite tree,
in this park called Meridian Hill,
called Malcolm X, that you call
the "Tomb of Sorrow"
(and claim to be its gatekeeper);
in the cool air lingering after the rain,
the men return to the Wailing Wall
to throw laughter and sad glances
into the fountains below,
or they scream out

for a stud by any name,
their beautiful asses
rimmed by the moon.

Gunshots ring out above our heads
as we cock dance
beneath your favorite tree.
There are no invectives
to use against us.
We are exhausted
from dreaming wet dreams,
afraid of the passion
that briefly consoles us.
I ask no more of you
than I ask of myself:
no more guilt, no more pity.
Occult risks await us
at the edge of restraint.

These are meaningless kisses
(aren't they?)
that we pass back and forth
like poppers and crack pipes,
and for a fleeting moment,
in a flash of heat and consent,
we release our souls
to hover above our bodies;
we believe our shuddering orgasms
are transcendental;
our loneliness manifests itself

as seed we cannot take
or give.

Gunshots ring out above our heads,
a few of us are seeking romance,
others a piece of ass,
some—a stroke of dick.
The rest of us are killing.
The rest of us get killed.

II

When I die,
honey chil',
my angels
will be tall
Black drag queens.
I will eat their stockings
as they fling them
into the blue
shadows of dawn.
I will suck
their purple lips
to anoint my mouth
for the utterance of prayers.

My witnesses
will have to answer
to go-go music.
Dancing and sweat

will be required
at my funeral.

Someone will have to answer
the mail I leave,
the messages
on my phone service;
someone else
will have to tend
to the aching
that drove me
to seek soul.

Everything different
tests my faith.
I have stood in places
where the absence of light
allowed me to live longer,
while at the same time
it rendered me blind.

I struggle against
plagues, plots,
pressure, paranoia.
Everyone wants a price
for my living.

When I die,
my angels,
immaculate

Black diva
drag queens,
all of them
sequined
and seductive,
some of them
will come back
to haunt you,
I promise,
honey chil'.

III

You stood beneath a tree
guarding moonlight,
clothed in military fatigues,
black boots, shadows,
winter rain, midnight,
jerking your dick slowly,
deliberately calling attention
to its proud length
and swollen head,
a warrior dick,
a dick of consequences
nodded knowingly at me.

You were stirring it
when I approached,
making it swell more,
allowing raindrops

escaping through
leaves and branches
to bounce off of it
and shatter like doubt.

Among the strangest gifts
I received from you
(and I returned them all)—
a chest of dark, ancient wood,
inside: red velvet cushions,
coins, paper money
from around the world.
A red book of hand-drawn runes,
a kufi, prayer beads,
a broken timepiece—
the stench of dry manure.

And there were other things
never to be forgotten—
a silver horse head
to hold my chain of keys,
a Christian sword,
black candles,
black dolls
with big dicks
and blue dreads
that you nailed
above my bed
to ensure fidelity.
A beer bottle filled
with hand-drawn soap,

a specificity—
a description of your life,
beliefs, present work,
weight and height;
declarations of love
which I accepted,
overlooking how I disguised
my real motivations—
a desire to keep
some dick at home
and love it as best I can.

I was on duty to your madness
like a night nurse
in a cancer ward.
Not one alarm went off
as I lay with you, Succubus.
I've dreamed of you
standing outside my soul
beneath a freakish tree,
stroking your dick
which is longer
in the dream, but I,
unable to be moved
and enchanted
rebuke you.
I vomit up your snake
and hack it to pieces,
laughing as I strike.

No, I was not
your pussy,
she would be
your dead wife.
I believe you
dispatched her soul
or turned her into a cat.
I was your man lover,
gambling dangerously
with my soul.
I was determined to love you
but you were haunted
by Vietnam,
taunted by demons.
In my arms you dreamed
of tropical jungles,
of young village girls
with razors embedded
in their pussies,
lethal chopsticks
hidden in their hair,
their nipples clenched
like grenade pins
between your grinding teeth.

You rocked and kicked
in your troubled sleep
as though you were fucking
one of those dangerous cunts,
and I was by your side

unable to hex it away,
or accept that peace
means nothing to you,
and the dreams you suffer
may be my only revenge.

IV

It was an end to masturbation.
That's what I was seeking.
I couldn't say it then, no,
I couldn't say it then.

When you told me
your first lover,
a white man,
wanted you to spit,
shit, piss on,
fist-fuck and
throw him down stairs,
alarms should have
blared forth
like hordes
of screaming queens.

When you said
in the beginning
you beat up Black men
after you fucked them,
when you said

in the last year
you were buying crack
for Black men
who let you fuck 'em,
alarms should have
deafened me for life.

When you told me
you once tied a naked man
between two trees
in an isolated,
wooded area,
debased him,
leaving him there
for several days,
then sent others
to rape him and feed him,
my head should have exploded
into shrapnel
and killed us both.

When you swore you loved me
and claimed to be sent here
to protect me,
I should have put bullets
in my temple
or flaming swords
up my ass.

Feeling my usual
sexual vexations,
I came here then,
seeking only pleasure,
dressed for the easy seduction.
I never considered
carrying a cross.
I had no intention
of being another queen
looking out
at the morning rain
from the Wailing Wall,
hoping to spy a brutish man
with a nearby home.

Slouching through Homo Heights,
I came to the Tomb of Sorrow
seeking penetration and Black seed.
My self-inflicted injuries occurred
when I began loving you
and trusting you.

V

Through some other
set of eyes
I have to see you
homeboy,
fantasy charmer,
object of my desire,

my scorn,
abuser of my affections,
curse, beauty,
tough/soft young men,
masked men,
cussing men,
sweet swaggering
buffalo soldiers.

Through some other
set of eyes
I must recognize
our positions
are often equal.
We are worth more
to each other
than twenty dollars,
bags of crack,
bullets piercing our skulls.
I can't hope to help
save us from destruction
by using my bed
as a pagan temple,
a false safe house.
There are other ways
to cross the nights,
to form lasting bonds;
there are other desires
as consuming as flesh.

There are ways
to respect our beauty.

Through some other set
of common eyes
I have to behold you
again, homeboy.
I rummage through
ancestral memories
in search of the
original tribes
that fathered us.
I want to remember
the exact practices
of civility
we agreed upon.
I want us to remember
the nobility of decency.

At the end of the day,
through some other vision,
perhaps the consequence
of growing firm and older,
I see the thorns of the rose
are not my enemy.
I strive to see this
in each of us—
O ancient petals,
O recent blooms.

Aunt Ida Pieces a Quilt (1989)

Melvin Dixon

You are right, but your patch isn't big enough

—Jesse Jackson

When a cure is found and the last panel is sewn into place, the Quilt will be displayed in a permanent home as a national monument to the individual, irreplaceable people lost to AIDS—and the people who knew and loved them the most

—Cleve Jones, founder, The NAMES Project

They brought me some of his clothes. The hospital
gown.
Those too-tight dungarees, his blue choir robe
with the gold sash. How that boy could sing!
His favorite color in a necktie. A Sunday shirt.
What I'm gonna do with all this stuff?
I can remember Junie without this business.
My niece Francine say they quilting all over the country.
So many good boys like her boy, gone.

At my age I ain't studying no needle and thread.
My eyes ain't so good now and my fingers lock in a fist,

they so eaten up with arthritis. This old back
don't take kindly to bending over a frame no more.
Francine say ain't I a mess carrying on like this.
I could make two quilts the time I spend running my
mouth.

Just cut his name out the cloths, stitch something nice
about him. Something to bring him back. You can do it,
Francine say. Best sewing our family ever had.
Quilting ain't that easy, I say. Never was easy.
Y'all got to help me remember him good.

Most of my quilts was made down South. My Mama
and my Mama's Mama taught me. Popped me on the tail
if I missed a stitch or threw the pattern out of line.
I did "Bright Star" and "Lonesome Square" and "Rally
Round,"
what many folks don't bother with nowadays. Then Elmo
and me
married and came North where the cold in Connecticut
cuts you like a knife. We was warm, though.
We had sackcloth and calico and cotton. 100% pure.
What they got now but polyester-rayon. Factory made.

Let me tell you something. In all my quilts there's a secret
nobody knows. Every last one of them got my name Ida
stitched on the backside in red thread.

That's where Junie got his flair. Don't let anybody
fool you.

When he got the Youth Choir standing up and singing
the whole church would rock. He'd throw up his hands
from them wide blue sleeves and the church would hush
right down to the funeral parlor fans whisking the air.
He'd toss his head back and holler and we'd all cry holy.

And never mind his too-tight dungarees.
I caught him switching down the street one Saturday
night,
and I seen him more than once. I said, Junie,
You ain't got to let the whole world know your business.
Who cared where he went when he wanted to have fun.
He'd be singing his heart out come Sunday morning.

When Francine say she gonna hang this quilt in the
church
I like to fall out. A quilt ain't no show piece,
it's to keep you warm. Francine say it can do both.
Now I ain't so old fashioned I can't change,
but I made Francine come over and bring her daughter
Belinda. We cut and tacked his name, JUNIE.
Just plain and simple. "JUNIE, our boy."
Cut the J in blue, the U in gold. N in dungarees
just as tight as you please. The I from the hospital gown
and the white shirt he wore First Sunday. Belinda
put the necktie E in the cross stitch I showed her.

Wouldn't you know we got to talking about Junie.
We could smell him in the cloth.
Underarm. Afro-Sheen pomade. Gravy stains.

I forgot all about my arthritis.
When Francine left me to finish up, I swear
I heard Junie giggling right along with me
as I stitched Ida on the backside in red thread.

Francine say she gonna send this quilt to Washington
like folks doing from all across the country,
so many good people gone. Babies, mothers, fathers,
and boys like our Junie. Francine say
they gonna piece this quilt to another one,
another name and another patch
all in a larger quilt getting larger and larger.

Maybe we all like that, patches waiting to be pieced.
Well, I don't know about Washington.
We need Junie here with us. And Maxine,
she cousin May's husband's sister's people,
she having a baby and here comes winter already.
The cold cutting like knives. Now where did I put that
needle?

FOR COLORED BOYS WHO HAVE CONSIDERED S-CURLS WHEN THE HOT COMB WAS ENUF
(1990)

Marvin K. White

HOW DO I GET IN TOUCH WITH
MY BLACKNESS?

"BLACKNESS, WHERE ARE YOU?"
I HAVE KENTE CLOTHED
MYSELF INTO A KNOT
I WEAR ENOUGH BEADS
TO CORNER THE WORLDS
MARKET ON CLAY.
MY BUTTONS ARE
AFRO-CENTERED POLITICALLY CORRECT
STATEMENTS OF OPPRESSION INSPIRED BY
CONSPIRACY THEORIES.

"HEY FUCKIN' BLACKNESS"
MY HAIR IS RELAXER FREE
TWISTS, BRAIDS, AND DREADS
I WEAR. ADORNED WITH SHELLS
I HAVE DUSTED OFF
MY DASHIKI AND I ONLY ACCESSORIZE
IN RED, BLACK, AND GREEN

"YO, LISTEN GODDAMNED BLACKNESS"

I KNOW WHO
LADYSMITH BLACK MAMBAZA ARE
I CAN COUNT TO TEN
IN SWAHILI
MOJO MEANS ONE
MOTHERFUCKER
NO MORE EURO-CAPITALIST
HOLIDAYS—KWAANZA ME TO AFRICA

"COME IN BLACKNESS—EARTH TO BLACK-
NESS"
I RIDE SUBWAYS
READING THE KORAN
AND "BLACK ATHENA"
GIVING MY SEAT TO
OUR OLD BLACK WOMEN
WEIGHED DOWN
WITH YEARS OF GROCERIES.
I GIVE THAT
"YEAH, BROTHER" LOOK
TO THE YOUNG DUDE
WHO WEARS HIS KINGDOM
ON HIS HEAD
I BUY SEMI-EXOTIC OILS
FROM BROTHERS IN WHITE

"EXCUSE ME, HAVE YOU SEEN MY BLACK-
NESS?"
I, I, I, REFUSE TO REPORT
MY MUGGING,

I REALIZE IT'S NOT
BLACK ON BLACK CRIME
BUT BLACK ON BLACK VICTIM
I BLAME "THE MAN"
AS I RUN WILDLY
DOWN THE STREET
BEING CHASED BY
ANGRY BOYS IN MEN'S BODIES
SHOUTING "FAGGOT!"
I TRY SHIFTING MY WEIGHT
ONTO MY RIGHT LEG
TO WALK WITH A STREET LIMP
AND NOT THREATEN THEIR MANHOOD
I SHOUT OUT
"WE GOT TO LOVE ONE ANOTHER"
AS FISTS FIND PLACES
ON MY BODY TO PUMMEL
PLACES WHICH NEVER FELT PAIN,
NOR SCARS.

I CAN'T
I DON'T
BLAME MY FATHER FOR LEAVING
HE'S BEEN DOWN
AND TRODDEN ALL HIS LIFE
ESCAPE WAS RELATIVE
HE WANTED TO BE A MAN
I KNOW THAT DRUGS
BEING PUSHED OUTSIDE
MY WINDOW

AREN'T BLACK DRUGS
BUT INSTEAD
THE GOVERNMENT'S ARMY
OF PUSHERS AND DEALERS
DISGUISED AS FBI AND SOCIAL WORKERS
INFILTRATING AND ASSAULTING
MY NEIGHBORHOOD
"LOOK THERE'S ONE NOW!"

"BLACK DON'T FAIL ME NOW"
I DON'T SEE
BLACK WOMEN HAVING BABIES
14 OR 40
AS ANYTHING BUT NATURAL
DON'T BELIEVE THE WHITE WOMAN'S
REPRODUCTIVE RIGHTS ISSUE
AS ANYTHING BUT GENOCIDE
AGAINST THE BLACK RACE
"SURVIVAL OF THE FETUS!"

"ALLI, ALLI OUT BLACKNESS, COME FREE,
FREE, FREE!"

ASALAMALAKUM
HOTEP BROTHER
SAY IT LOUD
BLUES
BARBEQUE
GET CHRISTY LOVE
AMAZING GRACE

NELSON MANDELA
RAP MUSIC
AIDS
GHETTO
THE JEFFERSONS
VIRGINIA
SOUTH AFRICA
RUN JESSE RUN
BISCUITS AND GRAVY
CORN ROWS
MOTOWN
CIVIL RIGHTS
JAY JAY, THELMA, MICHAEL
FLORIDA, JAMES, WILONA
BOOKMAN AND PENNY
KOVATIS
AUDREY, LANGSTON, AND ZORA
SEGREGATION
SPIKE LEE
CONK
PYRAMID
SOCK IT TO ME CAKE
BASKETBALL
PEANUT BUTTER
ARETHA
MOREHOUSE
BELOVED
DIOP
AILEY
CIVIL WAR

FREEDOM
KUMBAYA
SONNYS BLUES
SYLVIAS
LIVE AID
WE INTERRUPT THIS . . .
WE SHALL OVER COMMME . . .
WHOSE GOT HIS OWN . . .
40 ACRES AND A MULE . . .
WAS BLIND AND NOW I SEE . . .
MMPH, MPH, MMPH

I'M GOING OUT LIKE A FUCKING METEOR (1991)

Craig G. Harris

> *I want to live the rest of my life, however long or short, with as much sweetness as I can decently manage, loving all the people I love, and doing as much as I can of the work I still have to do. I am going to write fire until it comes out of my ears, my eyes, my noseholes—everywhere. Until it's every breath I breathe. I'm going to go out like a fucking meteor!*
>
> —Audre Lorde

It is a beautifully warm Monday afternoon and I wake with good spirits to receive a telephone call from a former colleague in Washington, D.C. We talk about my current situation, I crack jokes in the face of adversity, and we laugh hilariously like old times. After a few minutes, she tells me that someone is waiting outside her office, that she must run but had just wanted to holler at me for a second. She tells me that I haven't changed a bit and that she loves me. She'll keep in touch.

I remember that today is the last day I can remit my rent check without penalty of a five percent late fee. I find my checkbook and cringe as I write the check. When I signed the lease almost two years ago, I knew full well that the rent was outrageous. But now, my hand shakes a little more nervously each month as I sign the check.

I take the check to the management office on my way to the corner *bodega*. I notice that somehow I have only one dollar bill in my wallet and realize I must stop at the automatic teller machine before I can buy milk, juice, and butter for breakfast. Two twenties are ejaculated from the machine along with a receipt. The record indicates that the current balance of my checking account is only four dollars more than the amount of the check I have just given to my property management. That doesn't worry me as much as the fact that my savings account is at a zero balance, and pay day isn't until Friday.

I head to the *bodega*. I buy a pint of half-and-half, a can of papaya nectar and a pack of cigarettes. I hand the Arab woman behind the counter a twenty-dollar bill. She packs my groceries and hands me six dollars change. I stare at the change in my hand thinking that if I could really get around like I used to, I could have gotten a better bargain at Balducci's. Small matter. This place is grossly overpriced, but it is convenient.

By the time I return to my complex, the mail has been delivered. Despite appearances, my life has become so solitary that I am forced to look forward to this daily ritual. As I lock the box and peruse the envelopes, I am overjoyed to find that today's assortment contains two reimbursement checks from Blue Cross/Blue Shield.

I return to my apartment, pour my first cup of coffee, and sit with a cigarette to open the good news. The checks total three hundred and twenty-five dollars—an amount I have already paid my therapist and hematologist. This will carry me through the remainder of the week. I open the next envelope which is a three hundred and eighty dollar bill from my radiology oncologist. After reading every word on the bill three times, I conclude that these fees cannot be billed directly to my insurance carrier as I had been led to believe. I must remit payment and then submit a claim for reimbursement. The worst of it is that this bill only covers the cost of two radiology treatments and I receive four treatments per week. I lose my appetite and decide to skip breakfast, though I know quite well that my body is in desperate need of the vitamins and nutrients, calories and bulk. It is six hours later when I read the bill for a fourth time and realize that it can be directly submitted to Blue

Cross/Blue Shield. By this time, however, I have missed two meals and spent the day in a depressed mood.

I could bitch and complain. I could become depressed and withdrawn. But what good would either do? So I sit and contemplate my situation. I am one of the lucky ones. No matter how unfortunate my situation may seem, I know that I am a "privileged nigger." I know this because not only have I worked every day of my life, but for the last seven years I have worked in various positions in HIV prevention and service delivery. I have a good job. I have health insurance coverage. I have access to the most updated medical information and a stellar medical team. In no way could I compare my case to Evelyn, a former client.

I met Evelyn shortly after returning to New York in the spring of 1988 to assume the position of executive director of the Minority Task Force on AIDS. Evelyn had been diagnosed with Lupus in addition to HIV disease. Her drug habit was one she had great difficulty shaking. She was only somewhat literate, and dependent on social services as her man had left her to marry another woman. She had a five-year-old son, but couldn't depend on the father for child care because his wife was afraid that the young boy would infect her infant. Bureaucratic systems both baffled and intimidated Evelyn.

Through Evelyn I gained my first real insights into the horrors of the American health care and social services systems. It is not that I was totally naive until this time. Like most progressive activists, I had a conceptual handle on such injustices, but had really never encountered them first hand. I had that opportunity the day that Evelyn came into my office sobbing, interrupting my work on a grant proposal which, if approved, would allow the Task Force to increase its over-stressed staff of two. Evelyn explained to me that she had no money, her food stamps had been cut off, and no one at the local welfare office could explain why.

I called the welfare office, explained my position and politely requested to speak with a manager. That request was initially denied by the most surly public servant I have ever encountered. She told me that Evelyn's food stamps had been discontinued because she was "too stupid" to know how to fill out the forms. I informed her that I would be happy to send someone to the office to pick up the forms. I would then complete the forms for Evelyn and have them returned by the close of business. The clerk told me that they didn't operate that way. That I couldn't push through the process, and that Evelyn would have to make an appointment later in the month to pick up the forms.

I realized it was now time for me to demonstrate my trilingual roots (I am fluent in Anglo, Afro, and Homo). "Look girlfriend," I told her, "I run this muthafuckin' agency and I would strongly suggest that you go find someone in a comparable position at yours quick, fast, and in a hurry, because you're dancing on my last damn nerve and your office is only nine blocks from mine. I will not hesitate to jump into a gypsy cab and before you can blink, suck your teeth, roll your eyes and head, I'll be whipping your ass all up and down 125th Street." Within moments, a supervisor was on the line and the situation was corrected. Nonetheless, when I returned home that evening I cried at the day's events, knowing that there were a lot more Evelyns out there and more often than not, they do not have advocates for their cause.

On January 29, 1991, my hematologist informed me of my diagnosis of pulmonary Kaposi's sarcoma. He compassionately explained to me that I would probably have to undergo aggressive chemotherapy treatments for several months. When I complained, he explained that the most recent studies from San Francisco indicated that left untreated, the average post-diagnosis life expectancy of someone with my condition was three months. He ordered blood to be drawn, X-rays, and a Gallium scan. On the way home, I stopped at a liquor store and purchased a bottle of Haig & Haig

Pinch scotch. I also stopped at Li-Lac Chocolates and purchased a pound of champagne truffles.

Back at my apartment, I poured myself a drink, and placed a half-dozen of the chocolates on a china dish. I surveyed my mail, paid bills, renewed my subscription to *OUT/LOOK*, and proceeded to conduct my personal business. I played back my telephone messages and copied the numbers of callers onto a message pad. I had received a call from my friend Lauri, with whom I co-chair the African-American Alumnae/i of Vassar College.

Positioned with my scotch, chocolate, cigarettes, and my Vassar file, I returned the call. Lauri and I discussed pending business, divided up assignments, and made lists of the items we would fax to each other the next day from our offices. With all business efficiently taken care of, the conversation became more social.

"So, how are you doing anyway?"

"Okay, I guess. But my doctor diagnosed me with AIDS today. Pulmonary Kaposi's sarcoma, more specifically."

"What? And you let me go on like that about business? Why didn't you stop me?"

"Well, you know, the shit has to get done and life does go on—"

After I finished talking with Lauri, I started to make a few of the perceived obligatory calls to inform people of my condition. The first call was to George. George and I have worked together with these issues for numerous years. I suppose that's why I expected him to react to the news in a very enlightened, professional manner (whatever that might be). George listened to the details and then asked me what I was doing. I explained to him that I was having cocktails and eating chocolate. He told me that I was in denial.

"No, I'm not in denial. I just told you I'm drinking scotch, eating chocolates, and I have AIDS. That's not denial, George."

I firmly believe that every individual has the right to select a support group which works for them. Mine, for the moment, happened to consist of Benson & Hedges menthol lights, twelve-year-old whiskey, and expensive confections. Without them I don't know how I would have made it through that first night. With them I managed to call my brother, some cousins, and assorted friends realizing that each time, I'd have to assist them in dealing with their issues before they could assist me in dealing with mine. Disclosure is a very tedious task.

After completing the calls, I turned on the television set hoping to find something other than coverage of the war in the Middle East which our country had entered into thirteen days earlier. I had no idea that I would find President George Bush delivering his State of the Union Address. It seemed as though he talked forever about the wonderful job the troops were doing in Kuwait. He insisted upon referring to Saddam Hussein only by his first name, which he consistently mispronounced. He tried to assure us that adding to the devastation in the Persian Gulf was what made the United States a great country—the greatest!

President Bush dedicated only a short portion of his speech to domestic issues. Somehow he managed to work AIDS, illiteracy, and homelessness into one sentence and indicated that the government really couldn't solve these problems. He did not, however, make the logical leap proposing combined efforts on the part of government, private industry, philanthropic societies, etc. Wizard political electrician that he is, Bush suggested that U.S. citizens become a thousand points of light to tackle these dark, despairing social ills, and recommended that each American visit a person with AIDS.

I was too plucked to even get angry. I just turned off the set thinking to myself, "Darling, the last thing I need right now is company. What I could really use is the assurance that you are doing everything within your means to ensure that Anthony Fauci and his buddies at NIH [National Institutes of Health] are getting all the perks they desire. I don't care what it takes, keep that buckaroo happy and hovering over a petri dish!"

Feces, or the lack thereof, figures prominently in my life these days. Like many other individuals infected with HIV, shit has become a friend, a confidant, a significant other, an adversary, an enemy, and a nemesis. It is rarely a source of pleasure. Recently, it has had an almost liquid consistency which burns vehemently upon exit—leaving my rectum with a sensation similar to those occasions when I attempted to accommodate suitors who were larger than life.

The rotation of chemotherapy drugs (Doxorubicin, Bleomycin and Vincristine) which I receive weekly may be the cause of the unrelenting constipation or uncontrollable diarrhea. I must schedule events according to these side-effects with little advance warning. On several occasions, I have had to forego parties or dates to go dancing because my bowels were so incredibly constipated that it caused severe pains in my abdomen and back, making it difficult to walk or even stand for an extended period of time. At other times, warnings of upcoming diarrhea have caused me to reschedule appointments, calling ahead to say that I'd be late. On these occasions, I have sat on the toilet with a book, counting time by the quarter hour and carefully investigating anything that lands in the lavender water so that I will be able to report it to my physicians.

Yes, my shit has become something I study. My shit has become an anticipated activity. My shit has become a topic I have had to learn to become comfortable discussing with my service providers. My shit is no longer a private matter. In fact, my shit, at times, has gone quite public.

A few weeks ago, after a relaxing weekend, I spent Monday morning and afternoon at the computer and taking care of other business from my home office. I organized all my files and computer discs with the intent of stopping at my office between my 6:30 cobalt radiation treatment and my 8:30 appointment with my therapist. Preparing to go into the city, I showered and dressed in a Senegalese suit I had taken out of the cleaners over the weekend. I looked into the mirror and found it to be one of those days when I felt somewhat good about the way I looked, despite minimal weight loss and skin imperfections. As I boarded the PATH train at about 5:45, I thought to myself that my timing, so far, was pretty good. I was pleased at the thought that I had completed a great deal at home and should have just enough time for printing, xeroxing, and transmittals between appointments.

Between the Pavonia Newport and Christopher Street Stations I felt a churning and heard a bubbling in my abdomen. First, I thought it was just a case of gas. That happens quite frequently. Then I panicked, remembering that as often as not, it is impossible to distinguish gas from pending defecation until after the fact. Then it happened. I felt the mass of shit filling the scant space between my hips and cotton briefs—a feeling of outrageous discomfort, not particularly because of the tactile sensation, but rather because of the social awkwardness.

Situations such as this really challenge one's problem-solving abilities. I exited the train station at Christopher Street, then thought that this was a poor choice because of the potential number of friends and associates I might bump into in that area. Thoughts flashed quickly, what ifs, and how tos. I stepped out of myself in order to address myself in the second person.

"Take a taxi home—You can't take a taxi to New Jersey, you only have two dollars in your wallet—Get to a bank machine—No, don't use the one at Sheridan Square, you'll definitely be spotted there—Use the Chase on Eighth at 12th, no one is ever around there—Check yourself, is it showing through?—Okay, honey, you're at the bank, it's gonna be okay—No, no, take out more money—Yeah, eighty dollars is good, that will get you out of this one—Now, find a nice restaurant that will let you use their men's room—Clean up—Hide the soiled briefs in paper towels before you place them in the trash can—Find a discount store on 14th Street so you can get yourself a new pair of underwear and a washcloth—Okay, so they didn't sell washcloths, you got the underwear, you're gonna be okay—Call your radiology technician and see if she'll wait—She won't wait? Oh well—Take a taxi to your office, it's late enough that almost everyone is gone—Sit on one hip in the taxi, and tip well—Smile really friendly at your office's security guard, they'll never suspect anything—Beeline it to the men's room—Take your time to wash up more thoroughly—Change into the clean underwear—There, that's better—Now, go salvage the rest of your evening, honey, 'cause you haven't seen the worst of it."

I went to my desk, printed from my computer files, xeroxed, addressed envelopes, read my mail, etc. I completed all the tasks I had planned. Then I took a taxi to my therapist's. I didn't tell about the incident. We spent the hour discussing other issues. After all, with how many people do I have to sit and chat casually about my shit?

During my second visit to my hematologist, he prescribed a number of medications. Aside from the antiviral, Retrovir, I was instructed to purchase Myambutol tablets, Zovirax capsules, and a five-day supply of Vepesid oral chemotherapy capsules. I went to a nearby pharmacist who had been recommended by my physician, hoping that he would assign the costs to my insurance carrier.

When I presented the prescriptions to the pharmacist and asked about assignment, he explained to me that he couldn't do this with Blue Cross/Blue Shield, but that there shouldn't be a problem. If necessary, I could write a check. Thinking to myself that I don't possess any major credit cards, carry a New York State driver's license but live in New Jersey, and have no identification which bears any reasonable resemblance to my current blond bombshell look, I figured there could be a problem if the acceptance of my check were to be based on any of these qualifiers.

The pharmacist packaged the drugs and used an electric calculator to tally the costs. When he reached the balance, he looked up at me with a smile and said, "Mr. Harris, that will be $1,329.55. Oh, and you can post-date the check."

"THIRTEEN HUNDRED AND TWENTY-NINE DOLLARS! AND I CAN POST-DATE THE CHECK? UNTIL WHEN?"

I picked my chin up from the counter and nervously wrote the check. The lack of identification wasn't a problem. The pharmacist explained to me that he didn't have to see any ID because he was fully aware that my doctor didn't see "riff-raff." But what if I was one of the many who received medical attention in a clinic or emergency room? What if I didn't have health insurance coverage which would reimburse me eventually? Thirteen hundred dollars for four prescriptions. And I knew that this was only the beginning. There would be lots more drugs to be bought.

I told this story to a friend, who suggested that I might be eligible for free AZT under the ADAP program. I explained that only New York State residents are eligible for this program and that New Jersey has nothing similar. It was around this time that I realized that while I have worked for the Gay Men's Health Crisis, the world's oldest and largest AIDS education, advocacy and service provider for over two years, I was not eligible to become a client because GMHC only services residents of the five boroughs of New York City.

Access becomes a relative issue. I am thankful for the privileges I have. I resent the fact that these are not readily available to the bulk of people of color dealing with HIV disease. I am angry that because of the differences in the manner in which local municipalities and state health agencies set health policies, I am cut off from certain benefits as a result of the county of my residence. And sure, there are times when I can beat the system, but the real solution will only come when the system is destroyed, demolished!

I suppose that my romantic and sexual involvements have not diminished considerably over the past few years. It's difficult to assess this situation, however, as HIV has totally warped our perspectives on sexuality—both individually and collectively.

Without a clear understanding of safer-sex guidelines, so many have adopted the practice of celibacy (which frequently manifests itself in drunken or drug-induced forays of unsafe sex that are lamented the morning after) or the limiting of sexual partners on the basis of medical membership in my "church." Despite increasing rates of HIV infection and venereal diseases, it seems that no one is having sex, or at least they're not talking about it. I, for one, couldn't prove them wrong.

I was able to successfully dissolve a lover relationship during the winter of 1988. During the three years that followed, I spent a great deal of time contemplating what went wrong, and why the relationship lasted much longer than it should have. I've concluded that at age 30, I was determined to settle down, and that I had enough false confidence in myself to have believed that I could make that union work. But the obstacles of fear of intimacy, co-dependence, lack of commitment, political differences, and poor communication were too much to overcome.

The question I have asked myself most about that relationship is why I tolerated so much so long. My basic rule is: one strike, you're out, and preferably far, far away. The answer I have come up with is laziness. It is a real chore to acquire and maintain a loving, working relationship during the age of AIDS. Fear of HIV and it's related problems have entered every recess of our consciousness, constructing even more barriers than those which already existed for gay men of African descent. The stamina to keep searching, to keep trying, is very difficult to muster. More frequently, I am inclined to agree with the lyrics of an old Mary Clayton tune, "love me or let me be lonely."

Entering into a conversation with each new sexual partner regarding one's personal interpretation of safer sex and sexual boundaries is a very emotionally loaded situation. In it, one usually uncovers one's personal sexual history, political viewpoints, medical knowledge, fantasies, and fears. Of course, I contend that communication need not take the form of conversation, and in certain situations (baths, tearooms, parks) such chatter would be totally inappropriate. In many anonymous sexual situations, actions speak much louder. But in dating situations, the silence around such issues is noticeably deliberate.

Since my diagnosis, I have shared details of my health with two men whom I am attracted to. The initial news of my illness and subsequent updates have been met with compassion and consideration. Both of these men have been a major part of my support system, offering varying levels of affection. I have not had sex with either of them. At least I don't think I have. One of the strange things about this era is that we interpret sex very differently now, and do not always reach a consensus. The lines become fuzzy and we never know if we have crossed them. Was this a sexual act? Was anyone penetrated? Did anyone have an orgasm? Are we having fun yet?

No. I'm not having fun. Six months of unintentional celibacy is not fun. But, rather than push harder to solidify either of my two existing relationships (neither of these men is looking for what I am looking for within a relationship), or to seek other suitors, I try to satisfy myself with video lovers who don't ask questions, shy away from the intricate details of my body's malfunctions, or tell me during intimate moments that they are really having difficulty dealing with my "terminal illness."

This approach is not without its merits. When I become fatigued in the middle of the act, I can always push a pause button on the remote and resume activity with a second wind at any time. I do not have to fear arguments about why I decided not to take my medication this morning. I do not have to explain why the soreness of my rectal tissue will not allow penetration.

On the other hand, I haven't been held tightly in bed in four months. I haven't been allowed to curl up with my back against another's chest and feel his arms around me. I haven't been awakened by a light kiss on my eyelashes. I have not shared a bath or received a massage from someone who cares from more than a professional perspective. My sex life has been sanitized far beyond the impact of the intrusion of latex props.

I do not at all feel lonely. There are always enough telephone interruptions, cards, and even occasional floral arrangements sent by friends. My family has been there for me constantly, offering support, money, transportation, and hands to hold for support during medical procedures. My many friends are good to me. But I still feel alone.

I feel alone on Friday nights when I want to celebrate making it through the seven medical appointments of the week. I feel alone on Monday evenings when I stop at a flower stand on the way from my therapist. I feel alone when I am particularly pleased with a new poem or essay I have just finished, but there is no one I can immediately turn to share these words with. I feel alone most when I realize that through the years I have become strong. I have become stronger than would be necessary if I had a shoulder to sob on, arms that reassured me, lips that passed on a reason to live.

I'm not waiting for a cure. I'm not looking for a miracle. I am not resisting the inevitable. I will die. I will die much sooner than I would like to accept, and there is little I can do about this fact. Kübler-Ross can call that acceptance if she wants, but in doing so, I believe she minimizes one's will to fight. It is precisely because I know I will die that I work even more diligently for the causes I believe in.

It is within this framework that I make decisions about my medical care. It is within this framework that I have made decisions to increase my activities or lessen my involvement in certain organizations. It is within this framework that I continue to plan and conduct HIV prevention programs for African-American gay men. It is this philosophy which has caused me to renew work on a manuscript of poetry and fiction, which was begun over two years ago.

It is all about the quality of life I have found. My quality of life is a control issue. I refuse to be controlled by a daily regimen of oral medications and radiation therapy, controlled by weekly chemotherapy treatments, controlled by the increasing number of side-effects, fatigue or depression, medical bills or reimbursement checks. I refuse to be controlled by limitations imposed upon me by my race/ethnicity, class, sexual orientation, and health.

I have made a commitment to relinquish control only as a last resort. I want to live the rest of my life with an energy that ignites and irritates, burns and bubbles, soothes and inspires until it bursts from this atmosphere, dissipating into the cosmos.

BLACK MACHO REVISITED: REFLECTIONS OF A SNAP! QUEEN (1991)

Marlon Riggs

N egro faggotry is in fashion.
    SNAP!
Turn on your television and camp queens greet you in living color.
SNAP!
Turn to cable and watch America's most bankable modern minstrel
expound on getting "fucked in the ass" or his fear of faggots.
SNAP!
Turn off the TV, turn on the radio: Rotund rapper Heavy D, the
self-styled "overweight lover MC," expounds on how *his* rap will
make you "happy like a faggot in jail." Perhaps to preempt questions
about how he would know—you might wonder what kind of
"lover" he truly is—Heavy D reassures us that he's just "extremely
intellectual, not bisexual."

Jelly-roll SNAP!

    Negro faggotry is in vogue. Madonna commodified it into a
commercial hit. Mapplethorpe photographed it and art galleries
drew fire and record crowds in displaying it. Black macho movie
characters dis'—or should we say dish?—their antagonists with
unkind references to it. Indeed references to, and representations of,
Negro faggotry seem a rite of passage among contemporary black
male rappers and filmmakers.
    Snap-swish-and-dish divas have truly arrived, giving Beauty Shop

drama at center stage, performing the read-and-snap two-step as they sashay across the movie screen, entertaining us in the castles of our homes—like court jesters, like eunuchs—with their double entendres and dead-end lusts, and above all, their relentless hilarity in the face of relentless despair. Negro faggotry is the rage! Black gay men are not. For in the cinematic and television images of and from black America as well as the lyrics and dialogue that now abound and *seem* to address my life as a black gay man, I am struck repeatedly by the determined, unreasoning, often irrational desire to discredit my claim to blackness and hence to black manhood.

In consequence the terrain black gay men navigate in the quest for self and social identity is, to say the least, hostile. What disturbs—no, enrages me, is not so much the obstacles set before me by whites, which history conditions me to expect, but the traps and pitfalls planted by my so-called brothers, who because of the same history should know better.

I am a Negro faggot, if I believe what movies, TV, and rap music say of me. My life is game for play. Because of my sexuality, I cannot be black. A strong, proud, "Afrocentric" black man is res-olutely heterosexual, not *even* bisexual. Hence I remain a Negro. My sexual difference is considered of no value; indeed it's a testament to weakness, passivity, the absence of real guts—balls. Hence I remain a sissy, punk, faggot. I cannot be a black gay man because by the tenets of black macho, black gay man is a triple negation. I am consigned, by these tenets, to remain a Negro faggot. And as such I am game for play, to be used, joked about, put down, beaten, slapped, and bashed, not just by illiterate homophobic thugs in the night, but by black American culture's best and brightest.

In a community where the dozens, signifying, dis'ing, and *dishing* are revered as art form, I ask myself: What does this obsession with Negro faggotry signify? What is its significance?

What lies at the heart, I believe, of black America's pervasive cultural homophobia is the desperate need for a convenient Other *within* the community, yet not truly *of* the community, an Other to which blame for the chronic identity crises afflicting the black male psyche can be readily displaced, an indispensable Other which functions as the lowest common denominator of the abject, the base line of transgression beyond which a Black Man is no longer a man, no longer black, an essential Other against which black men and boys maturing, struggling with self-doubt, anxiety, feelings of political, economic, social, and sexual inadequacy—even impotence—can always measure themselves and by comparison seem strong, adept, empowered, superior.

Indeed the representation of Negro faggotry disturbingly parallels and reinforces America's most entrenched racist constructions around African American identity. White icons of the past signifying "Blackness" share with contemporary icons of Negro faggotry a manifest dread of the deviant Other. Behind the Sambo and the SNAP! Queen lies a social psyche in torment, a fragile psyche threatened by deviation from its egocentric/ethnocentric construct of self and society. Such a psyche systematically defines the Other's "deviance" by the essential characteristics which make the Other distinct, then invests those differences with intrinsic defect. Hence: Blacks are inferior because they are not white. Black gays are unnatural because they are not straight. Majority representations of both affirm the view that blackness and gayness constitute a fundamental rupture in the order of things, that our very existence is an affront to nature and humanity.

From black gay men, this burden of (mis)representation is compounded. We are saddled by historic caricatures of the black male, now fused with newer notions of the Negro faggot. The resultant dehumanization is multilayered, and profound.

What strikes me as most insidious, and paradoxical, is the degree to which popular African American depictions of us as black gay men so keenly resonate American majority depictions of us, as black people. Within the black gay community, for example, the SNAP! contains a multiplicity of coded meanings: as in—SNAP!—"Got your point!" Or—SNAP!—"Don't even try it." Or—SNAP!— "You *fierce!*" Or—SNAP!—"Get out my face." Or—SNAP!— "Girlfriend, *pleeeease.*" The snap can be as emotionally and politically charged as a clenched fist, can punctuate debate and dialogue like an exclamation point, a comma, an ellipse, or altogether negate the need for words among those who are adept at decoding its nuanced meanings.

But the particular appropriation of the snap by Hollywood's Black Pack deflates the gesture into rank caricature. Instead of a symbol of communal expression and, at times, cultural defiance, the snap becomes part of a simplistically reductive Negro faggot identity: It functions as a mere signpost of effeminate, cute, comic homosexuality. Thus robbed of its full political and cultural dimension, the snap, in this appropriation, descends to stereotype.

Is this any different from the motives and consequences associated with the legendary white dramatist T.D. Rice, who more than 150 years ago appropriated the tattered clothes and dance style of an old crippled black man, then went on stage and imitated him, thus shaping in the popular American mind an indelible image of blacks as simplistic and poor yet given, without exception, to "natural" rhythm and happy feet?

A family tree displaying dominant types in the cultural iconography of black men would show, I believe, an unmistakable line of descent from Sambo to the SNAP! Queen, and in parallel lineage, from the Brute Negro to the AIDS-infected Black Homo-Con-Rapist.

What the members of this pantheon share in common is an extreme displacement and distortion of sexuality. In Sambo and the SNAP! Queen sexuality is repressed, arrested. Laughter, levity, and a certain childlike disposition cement their mutual status as comic eunuchs. Their alter egos, the Brute Black and the Homo Con, are but psycho-social projections of an otherwise tamed sexuality run amuck—bestial, promiscuous, pathological.

Contemporary proponents of black macho thus converge with white supremacist D.W. Griffith in their cultural practice, deploying similar devices toward similarly dehumanizing ends. In their constructions of "unnatural" sexual aggression, Griffith's infamous chase scene in *Birth of a Nation*, in which a lusting "Brute Negro" (a white actor in blackface) chases a white Southern virgin to her death, displays a striking aesthetic kinship to the homophobic jail rap—or should I say, attempted rape?—in Reginald and Warrington Hudlin's *House Party*.

The resonances go deeper.

Pseudoscientific discourse fused with popular icons of race in late nineteenth-century America to project a social fantasy of black men, not simply as sexual demons, but significantly, as intrinsically corrupt. Diseased, promiscuous, destructive—of self and others— our fundamental nature, it was widely assumed, would lead us to extinction.

Against this historical backdrop consider the highly popular comedy routines of Eddie Murphy, which unite Negro faggotry, "Herpes Simplex 10"—and AIDS—into an indivisible modern icon of sexual terrorism. Rap artists and music videos resonate this perception, fomenting a social psychology that blames the *victim* for his degradation and death.

The sum total of primetime fag pantomimes, camp queens as culture critics, and the proliferating bit-part swish-and-dish divas who like ubiquitous black maids and butlers in fifties Hollywood films move along the edges of the frame, seldom at the center, manifests the persistent psychosocial impulse toward control, displacement, and marginalization of the black gay Other. This impulse, in many respects, is no different than the phobic, distorted projections which motivated blackface minstrelsy.

This is the irony: There are more black male filmmakers and rap artists than ever, yet their works display a persistently narrow, even monolithic, construction of black male identity.

"You have to understand something," explained Professor Griff of the controversial and highly popular rap group Public Enemy, in an interview. "In knowing and understanding black history, African history, there's not a word in any African language which describes homosexual, y'understand what I'm saying? You would like to make them part of the community, but that's something brand new to black people."

And so black macho appropriates African history, or rather, a deeply reductive, mythologized view of African history, to rationalize homophobia. Pseudoacademic claims of "Afrocentricity" have now become a popular invocation when black macho is pressed to defend its essentialist vision of the race. An inheritance from Black Cultural Nationalism of the late sixties, and Negritude before that, today's Afrocentrism, as popularly theorized, premises an historical narrative which runs thus: Before the white man came, African men were strong, noble, protectors, providers, and warriors for their families and tribes. In precolonial Africa, men were truly men. And women—were women. Nobody was lesbian. Nobody was feminist. Nobody was gay.

This distortion of history, though severe, has its seductions. Given the increasingly besieged state of black men in America, and the nation's historic subversion of an affirming black identity, it is no wonder that a community would turn to pre-Diasporan history for metaphors of empowerment. But the embrace of the African warrior ideal—strong, protective, impassive, patriarchal—has cost us. It has sent us down a perilous road of cultural and spiritual redemption, and distorted or altogether deleted from the historical record the multiplicity of identities around color, gender, sexuality, and class, which inform the African and African American experience.

It is to me supremely revealing that in black macho's popular appropriation of Malcolm X (in movies, music, rap videos), it is consistently Malcolm *before Mecca*—militant, macho, "by any means necessary" Malcolm—who is quoted and idolized, not Malcolm *after* Mecca, when he became more critical of himself and exclusivist Nation of Islam tenets, and embraced a broader, multicultural perspective on nationalist identity.

By the tenets of black macho, true masculinity admits little or no space for self-interrogation or multiple subjectivities around race. Black macho prescribes an inflexible ideal: Strong black men— "Afrocentric" black men—don't flinch, don't weaken, don't take blame or shit, take charge, step-to when challenged, and defend themselves without pause for self-doubt.

Black macho counterpoises this warrior model of masculinity with the emasculated Other: the Other as punk, sissy, Negro faggot, a status with which any man, not just those who in fact are gay, can be, and are, branded should one deviate from rigidly prescribed codes of hyper-masculine conduct.

"When I say Gamma, you say Fag. Gamma. Fag. Gamma. Fag." In the conflict between the frat boys and the "fellas" in Spike Lee's *School Daze*, verbal fag-bashing becomes the weapon of choice in the fellas' contest for male domination. In this regard Lee's movie not only resonates a poisonous dynamic in contemporary black male relations but worse, Lee glorifies it.

Spike Lee and others like him count on the complicit silence of those who know better, who know the truth of their own lives as well as the diverse truths which inform the total black experience.

Notice is served. Our silence has ended. SNAP!

COMFORT (1991)

Don Charles

When you looked and
    saw my Brown skin
Didn't it make you
    feel comfortable?

Didn't you remember that
    old blanket
You used to wrap up in
    when the nights got cold?

Didn't you think about that
    maplewood table
Where you used to sit and
    write letters to your daddy?

Didn't you almost taste that
    sweet gingerbread
Your granny used to make?
    (And you *know* it was good.)

When you looked and
    saw my Brown eyes

Didn't they look just like
home?

THE FOUNDATIONS OF THE EARTH (1992)

Randall Kenan

I

Of course they didn't pay it any mind at first: just a tractor—one of the most natural things in the world to see in a field—kicking dust up into the afternoon sky and slowly toddling off the road into a soybean field. And fields surrounded Mrs. Maggie Mac-Gowan Williams's house, giving the impression that her lawn stretched on and on until it dropped off into the woods far by the way. Sometimes she was certain she could actually see the earth's curve—not merely the bend of the small hill on which her house sat but the great slope of the sphere, the way scientists explained it in books, a monstrous globe floating in a cold nothingness. She would sometimes sit by herself on the patio late of an evening, in the same chair she was sitting in now, sip from her Coca-Cola, and think about how big the earth must be to seem flat to the eye.

She wished she were alone now. It was Sunday.

"Now, I wonder what that man is doing with a tractor out there today?"

They sat on Maggie's patio, reclined in that after-Sunday-dinner way—Maggie; the Right Reverend Hezekiah Barden, round and pompous as ever; Henrietta Fuchee, the prim and priggish music teacher and president of the First Baptist Church Auxiliary Council; Emma Lewis, Maggie's sometimes housekeeper; and Gabriel, Mrs. Maggie Williams's young, white, special guest—all looking out lazily into the early summer, watching the sun begin its slow downward arc, feeling the baked ham and the candied sweet potatoes and the fried chicken with the collard greens and green beans and beets settle in their bellies, talking shallow and pleasant talk, and sipping their Coca-Colas and bitter lemonade.

"Don't they realize it's Sunday?" Reverend Barden leaned back in his chair and tugged at his suspenders thoughtfully, eyeing the tractor as it turned into another row. He reached for a sweating glass of lemonade, his red bow tie afire in the penultimate beams of the day.

"I . . . I don't understand. What's wrong?" Maggie could see her other guests watching Gabriel intently, trying to discern why on earth he was present at Maggie MacGowan Williams's table.

"What you mean, what's wrong?" The Reverend Barden leaned forward and narrowed his eyes at the young man. "What's wrong is: it's Sunday."

"So? I don't . . ." Gabriel himself now looked embarrassed, glancing to Maggie, who wanted to save him but could not.

" 'So?' 'So?' " Leaning toward Gabriel and narrowing his eyes, Barden asked: "You're not from a church-going family, are you?"

"Well, no. Today was my first time in . . . Oh, probably ten years."

"Uh-huh." Barden corrected his posture, as if to say he pitied Gabriel's being an infidel but had the patience to instruct him. "Now you see, the Lord has declared Sunday as His day. It's holy. 'Six days shall thou labor and do all thy work: but the seventh day is the sabbath of the Lord thy God: in it thou shalt not do any work, thou, nor thy son, nor thy daughter, thy manservant, nor thy maidservant, nor thy cattle, nor thy stranger that is within thy gates: for in six days the Lord made heaven and earth, the sea, and all that in them is, and rested the seventh day: wherefore, the Lord blessed the sabbath day, and hallowed it.' Exodus. Chapter twenty, verses nine and ten."

"Amen." Henrietta closed her eyes and rocked.

"Hez." Maggie inclined her head a bit to entreat the good Reverend to desist. He gave her an understanding smile, which made her cringe slightly, fearing her gesture might have been mistaken for a sign of intimacy.

"But, Miss Henrietta—" Emma Lewis tapped the tabletop, like a judge in court, changing the subject. "Like I was saying, I believe that Rick on *The Winds of Hope* is going to marry that gal before she gets too big with child, don't you?" Though Emma kept house for Maggie Williams, to Maggie she seemed more like a sister who came three days a week, more to visit than to clean.

"Now go on away from here, Emma." Henrietta did not look up from her empty cake plate, her glasses hanging on top of her sagging breasts from a silver chain. "Talking about that worldly foolishness on TV. You know I don't pay that mess any attention." She did not want the Reverend to know that she secretly watched afternoon soap operas, just like Emma and all the other women in the congregation. Usually she gossiped to beat the band about this rich heifer and that handsome hunk whenever she found a fellow TV-gazer. Buck-toothed hypocrite, Maggie thought. She knew the truth: Henrietta, herself a widow now on ten years, was sweet on the widower minister, who in turn, alas, had his eye on Maggie.

"Now, Miss Henrietta, we was talking about it t'other day. Don't you think he's apt to marry her soon?" Emma's tone was insistent.

"*I don't know,* Emma." Visibly agitated, Henrietta donned her glasses and looked into the fields. "I wonder who that is anyhow?"

Annoyed by Henrietta's rebuff, Emma stood and began to collect the few remaining dishes. Her purple-and-yellow floral print dress hugged her ample hips. "It's that ole Morton Henry that Miss Maggie leases that piece of land to." She walked toward the door, into the house. "He ain't no God-fearing man."

"Well, that's plain to see." The Reverend glanced over to Maggie. She shrugged.

They are ignoring Gabriel, Maggie thought. She had invited them to dinner after church services thinking it would be pleasant for Gabriel to meet other people in Tims Creek. But generally they chose not to see him, and when they did it was with ill-concealed scorn or petty curiosity or annoyance. At first the conversation seemed civil enough. But the ice was never truly broken, questions still buzzed around the talk like horseflies, Maggie could tell. "Where you from?" Henrietta had asked. "What's your line of work?" Barden had asked. While Gabriel sat there with a look on his face somewhere between peace and pain. But Maggie refused to believe she had made a mistake. At this stage of her life she depended on no one for anything, and she was certainly not dependent on the approval of these self-important fools.

She had been steeled by anxiety when she picked Gabriel up at the airport that Friday night. But as she caught sight of him stepping from the jet and greeted him, asking about the weather in Boston; and after she had ushered him to her car and watched him slide in, seeming quite at home; though it still felt awkward, she thought: I'm doing the right thing.

II

"Well, thank you for inviting me, Mrs. Williams. But I don't understand . . . Is something wrong?"

"Wrong? No, nothing's wrong, Gabriel. I just thought it'd be good to see you. Sit and talk to you. We didn't have much time at the funeral."

"Gee . . . I—"

"You don't want to make an old woman sad, now do you?"

"Well, Mrs. Williams, if you put it like that, how can I refuse?"

"Weekend after next then?"

There was a pause in which she heard muted voices in the wire.

"Okay."

After she hung up the phone and sat down in her favorite chair in the den, she heaved a momentous sigh. Well, she had done it. At last. The weight of uncertainty would be lifted. She could confront him face to face. She wanted to know about her grandboy, and Gabriel was the only one who could tell her what she wanted to know. It was that simple. Surely, he realized what this invitation meant. She leaned back looking out the big picture window onto the tops of the brilliantly blooming crepe myrtle trees in the yard, listening to the grandfather clock mark the time.

III

Her grandson's funeral had been six months ago, but it seemed much longer. Perhaps the fact that Edward had been gone away from home so long without seeing her, combined with the weeks and days and hours and minutes she had spent trying not to think about him and all the craziness that had surrounded his death, somehow lengthened the time.

At first she chose to ignore it, the strange and bitter sadness that seemed to have overtaken her every waking moment. She went about her daily life as she had done for thirty-odd years, overseeing her stores, her land, her money; buying groceries, paying bills, shopping, shopping; going to church and talking to her few good living friends and the few silly fools she was obliged to suffer. But all day, dusk to dawn, and especially at night, she had what the field-workers called "a monkey on your back," when the sun beats down so hot it makes you delirious; but her monkey chilled and angered her, born not of the sun but of a profound loneliness, an oppressive emptiness, a stabbing guilt. Sometimes she even wished she were a drinking woman.

The depression had come with the death of Edward, though its roots reached farther back, to the time he seemed to have vanished. There had been so many years of asking other members of the family: Have you heard from him? Have you seen him? So many years of only a Christmas card or birthday card a few days early, or a cryptic, taciturn phone call on Sunday mornings, and then no calls at all. At some point she realized she had no idea where he was or how to get in touch with him. Mysteriously, he would drop a line to his half-sister, Clarissa, or drop a card without a return address. He was gone. Inevitably, she had to ask: Had she done something evil to the boy to drive him away? Had she tried too hard to make sure he became nothing like his father and grandfather? I was as good a mother as a woman can claim to be, she thought: from the cradle on he had all the material things he needed, and he certainly didn't want for attention, for care; and I trained him proper, he was a well-mannered and upright young fellow when he left here for college. Oh, I was proud of that boy, winning a scholarship to Boston University. Tall, handsome like his granddad. He'd make somebody a good . . .

So she continued picking out culprits: school, the cold North, strange people, strange ideas. But now in her crystalline hindsight she could lay no blame on anyone but Edward. And the more she remembered battles with the mumps and the measles and long division and taunts from his schoolmates, the more she became aware of her true anger. He owes me respect, damn it. The least he can do is keep in touch. Is that so much to ask?

But before she could make up her mind to find him and confront him with her fury, before she could cuss him out good and call him an ungrateful, no-account bastard just like his father, a truck would have the heartless audacity to skid into her grandchild's car one rainy night in Springfield and end his life at twenty-seven, taking that opportunity away from her forever. When they told her of his death she cursed her weakness. Begging God for another chance. But instead He gave her something she had never imagined.

Clarissa was the one to finally tell her. "Grandma," she had said, "Edward's been living with another man all these years."

"So?"

"No, Grandma. Like man and wife."

Maggie had never before been so paralyzed by news. One question answered, only to be replaced by a multitude. Gabriel had come with the body, like an interpreter for the dead. They had been living together in Boston, where Edward worked in a bookstore. He came, head bowed, rheumy-eyed, exhausted. He gave her no explanation; nor had she asked him for any, for he displayed the truth in his vacant and humble glare and had nothing to offer but the penurious tribute of his trembling hands. Which was more than she wanted.

In her world she had been expected to be tearless, patient, comforting to other members of the family; folk were meant to sit back and say, "Lord, ain't she taking it well. I don't think I could be so calm if my grandboy had've died so young." Magisterially she had done her duty; she had taken it all in stride. But her world began to hopelessly unravel that summer night at the wake in the Raymond Brown Funeral Home, among the many somber-bright flower arrangements, the fluorescent lights, and the gleaming bronze casket, when Gabriel tried to tell her how sorry he was . . . How dare he? This pathetic, stumbling, poor trashy white boy, to throw his sinful lust for her grandbaby in her face, as if to bury a grandchild weren't bad enough. Now this abomination had to be flaunted.— Sorry, indeed! The nerve! Who the hell did he think he was to parade their shame about?

Her anger was burning so intensely that she knew if she didn't get out she would tear his heart from his chest, his eyes from their sockets, his testicles from their sac. With great haste she took her leave, brushing off the funeral director and her brother's wives and husband's brothers—they all probably thinking her overcome with grief rather than anger—and had Clarissa drive her home. When she got to the house she filled a tub with water as hot as she could stand it and a handful of bath oil beads, and slipped in, praying her hatred would mingle with the mist and evaporate, leaving her at least sane.

Next, sleep. Healing sleep, soothing sleep, sleep to make the world go away, sleep like death. Her mama had told her that sleep was the best medicine God ever made. When things get too rough— go to bed. Her family had been known as the family that retreated to bed. Ruined crop? No money? Get some shut-eye. Maybe it'll be better in the morning. Can't be worse. Maggie didn't give a damn where Gabriel was to sleep that night; someone else would deal with it. She didn't care about all the people who would come to the house after the wake to the Sitting Up, talking, eating, drinking, watching over the still body till sunrise; they could take care of themselves. The people came; but Maggie slept. From deeps under deeps of slumber she sensed her granddaughter stick her head in the door and whisper, asking Maggie if she wanted something to eat. Maggie didn't stir. She slept. And in her sleep she dreamed.

She dreamed she was Job sitting on his dung heap, dressed in sackcloth and ashes, her body covered with boils, scratching with a stick, sending away Eliphaz and Bildad and Zophar and Elihu, who came to counsel her, and above her the sky boiled and churned and the air roared, and she matched it, railing against God, against her life—*Why? Why? Why did you kill him, you heartless old fiend? Why make me live to see him die? What earthly purpose could you have in such a wicked deed? You are God, but you are not good. Speak to me, damn it. Why? Why? Why?* Hurricanes whipped and thunder ripped through a sky streaked by lightning, and she was lifted up, spinning, spinning, and Edward floated before her in the rushing air and quickly turned around into the comforting arms of Gabriel, winged, who clutched her grandboy to his bosom and soared away, out of the storm. Maggie screamed and the winds grew stronger, and a voice, gentle and sweet, not thunderous as she expected, spoke to her from the whirlwind: *Who is this that darkeneth counsel by words without knowledge? Gird up now thy loins like a man; for I will demand of thee, and answer them me. Where wast thou when I laid the foundations of the earth? Declare if thou hast understanding* . . . The voice spoke of the myriad creations of the universe, the stupendous glory of the Earth and its inhabitants. But Maggie was not deterred in the face of the maelstrom, saying: *Answer me, damn you: Why?,* and the winds began to taper off and finally halted, and Maggie was alone, standing on water. A fish, what appeared to be a mackerel, stuck its head through the surface and said: *Kind woman, be not aggrieved and put your anger away. Your arrogance has clouded your good mind. Who asked you to love? Who asked you to hate?* The fish dipped down with a plip and gradually Maggie too began to slip down into the water, down, down, down, sinking, below depths of reason and love, down into the dark unknown of her own mind, down, down, down.

Maggie MacGowan Williams woke the next morning to the harsh chatter of a bluejay chasing a mocking-bird just outside her window, a racket that caused her to open her eyes quickly to blinding sunlight. Squinting, she looked about the room, seeing the chest of drawers that had once belonged to her mother and her mother's mother before that, the chairs, the photographs on the wall, the television, the rug thickly soft, the closet door slightly ajar, the bureau, the mirror atop the bureau, and herself in the mirror, all of it bright in the crisp morning light. She saw herself looking, if not refreshed, calmed, and within her the rage had gone, replaced by a numb humility and a plethora of questions. Questions. Questions. Questions.

Inwardly she had felt beatific that day of the funeral, ashamed at her anger of the day before. She greeted folk gently, softly, with a smile, her tones honey-flavored but solemn, and she reassumed the mantle of one-who-comforts-more-than-needing-comfort.

The immediate family had gathered at Maggie's house—Edward's father, Tom, Jr.; Tom, Jr.'s wife, Lucille; the grandbaby,

Paul (Edward's brother); Clarissa. Raymond Brown's long black limousine took them from the front door of Maggie's house to the church, where the yard was crammed with people in their greys and navy blues, dark browns, and deep, deep burgundies. In her new humility she mused: When, oh when will we learn that death is not so somber, not something to mourn so much as celebrate? We should wear fire reds, sun oranges, hello greens, ocean-deep blues, and dazzling, welcome-home whites. She herself wore a bright dress of saffron and a blue scarf. She thought Edward would have liked it.

The family lined up and Gabriel approached her. As he stood before her—raven-haired, pink-skinned, abject, eyes bloodshot—she experienced a bevy of conflicting emotions: disgust, grief, anger, tenderness, fear, weariness, pity. Nevertheless she *had* to be civil, *had* to make a leap of faith and of understanding. Somehow she felt it had been asked of her. And though there were still so many questions, so much to sort out, for now she would mime patience, pretend to be accepting, feign peace. Time would unravel the rest.

She reached out, taking both his hands into her own, and said, the way she would to an old friend: "How have you been?"

IV

"But now, Miss Maggie . . ."

She sometimes imagined the good Reverend Barden as a toad-frog or an impotent bull. His rantings and ravings bored her, and his clumsy-advances repelled her; and when he tried to impress her with his holiness and his goodness, well . . .

". . . that man should know better than to be plowing on a Sunday. Sunday! Why, the Lord said . . ."

"Reverend, I know what the Lord said. And I'm sure Morton Henry knows what the Lord said. But I am not the Lord, Reverend, and if Morton Henry wants to plow the west field on Sunday afternoon, well, it's his soul, not mine."

"But, Maggie. Miss Maggie. It's—"

"Well,"—Henrietta Fuchee sat perched to interject her five cents into the debate—"but, Maggie. It's your land! Now, Reverend, doesn't it say somewhere in Exodus that a man, or a woman in this case, a woman is responsible for the deeds or misdeeds of someone in his or her employ, especially on her property?"

"But he's not an emplo—"

"Well,"—Barden scratched his head—"I think I know what you're talking about, Henrietta. It may be in Deuteronomy . . . or Leviticus . . . part of the Mosaic Law, which . . ."

Maggie cast a quick glance at Gabriel. He seemed to be interested in and entertained by this contest of moral superiority. There was certainly something about his face . . . but she could not stare. He looked so *normal* . . .

"Well, I don't think you should stand for it, Maggie."

"Henrietta? What do you . . . ? Look, if you want him to stop, *you* go tell him what the Lord said. I—"

The Right Reverend Hezekiah Barden stood, hiking his pants up to his belly. "Well, *I* will. A man's soul is a valuable thing. And I can't risk your own soul being tainted by the actions of one of your sharecroppers."

"My soul? Sharecropper—he's not a sharecropper. He leases that land. I—wait! . . . Hezekiah! . . . This doesn't . . ."

But Barden had stepped off the patio onto the lawn and was headed toward the field, marching forth like old Nathan on his way to confront King David.

"Wait, Reverend." Henrietta hopped up, slinging her black pocket-book over her left shoulder. "Well, Maggie?" She peered at Maggie defiantly, as if to ask: *Where do you stand?*

"Now, Henrietta, I—"

Henrietta pivoted, her moral righteousness jagged and sharp as a shard of glass. "Somebody has to stand up for right!" She tromped off after Barden.

Giggling, Emma picked up the empty glasses. "I don't think ole Morton Henry gone be too happy to be preached at this afternoon."

Maggie looked from Emma to Gabriel in bewilderment, at once annoyed and amused. All three began to laugh out loud. As Emma got to the door she turned to Maggie. "Hon, you better go see that they don't get into no fistfight, don't you think? You know that Reverend don't know when to be quiet." She looked to Gabriel and nodded knowingly. "You better go with her, son," and was gone into the house; her molasses-thick laughter sweetening the air.

Reluctantly Maggie stood, looking at the two figures—Henrietta had caught up with Barden—a tiny cloud of dust rising from their feet. "Come on, Gabe. Looks like we have to go referee."

Gabriel walked beside her, a broad smile on his face. Maggie thought of her grandson being attracted to this tall white man. She tried to see them together and couldn't. At that moment she understood that she was being called on to realign her thinking about men and women, and men and men, and even women and women. Together . . . the way Adam and Eve were meant to be together.

V

Initially she found it difficult to ask the questions she wanted to ask. Almost impossible.

They got along well on Saturday. She took him out to dinner; they went shopping. All the while she tried with all her might to convince herself that she felt comfortable with this white man, with this homosexual, with this man who had slept with her grandboy. Yet he managed to impress her with his easygoing manner and openness and humor.

"Mrs. W." He had given her a *nickname*, of all things. No one had given her a nickname since . . . "Mrs. W., you sure you don't want to try on some swimsuits?"

She laughed at his kind-hearted jokes, seeing, oddly enough, something about him very like Edward; but then that thought would make her sad and confused.

Finally that night over coffee at the kitchen table she began to ask what they had both gingerly avoided.

"Why didn't he just tell me?"

"He was afraid, Mrs. W. It's just that simple."

"Of what?"

"That you might disown him. That you might stop . . . well, you know, loving him, I guess."

"Does your family know?"

"Yes."

"How do they take it?"

"My mom's fine. She's great. Really. She and Edward got along swell. My dad. Well, he'll be okay for a while, but every now and again we'll have these talks, you know, about cures and stuff and sometimes it just gets heated. I guess it'll just take a little more time with him."

"But don't you *want* to be normal?"

"Mrs. W., I *am*. Normal."

"I see."

They went to bed at one-thirty that morning. As Maggie buttoned up her nightgown, Gabriel's answers whizzed about her brain; but they brought along more damnable questions and Maggie went to bed feeling betrayal and disbelief and revulsion and anger.

In church that next morning with Gabriel, she began to doubt the wisdom of having asked him to come. As he sat beside her in the pew, as the Reverend Barden sermonized on Jezebel and Ahab, as the congregation unsuccessfully tried to disguise their curiosity—("What is that white boy doing here with Maggie Williams? Who is he? Where he come from?")—she wanted Gabriel to go ahead and tell her what to think: *We're perverts* or *You're wrong-headed, your church has poisoned your mind against your own grandson; if he had come out to you, you would have rejected him. Wouldn't you?* Would she have?

Barden's sermon droned on and on that morning; the choir sang; after the service people politely and gently shook Gabriel's and Maggie's hands and then stood off to the side, whispering, clearly perplexed.

On the drive back home, as if out of the blue, she asked him: "Is it hard?"

"Ma'am?"

"Being who you are? What you are?"

He looked over at her, and she could not meet his gaze with the same intensity that had gone into her question. "Being gay?"

"Yes."

"Well, I have no choice."

"So I understand. But is it hard?"

"Edward and I used to get into arguments about that, Mrs. W." His tone altered a bit. He spoke more softly, gently, the way a widow speaks of her dead husband. Or, indeed, the way a widower speaks of his dead husband. "He used to say it was harder being black in this country than gay. Gays can always pass for straight; but blacks can't always pass for white. And most can never pass."

"And what do you think now?"

"Mrs. W., I think *life* is hard, you know?"

"Yes. I know."

VI

Death had first introduced itself to Maggie when she was a child. Her grandfather and grandmother both died before she was five; her father died when she was nine; her mother when she was twenty-five; over the years all her brothers except one. Her husband ten years ago. Her first memories of death: watching the women wash a cold body: the look of brown skin darkening, hardening: the corpse laid out on a cooling board, wrapped in a winding-cloth, before interment: fear of ghosts, bodyless souls: troubled sleep. So much had changed in seventy years; now there were embalming, funeral homes, morticians, insurance policies, bronze caskets, a bureaucratic wall between deceased and bereaved. Among the many things she regretted about Edward's death was not being able to touch his body. It made his death less real. But so much about the world seemed unreal to her these dark, dismal, and gloomy days. Now the flat earth was said to be round and bumblebees were not supposed to fly.

What was supposed to be and what truly was. Maggie learned these things from magazines and television and books; she loved to read. From her first week in that small schoolhouse with Miss Clara Oxendine, she had wanted to be a teacher. School: the scratchy chalkboard, the dusty-smelling textbooks, labyrinthine grammar and spelling and arithmetic, geography, reading out loud, giving confidence to the boy who would never learn to read well, correcting addition and subtraction problems, the taste and the scent of the schoolroom, the heat of the potbellied stove in January. She liked that small world; for her it was large. Yet how could she pay for enough education to become a teacher? Her mother would smile, encouragingly, when young Maggie would ask her, not looking up from her sewing, and merely say: "We'll find a way."

However, when she was fourteen she met a man named Thomas Williams, he sixteen going on thirty-nine. Infatuation replaced her dreams and murmured to her in languages she had never heard before, whispered to her another tale: *You will be a merchant's wife.*

Thomas Williams would come a-courting on Sunday evenings for two years, come driving his father's red Ford truck, stepping out with his biscuit-shined shoes, his one good Sunday suit, his hat cocked at an impertinent angle, and a smile that would make cold butter drip. But his true power lay in his tongue. He would spin yarns and tell tales that would make the oldest storyteller slap his knee and declare: "Hot damn! Can't that boy lie!" He could talk a possum out of a tree. He spoke to Maggie about his dream of opening his own store, a dry-goods store, and then maybe two or three or four. An audacious dream for a seventeen-year-old black boy, son of a farmer in 1936—and he promised, oh, how he promised, to keep Maggie by his side through it all.

Thinking back, on the other side of time and dreams, where fantasies and wishing had been realized, where she sat rich and alone, Maggie wondered what Thomas Williams could possibly have seen in that plain brown girl. Himself the son of a farmer with his own land, ten sons and two daughters, all married and doing well. There she was, poorer than a skinned rabbit, and not that pretty. Was he looking for a woman who would not flinch at hard work?

Somehow, borrowing from his father, from his brothers, working two, three jobs at the shipyards, in the fields, with Maggie taking in sewing and laundry, cleaning houses, saving, saving, saving, they opened their store; and were married. Days, weeks, years of days, weeks of days, weeks of inventory and cleaning and waiting on people and watching over the dry-goods store, which became a hardware store in the sixties while the one store became two. They were prosperous; they were respected; they owned property. At seventy she now wanted for nothing. Long gone was the dream of a schoolhouse and little children who skinned their knees and the teaching of the ABCs. Some days she imagined she had two lives and she preferred the original dream to the flesh-and-blood reality.

Now, at least, she no longer had to fight bitterly with her pompous, self-satisfied, driven, blaspheming husband, who worked seven days a week, sixteen hours a day, money-grubbing and mean though—outwardly—flamboyantly generous; a man who lost interest in her bed after her first and only son, Thomas, Jr., arrived broken in heart, spirit, and brain upon delivery; a son whose only true achievement in life was to illegitimately produce Edward by some equally brainless waif of a girl, now long vanished; a son who practically thrust the few-week-old infant into Maggie's arms, then flew off to a life of waste, sloth, petty crime, and finally a menial job in one of her stores and an ignoble marriage to a woman who could not conceal her greedy wish for Maggie to die.

Her life now was life that no longer had bite or spit or fire. She no longer worked. She no longer had to worry about Thomas's philandering and what pretty young thing he was messing with now. She no longer had the little boy whom Providence seemed to have sent her to maintain her sanity, to moor her to the Earth, and to give her vast energies focus.

In a world not real, is there truly guilt in willing reality to cohere through the life of another? Is that such a great sin? Maggie had turned to the boy—young, brown, handsome—to hold on to the world itself. She now saw that clearly. How did it happen? The mental slipping and sliding that allowed her to meld and mess and confuse her life with his, his rights with her wants, his life with her wish? He would not be like his father or his grandfather; he would rise up, go to school, be strong, be honest, upright. He would be; she would be . . . a feat of legerdemain; a sorcery of vicariousness in which his victory was her victory. He was her champion. Her hope.

Now he was gone. And now she had to come to terms with this news of his being "gay," as the world called what she had been taught was an unholy abomination. Slowly it all came together in her mind's eye: Edward.

He should have known better. I should have known better. I must learn better.

VII

They stood there At the end of the row, all of them waiting for the tractor to arrive and for the Reverend Hezekiah Barden to save the soul of Morton Henry.

Morton saw them standing there from his mount atop the green John Deere as it bounced across the broken soil. Maggie could make out the expression on his face: confusion. Three blacks and a white man out in the fields to see him. Did his house burn down? His wife die? The President declare war on Russia?

A big, red-haired, red-faced man, his face had so many freckles he appeared splotched. He had a big chew of tobacco in his left jaw and he spat out the brown juice as he came up the edge of the row and put the clutch in neutral.

"How you all today? Miss Maggie?"

"Hey, Morton."

Barden started right up, thumbs in his suspenders, and reared back on his heels. "Now I spect you're a God-fearing man?"

"Beg pardon?"

"I even spect you go to church from time to time?"

"Church? Miss Maggie, I—"

The Reverend held up his hand. "And I warrant you that your preacher—where do you go to church, son?"

"I go to—wait a minute. What's going on here? Miss Maggie—"

Henrietta piped up. "It's Sunday! You ain't supposed to be working and plowing fields on a Sunday!"

Morton Henry looked over to Maggie, who stood there in the bright sun, then to Gabriel, as if to beg him to speak, make some sense of this curious event. He scratched his head. "You mean to tell me you all come out here to tell me I ain't suppose to plow this here field?"

"Not on Sunday you ain't. It's the Lord's Day."

" 'The Lord's Day'?" Morton Henry was visibly amused. He tongued at the wad of tobacco in his jaw. "The Lord's Day." He chuckled out loud.

"Now it ain't no laughing matter, young man." The Reverend's voice took on a dark tone.

Morton seemed to be trying to figure out who Gabriel was. He spat. "Well, I tell you, Reverend. If the Lord wants to come plow these fields I'd be happy to let him."

"You . . ." Henrietta stomped her foot, causing dust to rise. "You can't talk about the Lord like that. You're using His name in vain."

"I'll talk about Him any way I please to." Morton Henry's face became redder by the minute. "I got two jobs, five head of children, and a sick wife, and the Lord don't seem too worried about that. I spect I ain't gone worry too much about plowing this here field on His day none neither."

"Young man, you can't—"

Morton Henry looked to Maggie. "Now, Miss Maggie, this is your land, and if you don't want me to plow it, I'll give you back your lease and you can pay me my money and find somebody else to tend this here field!"

Everybody looked at Maggie. How does this look, she couldn't help thinking, a black woman defending a white man against a black minister? Why the *hell* am I here having to do this? she fumed. Childish, hypocritical idiots and fools. Time is just slipping, slipping away and all they have to do is fuss and bother about other folk's business while their own houses are burning down. God save their souls. She wanted to yell this, to cuss them out and stomp away and leave them to their ignorance. But in the end, what good would it do?

She took a deep breath. "Morton Henry. You do what you got to do. Just like the rest of us."

Morton Henry bowed his head to Maggie, "Ma'am," turned to

the others with a gloating grin, "Scuse me," put his gear in first, and turned down the next row.

"Well—"

Barden began to speak but Maggie just turned, not listening, not wanting to hear, thinking: When, Lord, oh when will we learn? Will we ever? *Respect*, she thought. Oh how complicated.

They followed Maggie, heading back to the house, Gabriel beside her, tall and silent, the afternoon sunrays romping in his black hair. How curious the world had become that she would be asking a white man to exonerate her in the eyes of her own grandson; how strange that at seventy, when she had all the laws and rules down pat, she would have to begin again, to learn. But all this stuff and bother would have to come later, for now she felt so, so tired, what with the weekend's activities weighing on her three-score-and-ten-year-old bones and joints; and she wished it were sunset, and she alone on her patio, contemplating the roundness and flatness of the earth, and slipping softly and safely into sleep.

MIKE #2 (1992)

Robert E. Penn

M ike languished on the old sofa that dominated his tiny Village apartment. He stared listlessly at the ceiling, wondering. Fearing, worrying, asking, praying, crying without tears. What could he do now? What hadn't he already done that should have led him to a different space than here? Here in his head and heart somewhere so close to nothingness that he could not survive it, or so he thought, feared. Not alone at any rate. Now was the time, surely, to commit to bite the bullet, to merge and/or share for sure because there might be no other time to do it. There simply might not be time.

Playing hard to get all these years. Getting so many lays all these years. Taking the grovelling ones, turning away the ones of substance. They would always be around. Around for the long haul when Mike would be ready for a real relationship, a real partner, a person with whom to grow old.

If he didn't decide to get some woman pregnant just so that he could have a family like everyone else. So that he could fit in: she would fit in, too. There were five single women for every single man in New York. More than one would be willing to accept a part-time husband when the only alternative was no husband at all.

Choice was made now. He had made it without knowing it, he had made the choice—years ago. Yes. He had, in fact, made the choice years ago—but he would have preferred to leave the back (Ha! Back? More like front) door open for a quick escape. Ever present escape—easy way out, flip flopping back and forth from one to the other. One person to the other—one gender to the other. The ultimate flip—when some man gets too close, get a wife. No! Not anymore. He would no longer have that option. Well, he had that option. But it was no longer the solution it might otherwise have been. Because now he could no longer rely upon her to saddle him with child, to make him force him to choose—for all intents and appearances—straight family life.

Mike's neck snapped back and upside down as he strained to look behind him around the sofa's arm through the kitchen to the buzzer. He was expecting Lawrence, Rasta-looking brother he hadn't seen or called for months, until today.

He thought his line of vision might align with the button and thereby free him of the need to sit up, stand, walk over to the door, push the button, and talk to the person outside the building's front door. He spotted the button and started. He focused on it with all his might.

The meditation courses for which he spent hard-earned money had not yet raised his consciousness to the right level. All those hours of Zazen sitting cross-legged in utter pain (limbs asleep, blood frozen) had not paid off. Not yet, anyway. In more than one way, they hadn't taken him to Nirvana; hadn't spared his mortality and vulnerability; and hadn't even given him the power to move objects. All he wanted to do was to push a lousy 1/4-inch button.

"Who is it?"

"Lawrence. Expecting someone else?"

"No, only you, man. Sometimes kids pass by and push all the buttons just for the hell of it."

"It's freezing out here. You asked me over, remember?"

"Yeah, sure." He buzzed the door. "Come on in, man. Up three flights."

"I'm already breathless."

"That's how I like it! See you in a few."

* * *

Mike unlocked and cracked the door open, then rushed back to the living/bedroom and hurriedly straightened the spartan space. Several papers disappeared under the sofa. The Levolor mini-blinds were redirected to bounce the waning sunlight away from the faded upholstery onto the ceiling.

Mike smiled as he walked back to the kitchen and the welcoming door. His right ear twitched when he heard Lawrence's footsteps on the third-floor landing, his third-floor landing. His heart leapt or was it his *hara:* the center of gravity just above the base of the penis, the axis of his sexuality, nave of spirituality. He opened the door wide and leaned mock-seductively against the doorjamb. "You made it." Mike happily recognized the firm muscles he knew lay below Lawrence's layers of down and denim.

"Thank God I went to the gym today."

Lawrence's dreads shimmied around, his glowing face. "Hi!" He braced himself against Mike's chest and tiptoed up to kiss him. Feet flat again, he moved as close into his host as he could without crushing the flowers against the bottled water, the shrimp, and the fresh vegetables that shared the space of a paper bag in his left hand. They hugged a greeting. Face to face like this, Lawrence's eyelids brushed Mike's pouting lower lip; his forehead filled the hollow of Mike's cheek as if tailored. They looked perfect together: moderate bulk, medium build, great definition.

A certain concern for Lawrence's well-being pulled Mike away to a safe, bashful distance. "What's in the bag?"

"Flowers and—"

"For me? I love flowers."

"Doesn't everybody?"

"No. Or at least they won't all admit it."

"I knew you did."

"Come on in, man."

"A kitchen tub." Lawrence smiled. "I think I had you pegged for that, too."

"It's cheap." Mike took the flowers and put them in a cobalt-blue glass vase he filled with fresh bath water. "What's all that?"

"Dinner." Lawrence smiled as he set the bag on the counter. "Feel like cooking?"

"Not really, but—"

"We can do it together."

"I know."

Lawrence laughed. "Yes, that too."

"An evening of innuendo."

"Only innuendo?"

Mike wondered if he were really up to the task of confiding in Lawrence. He feared that, once informed, Lawrence would no longer find him attractive—physically or as a catch for the relationship. "Slow is what we agreed."

"That was months ago—and besides, it was my idea. If I'm ready to speed things up—well, you don't really have much to say about it, do you?"

"Some logic."

"Politics," he laughed. "You got any pasta?"

"Jackpot," intentionally brushing against Lawrence's side and back, he reached to open the cabinet above two wrought iron burners on the counter where Lawrence stood. Mike smiled. "That's about all I have."

"Don't cook much?"

"Get meals at work, mostly."

"You still waitering?"

"I send out hundreds of résumés."

"Something will come up. Do you have a skillet, or maybe a wok?"

"Yeah, a wok! Never used it."

"A virgin wok! Imagine that." Lawrence cruised Mike below the waist as he took the wok. He smiled, then lit the fire, chopped vegetables and cleaned shrimp in a flurry of activity. He instructed Mike to set the table and brought the piping hot food to it. They sat to eat.

Mike forgot his fears as they ate. It was delicious. He noticed a smile across Lawrence's face as he bit into his own creation. Mike imagined that Lawrence was a very proud person, happy to cook a fine meal, do a good workout, make love well. He was glad that he had called Lawrence, even if it were out of distress. No matter what happened now, whether he could confide or not, their time together had its rewards.

He played with his food for a few seconds in order to conceal the bemused infatuation that he felt. When he looked up to smile at Lawrence, he saw a near apparition: Lawrence's body was there, but his spirit, consciousness seemed to be far removed. Lawrence stared at a space on the wall behind Mike's sofa. What did he see? Mike craned to see if there was anything special, but only saw chipping paint.

Mike catalogued the expression on Lawrence's face under child-like, innocent, sweet, tender, loving and cross-referenced it to Lawrence under Special Friends and Potential Lovers.

Mike reached out toward Lawrence and felt a stillness within the radiance of his body, from his cranium to the bottom of his spine. He touched Lawrence's shoulder. "Lawrence. Man. Hello—you stopped mid-sentence."

Lawrence turned his gaze back to the present and to Mike. He wrested forth a shallow smile. "Sorry, I do that daydreaming, fantasies, sometimes I come up with great ideas that way. My boss loves it. My ads work, they really sell. Just then, I saw a cottage, roaring fireplace, you and me—on a bearskin rug. It was very romantic."

"You're romantic?"

"Yeah. Of course."

"I had no idea. You never called, I thought—"

Lawrence's entire face relaxed as he admitted, "You were often in my dreams."

Mike's expression iced over. Every muscle in his body flexed tight, tense. "I've gotta tell you something. It's the reason I called you over." What could he do now? Of all the times for Lawrence to choose to get romantic. Mike considered keeping his important secret, for fear that sharing it would shatter the affection he so desperately craved.

"Let's get comfortable, then you can tell me everything." Lawrence led Mike to the sofa, settled in, looked at Mike's chin, smiled, then took Mike's hands in his. "I'm all ears."

"I—I—I got some results from the doctor today. This is very difficult. I don't even know what I think about it yet, how are you going to feel about it?"

"I'm not going anywhere."

Mike smiled and, leaning very close to Lawrence's ear, he whispered. "My T-cells are down, man. I can't—"

"Excuse me for cutting you short, but if you're trying to tell me that you're HIV-positive, don't worry, I figured as much. We all took the same risks, all went through that period of not speaking to each other for fear that staying in contact with the old pier, bathhouse, and disco crowd would make us sick. I know guys who have sixteen T-4 cells and still look great—keeping busy—working out."

"Have you taken the test?"

"So far I've decided not to test. Well, I just can't bring myself to do it. I guess I know I'm positive, but I don't want my worst fears confirmed. I take good care of myself—"

"So do I, but it's not enough."

"Hey, don't slip into that shit. The virus didn't suddenly appear just to punish you. It's always been here. You'll be fine."

Mike had expected a more dramatic, frightened reaction from Lawrence. Disappointed, he jumped up. "What makes you think you know so much?"

"I learned a lot from a good buddy who died last year. He was proud to be gay and black; proud of his way of loving other men; proud that HIV was in him because it was. He accepted the virus as sort of a misguided tourist—you know, like the classic ugly American—too unconscious to realize it was killing what it came to visit. I accepted the reality of it without buying into negative stuff."

"You don't hate me?"

Lawrence smiled and reached up to Mike.

"You don't want to lose me?"

"Get serious."

Mike sat next to his friend again. Every sinew sighed and slackened. His torso relaxed into Lawrence's side.

Mike felt his friend's warmth and electricity flow into him and automatically passed his palm over Lawrence's crotch. The go-slow ended. "Will you hold me?" His smile stretched across his face. What a smile.

"I'll do more than that. Is this sofa, your bed?"

"Yeah."

"Want me to stay the night?"

"Yeah."

"Done."

"We don't have to do anything, but I got some free condoms at the Gay Health Clinic."

"I picked up some on the way over here, just in case."

Mike drew Lawrence to his feet, then pulled out the bed. "I haven't decided what to do about medication yet. Got the benefit forms and everything. It's confusing. My doctor wants me to start low-dose AZT."

"We can talk about that tomorrow. Tonight, well—" Lawrence smiled sensually. "Where are the sheets?"

"I'll get them."

"I'll help."

Mike approached Lawrence from behind and wrapped around him. They turned into one another and smiled. "Let's do this right. We've postponed it long enough." They kissed long and real.

"Yeah, right." Lawrence smiled deep into Mike's eyes. "I can look you in the eye tonight. Before, I was too nervous to simultaneously look you in the eye and smile. Too scared you were so perfect, so powerful that you'd absorb me, take all of me, and spit out the remains when you were done."

"That's what I thought you'd do to me!"

They laughed as they made the bed, undressed to their shorts and slid onto the bed. Mike tugged at Lawrence's briefs, coaxing. "Let me see, before we turn out the lights."

"You've already seen everything—in the showers, at the gym."

"I thought I was slicker than that." Mike tossed his head back, embarrassed, laughing. "But anyway, I didn't see up close."

Mike moaned throatily as he kissed Lawrence.

They stripped each other and rubbed their gym-calloused hands over each other's smooth legs. Their lips turned up in crescents. Their arms became feathers of a wing. Their torsos intertwined like tall, dark, strong trees.

Their fingers pulled each other close together, tight. Their shoulders brushed, struggling to meld. Their chests throbbed against each other. Their penises kissed.

Each felt the thrill of the very best high—heat and electricity move over and through his body, from crown to tail, each felt the hot bath of the other's saliva on his chest, thighs, and shaft.

They expressed their passion well that night and slept deeply, touching, embracing, loving.

FROM CAPTAIN SWING (1993)

Larry Duplechan

I'm here to see my father," I said to the same braided-haired nurse I'd seen the previous day. "Lance Rousseau." The nurse glanced at her wristwatch and then briefly down at the desk and said, "They givin' him his breakfast now. You can go on in if you want to."

Nigel said, "I'll wait over there," indicating the small waiting area.

Several long, deep yoga breaths failed to calm my racing heartbeat as I approached the door to my father's room. I should have hopped the first plane home when I had the chance, I thought. Well, maybe the first train.

"Please, Mr. Rousseau," came a plaintive female voice from within the room. "How can I feed you if you won't open your mouth?" From the doorway, I could see my father, propped up in bed with several pillows, his face set, jaw clenched, a food tray set before him. Bedside, perched on a high stool, spoon in hand, was a heavyset, caramel-colored young nurse's assistant.

"I said get away from me, girl," Lance growled through clenched teeth.

"Come on now, Mr. Rousseau," the woman repeated in a voice like honey-butter laced with arsenic, "just one bite."

"No!" Lance said, teeth together as if wired shut. "You eat it."

I smiled at the little drama, at my father's childish petulance, the woman's exasperation. Suddenly I was considerably less nervous. The brawny-armed disciplinarian who had left so many stripes on my thighs, the paragon of masculinity who had made me feel so inferior for so very long, the father who had turned me from his home—that man, or what was left of him—lay all but helpless in a hospital bed, refusing to eat his porridge. Fate had had to nearly flatten Lance Rousseau before I could feel I had anything resembling the upper hand, but this was definitely it.

"Let me give it a try," I said, stepping into the small, machine-dense room. The nurse's aide turned. Lance looked across the bed, across the room. Though Lance's eyes gave me nothing, I could have sworn I saw the threat of a smile pass, if briefly, across my father's tightly shut face. "I'm his son," I added for the woman's benefit. She looked at Lance, then back at me. Perhaps finding a family resemblance in my features, almost certainly happy to be relieved of duty, she shook the spoon clean, walked over, and handed it to me. "Good luck," she said, deadpan, and left the room.

Wiggling the spoon between my fingers, I strolled toward the bed. "Hello, Dad," I said, climbing onto the stool vacated by the nurse's aide. No visible or audible acknowledgment from the man in bed. So I said, "Hello, son, how nice of you to drop everything and schlep halfway across the United States to be treated like so much dog shit by your hateful homophobic asshole father. What a good, good son you are."

Lance blinked. I considered emptying the breakfast tray onto my father's head and fingerpainting obscenities across his hospital gown in strained squash, but thought better of it. I took a couple of yoga breaths and tried again.

"How are you feeling today, Dad?" I said. Lance continued to stare straight ahead. But after a moment, he said, "I'm dying. How the hell are you?"

I suppressed a smile. It wasn't much, but it was an answer. "Well," I said, "Garbo talks. How the hell am I, you ask. Well, let's see, now . . . my lover was killed by a hit-and-run over a year ago and I'm still in mourning. I'm given to screaming nightmares, I've been taking an extremely habit-forming prescription drug just to keep my mind from flying apart like a New Year's party favor, and I don't know if I'll ever love again. I'm in therapy with a shrink who looks like Opie, and who tells me there's no formal timetable for grief. And right at the moment, I'm sitting in a hospital room in the middle of Nowhere City, Louisiana, staring at my dying father, who doesn't want to see me. I'm fine." It crossed my mind to mention that I'd recently made something very like whoopie with Lance's nearly nineteen-year-old nephew, but chose not to just yet.

Finding no discernible reaction from Lance, I waved the spoon I still held, made a pop-eyed, twisted-lipped Baby Jane Hudson face, and barked à la Bette Davis, "Time ta eat-cha BREAK-fast!" I scooped up a spoonful of orangish-brownish mush from one of the larger compartments of the food tray and held it toward my father's tightly closed lips. Lance continued to stare straight ahead, across the room and seemingly through the open doorway and into the hall. I raised the spoon high, then brought it slowly down in a long, wavy line. "Open up the hangar," I singsonged, "here comes the airplane." No reaction. "Come on, Dad," I said softly. "I know it doesn't look so good, but I'm sure it's good for you. You need to rally your strength, you know."

"What for?" Lance said, opening his lips just enough to allow the words to escape. "I'm gonna die anyhow."

"So die, already!" I shouted, slamming the spoon down onto the tray, causing the food to splatter, leaving a little sprinkling of orangish-brownish spots on my father's hospital gown. "Don't just lie there, staring out into space, talking through your teeth, throwing people out, and pointedly not eating anything. Die if you're going to die. I'm sure they could use the room, and besides—I personally can't wait to do the hokey-pokey on your grave and get on with what is laughingly called my life. So just die, okay?"

I was trembling by the time I'd finished that little tirade. I crossed my arms tightly over my ribs and waited for it to pass. When, to my surprise, Lance opened his mouth wide, eyes closed like a man about to have his gums poked by a particularly clumsy dental hygienist, I scraped up another spoonful of food and carefully introduced it into my father's gaping mouth. Lance closed his lips around the spoon, frowning at the taste of it. When I had withdrawn the empty spoon, Lance said, "You talk just like your mother. You always did."

I lifted another spoonful from the tray and said, "I'll take that as a compliment, thanks. Open." Lance took another spoonful of the indeterminate mush, then said through barely parted lips, "How is your mother?"

"She's fine," I said. I seriously considered adding something about my mother finally finding a man who treated her as she deserved, but let it go for the moment. Among the grab bag of ill feelings I was harboring for my father, I held a special grudge for the sexual infidelities—some surreptitious, others carelessly exposed, some spitefully flaunted—which had driven Clara Rousseau away from her husband after twenty-one years of marriage. Now, nearly fifteen years later, I enjoyed the idea that my father, no longer the handsome bronze charmer, without wife and decidedly without paramour, might finally have lived to regret his past actions.

"She still living with that Jew?" Lance said.

"Yes," I said with some satisfaction. "She and Daniel are in Paris at the moment. Paris, France," I added, hoping the thought of the wife he'd so stupidly allowed himself to lose, summering in the city of *toujours l'amour* wiih a red-haired gynecologist seventeen years her junior, might cause my father some small pain. Nothing excruciating; a nice little sting would do. I smiled and said, "She's very, very happy." I watched my father's jaw muscles tighten and knew the sting had stung. I've seldom been one for kicking a man when he's down, but I have to admit I was really enjoying this.

The better part of a minute passed before Lance said, so softly I could just hear it, "I loved that woman."

I failed to stifle a quick, high, Chihuahua-bark of a laugh. "Well, you always did have the oddest little ways of showing your affection." I scooped up another spoonful of food, held it toward my father's face, and said, "More?"

"No," Lance said through his teeth, his eyes shut tight, as if the food ceased to exist as soon as he couldn't see it.

A long minute went by. Then two. Lance lay there thinking thoughts I could only have guessed at: the loss of a good wife? the impending loss of life? the blandness of his hospital breakfast? For my own part, I spent the silence thinking about a question, one I'd waited years to ask. Just considering it brought on a case of the trembles so strong I had to lay down the spoon. I took a good, long breath and went ahead. "On the general subject of people you allegedly loved," I said, crossing my arms again tightly across my front in a self-hug, "do—did you love me?"

"What?" Lance said, his expression unchanged.

"Nothing," I said quickly, feeling a fool for asking, feeling frustrated for having to ask. "Never mind."

Lance's sudden attack of deafness, whether genuine or feigned, gave me the opportunity to backpedal, to approach the love question a bit more slowly and quietly, like a rabbit in your dahlia garden. "You always favored David so much," I began. "Not that I blame you. What father wouldn't have? He was everything a father could want in a son. Unlike some of us." My heart beat like a West Hollywood dance club on a Saturday night, but I forced myself to continue. "And I know I never brought home any basketball trophies, but I did excel in some things—my grades, my clarinet. My singing. But I—" I felt my throat tighten; I swallowed hard. "God, I must sound like Tommy Smothers, here. 'Dad always liked you best.' But, see, I never quite felt like you valued the things I did as much as you valued what David did. I so wanted to feel like you were proud of me, too. For the things I accomplished. And that you loved me, too." I paused a moment, waiting for some reaction from my father: if not some small morsel of belated reassurance, at least some knee-jerk denial of ever having withheld his approval or his love.

There I sat. Open. Vulnerable. Utterly unacknowledged.

Finally, I heard my father take in a breath through slightly parted lips.

"Proud of you," he said, neither opening his eyes nor turning his face in my direction, his voice a harsh rasp, like steel wool against your skin. The phrase emerged without inflection, not quite a question, not exactly a statement. It occurred to me that my father might be attempting to tell me that he was, in fact, proud of me, and I felt a slight adrenaline kick at the thought.

"You made me sick," he said, slowly, deliberately, his meaning quite unequivocal, each word hitting me like a roundhouse right to the stomach. "Come sashaying into my house," he continued, his lips scarcely moving, "talking about 'I'm gay,' like you so damn happy you was a faggot. Like I'm supposed to be happy about it. Bringing some little sissified white boyfriend right *in* my house. Like it wasn't enough, my son was taking some white man up the butt— I had to *meet* him, too." He made a little snorting sound around the plastic nose piece. "Proud of you," he repeated, then added, "shit."

I gripped the sides of the stool I sat on, fighting the shakes, blinking rapidly against the tears. I was *not* going to cry. I refused to give him the satisfaction of making me cry. A minute, maybe ninety seconds, and several long, deep breaths later, the trembling subsided and I decided to trust my voice not to betray my pain. I decided to pass on the opportunity to mention that I was, in fact, quite happy to be gay; to remind him that the young man I so foolishly chose to bring home to meet the folks, was a strapping six-footer and anything but "sissified"; or to volunteer that, notwithstanding my father's remark about my taking it up the butt, I'm basically a top.

I spoke softly, slowly, as evenly as I could manage.

"Why, you ugly old half-dead *piece* of an evil muthafucka. I have never in my life asked you to be proud of my gayness. I am neither proud nor ashamed of being gay. Being gay is not in and of itself an accomplishment. However," and I swallowed around a lump of soreness, "let us forget the subject of pride for just a moment"—I sniffed a wet one—"and get back to this love thing. After all, whatever else I may be, I am your firstborn son. Your only living son. And I think it's a perfectly reasonable question to ask, so I'll ask it again, in case you missed it the first time around. Do you love me"—and I paused for a bit of dramatic effect before adding, "Father?"

Lance made no sound, save for the soft hiss of his slow, even breathing.

I waited.

Then I waited a little longer.

"Dad?" I leaned in toward my father's ear. "Dad?" Lance's only reply was his familiar, flutteringly glottal snore—a sound not unlike an old Volkswagen Beetle with serious muffler problems, taking a steep incline—the snore both David and I myself had inherited. While no longer the roar it had been in Lance's robust youth (when it resembled a Mack truck with no muffler at all), it was still a formidable sound, more than capable of filling a small hospital room.

"Perfect," I said aloud, taking my leave of Lance, the room, the snore.

Nigel looked up from a magazine as I approached. "How'd it go?" he asked.

"Oh, fine," I said. "I force-fed him three mouthfuls of baby food, then sang him to sleep."

Nigel's thick, black eyebrows rose and Nigel followed them up to a standing position. "You sang?"

"No," I said. "Could we go get some breakfast? I'd absolutely kill for a cheese omelette."

"How 'bout Anna Lee's?" Nigel said. I shot him a look—I was in no mood. "For breakfast, Captain," Nigel said, raising a shielding hand, "for breakfast. Anna Lee can bum her some grits and eggs and she'll sling it our way free-for-nothin'. Okay?" He smiled that smile.

FROM FRAGMENTS THAT REMAIN (1993)

Steven Corbin

M y sons's not going anywhere with those two . . . freaks!"
"Would you lower your voice. They ain't deaf, you know."
"They're not normal either . . . and I've told you before, there's no
such word as 'ain't.' "

"You understand what I'm saying. He told you all about it. You
already said it was okay."

Skylar was embarrassed for his Uncle Aubrey. Though the conversation had been conducted in the upstairs bedroom, every word
tumbled down the staircase, loud and clear. Skylar covered his ears,
but the words filtered through his fingers and penetrated his
eardrums.

Uncle Aubrey appeared relaxed. His legs crossed, he fanned himself nonchalantly with his fedora, the sheer curtains stirring from
the unusually hot June breeze. The oscillating electric fan blew hot
air as flies the size of kidney beans buzzed overhead. Uncle Aubrey's
friend George wasn't as calm. He paced the living room floor,
cursing under his breath, apparently annoyed and insulted by the
conversation bellowing from upstairs. When he heard the word
freaks, he looked at Uncle Aubrey, his mouth shaped in an O, gestic-
ulating with his hands, pointing upstairs with his thumb. Uncle
Aubrey grinned. His serenity put Skylar at ease. As it was, Skylar
was wondering if he was all dressed up on a Sunday afternoon with
no place to go.

Greenwich Village.

Skylar had never seen anything like it. Though a native New Yorker, he hadn't realized until then that he hadn't seen much of this wide and wondrous city. Outside Harlem and midtown, he'd barely explored the diverse neighborhoods. During the subway ride downtown on the A train, the dark tunnel was broken with an opening of yellow light. The conductor's voice announced Waverly Place. Uncle Aubrey tapped his nephew on the shoulder, and the three of them walked between the sliding doors onto the platform. Up several flights of stairs they climbed, the roaring of underground trains rumbling and shaking the foundations on which they stood. One last flight of stairs and they strolled out onto the sidewalk of Avenue of the Americas.

Skylar couldn't believe his eyes.

He'd never seen such . . . strange people. "See those men over there with the beards, earrings, berets, and sunglasses?" Uncle Aubrey explained, with the authority of a tour guide. "They're the last of what's called beatniks." They walked a block or so through the thick, slow-moving crowd, Skylar repeatedly bumping into passersby, his head constantly turning, neck craning, soaking up the sights.

"And this," Uncle Aubrey said, "is the Village. Never in your life will you ever see a place as fantastic as this." The streets teemed with so many people, Skylar imagined that every New Yorker was crammed into this neighborhood. Crowds were gathered at several spots, where opposing political viewpoints were being passionately put forth, as people cheered, clapped, or booed. They were debating civil rights, abortion, capital punishment, and something called Vietnam. Skylar had never heard those strange words before. Hadn't realized, until now, that his country was at war. His uncle pointed out a tall brick building with bars covering the windows. The Women's House of Detention, his uncle called it. A red-haired, freckled white girl in green pedal pushers and white sneakers, licking a strawberry ice cream cone, clutched her mother's skirt and pointed at Skylar. "Mommy, look! He has blue eyes!" Her mother slapped her pointed finger, and scolded her, whispering that it was bad manners to stare and point.

Scattered every few feet on the sidewalks were portrait artists, who sat before their easels capturing the likenesses of their subjects on paper with charcoal, pastels, and watercolors. Skylar was excited. He didn't understand why, but he was. A street poet recited verses aloud from a book. "He's reading Kerouac," Uncle Aubrey said. "One of my favorites." They stopped to listen. Skylar's attention strayed, his eyes studying a family of Negroes draped in dazzling African garb. The woman's hair was not straightened, long, flowing, and shiny with relaxer, like his mother's. Their hairstyles were identical. Coarse, bushy, thick.

"What's that?" Skylar asked his uncle.

"They're called Afros."

Skylar thought it looked horrendous. The little girl beside them, whose hair was a miniature version of that of the two adults, also wore a dashiki, beads, and sandals. The woman's ears were clipped with large wire hoops. Strings of multicolored beads looped, swung, and clicked about her neck. Skylar wasn't sure he liked it. But it was fascinating just the same.

They headed down Eighth Street, turned into MacDougal, and entered a park called Washington Square. The swaying trees danced to the clashing musical pulsations. Negro men played conga drums and bongos, while a chorus sang a South African chant, dancing as if possessed by ancient spirits. "They're singing that Miriam Makeba folk song she did on *The Ed Sullivan Show*," George said to Uncle Aubrey. At the fountain, before the structure resembling the Arc de Triomphe, another group sat in Indian squats. A long-haired man in sunglasses who called himself David Peel was backed by his band, the Lower East Side, as he sang risque songs entitled "I Do

My Balling in the Bathroom" and "Up Against the Wall, Motherfucker."

Uncle Aubrey and George laughed at the songs' lyrics, but Skylar
felt left out, missing the inside joke. It frustrated him not knowing
what balling meant. A hat was passed around among the spectators,
collecting donations. Skylar's eyes followed the strange-smelling cigarette, which strangers passed back and forth and drew deep puffs
from, holding their breath and speaking as though they were suffocating, their eyes red and glassy. There were dancers, jugglers, mimes,
men doing two-bit magic acts, a young mezzo-soprano standing on
a milk crate and singing opera. A circus. Not quite Barnum & Bailey
at Madison Square Garden, but strange, and wonderful. Skylar never
felt this much at home in his native Harlem.

"Now," Uncle Aubrey announced, affectionately wrapping an arm
around Skylar's shoulder, "we're going over to the East Village. You
like it so far, Sky?"

"Yes," Skylar said. "A lot."

"People here are free," his uncle said. "You can be what you want
and nobody cares."

They had crossed Second Avenue and St. Mark's Place before
entering a run-down theater called the Bijou. What a weird name, Skylar
thought, nibbling his Nathan's hot dog, sipping an Orange Julius. Uncle
Aubrey let him do as he pleased. Quite different from being out
with Daddy, who always reminded him: Don't do this—You can't
do that—Stand over here where I can see you. Skylar wished
Uncle Aubrey was his father. If for no other reason than, Uncle
Aubrey never used the word *don't*. It didn't seem to be part of his
vocabulary.

In the darkness of the theater, Skylar sat with a large container of
buttered popcorn and Bon Bons in his lap. With Daddy, he was
allowed one small box of popcorn which he had to share with
Kendall. Strains of orchestral music floated from the orchestra pit

to the ceiling as the stage curtains parted slowly. Weren't many people in the theater, and it was as if they had it to themselves.

Skylar couldn't believe what he was watching.

This Greenwich Village was bubbling over with surprises, one after another. His eyes bugged out of his head, watching a large white screen filled with faces as black as his. Skylar loved the movies. He'd seen what he believed to be hundreds of them. But this was different, new, unfamiliar. He'd never seen a movie with an all-colored cast of actors, singers, musicians, and dancers. When his family went to the drive-in, his parents brought along blankets. They anticipated the children falling asleep halfway through the picture, so the blanket was to keep them warm. Kendall fell asleep, invariably. Most times, Skylar would watch until the end, but he, too, fell asleep if the movie didn't hold his interest.

Compelling movies like *Imitation of Life* and *Psycho* had held his attention throughout. They were indelibly imprinted in his memory. The former, because he couldn't figure out why a white girl was calling a Negro woman Mama. The latter, due to the mentally disturbed man who dressed like, and spoke in the voice of, his dead mother. Skylar was forbidden to watch the shower scene. His mother held up the blanket across the length of the front seat, like a curtain. If he saw it, he would have nightmares, she explained. He construed that to mean it was the best part. Though he missed it, he liked the movie anyway. It was scarier than even Vincent Price's *House on Haunted Hill*.

This movie with the all-colored cast would keep him awake, he knew. He heard wet, smacking noises. When he turned, he could've sworn he saw Uncle Aubrey kissing George. And though the theatre was dark—he was almost certain, but could've been mistaken—it looked as if the two men were holding hands. Skylar decided he didn't like Uncle Aubrey's friend George.

Then it happened. On-screen, a beautiful woman, the complexion of his father and brother, the most breathtaking woman he'd ever seen, sang an unforgettable song. She was leaning against a window, her head tilted back, cocked gracefully to the side, bangs covering her forehead. Elegant and sultry, her hands enhanced the strange beauty of her sorrow with fluid, airy movements. Outside her window, rain poured and winds blew over her and her gauzy dress. It reminded Skylar of the living room curtains at home being blown by the summer breeze.

Skylar was mesmerized. An engaging melody poured like liquid gold from the divinely sculptured lips of this exquisite woman.

"That's Lena Horne," Uncle Aubrey leaned over and whispered, his chair creaking. Skylar heard but didn't hear, much too captivated by the novelty of it all. She sang of love, of her heart being broken by love. She moaned about there being no sun up in the sky. She swooned about the rainy weather, since she and her man ain't been together. When he heard her sing "ain't" in the lyric, he recalled Daddy scolding Mama, not three hours earlier, for using the same word. Daddy should see this lady, Skylar thought. Nothing she said, or sang, could possibly be wrong, grammatically or otherwise. When the song finished, Skylar exhaled. He hadn't realized he was holding his breath throughout each arresting verse.

The movie ended, screen going blank, curtains closing, house lights coming up. "See, didn't I tell you?" Uncle Aubrey said to him. "Your daddy said there's no such thing as a colored movie star. Now, you've just seen a whole movie full of them. Sky, you can be anything you want to be. You're a beautiful, bright, promising child. Let no one stand in your way of what you want to do . . . not even your father. Understand?"

Skylar nodded his head. He understood all too well. Daddy never said things like that to him. He said them, instead, to Kendall, who entertained aspirations of NFL stardom.

Skylar became somber. He thought the day had ended, that this wonderful Sunday afternoon out on the town in Greenwich Village with his favorite Uncle Aubrey and his friend George was over. When Uncle Aubrey mentioned that they had one more stop before boarding the A train back uptown, he was happy again. But he didn't understand Uncle Aubrey's warning of, "Promise me you won't tell your parents I brought you here. Not even your mother, okay?" Skylar agreed, unsure of what he was agreeing to.

They were in front of a building that flashed a yellow neon sign. GOLD BUG. Opening the door, they descended a long staircase into pitch darkness. Skylar was a little frightened, and held onto his uncle's sleeve. An old, crusty man, with facial pockmarks, sat in a booth collecting money, handing out tickets, like the ticket-taker at the Bijou. He stamped their hands with a mark detectable under a fluorescent light which meant, Skylar assumed, they were members of a secret club. Judy Garland was on the jukebox belting, "Sing Hallelujah, Come On Get Happy!" and several young and middle-aged men snapped their fingers, or bobbed their heads to the rhythm.

This place was strange. Dark, murky, not a woman in the joint. Uncle Aubrey's warning flashed back into his head. But as yet, he could see nothing to tell his parents about, even if he wanted to. Uncle Aubrey ordered two Jack Daniel's for George and himself, a Roy Rogers for Skylar. The bartender with the plucked eyebrows acted sissyish and pinched Skylar's cheek.

"You're the youngest customer we've ever had here at the Bug," he said. "And by far the cutest."

Skylar didn't like him. He smiled too much. And behaved more like a woman than a man. Skylar grew uncomfortable, fidgeting on the bar stool, spinning quarters and nickels on the counter. The men started dancing—with each other, mind you. Skylar didn't know what to make of this. Girls were allowed to dance with each other. Hold hands. Even kiss. That was socially acceptable and tolerable.

But not boys. If the kids uptown saw him doing this, he'd be called a faggot. Come to think of it, that's what they called him anyway. And they'd never seen him dance with anybody. After two sips of his soda, he doubled over, complaining, faking a stomachache. His uncle assured him they'd be leaving soon. "I promised your mama I'd have you back by dark, and I'm not in the mood to fight with that father of yours again today," Uncle Aubrey said, sipping his Jack Daniel's. "We fight so much, I should be getting paid for it." That being the case, Skylar thought, I should be rich.

When they finished with late-afternoon cocktails and were headed back toward the direction of the Sixth Avenue subway, Skylar decided that he was displeased. He didn't like George. Hated that place where the men danced together. Uncle Aubrey was talking to him, probing him about his observations of the entire day. Uncle Aubrey could tell, by Skylar's grunts and one-word replies, that the child was troubled about something. "What's wrong, Sky? Tell your Uncle Aubrey." Skylar wanted to speak his mind. But when glancing at George, he changed it. Uncle Aubrey excused himself, taking Skylar to the side in private conference.

"I don't want you to take me to that place again," he said, his big blue eyes glowing in the setting afternoon sun.

"Why?" Uncle Aubrey asked.

"Because . . . just because," Skylar said, shrugging his shoulders.

An early-evening storm was hovering. Warm drops of precipitation splashed on the sidewalk, the air heavy with the smell of the Atlantic Ocean. Uncle Aubrey, turning up his collar and lapels, stooped to look his nephew straight in the eye.

"Sky," he said, "everybody in the world isn't the same. Some of us are . . . different."

"Different how?" Skylar said.

Uncle Aubrey took his hand. "You know I love you, right? You're my favorite nephew, and I have two dozen if I have one, right? I would never tell you anything wrong. What I'm trying to say is . . . everybody's not meant to . . . grow up, get married, and have children."

"Is that why Daddy always calls you a . . . freak?" Skylar said, deliberately being a smart-ass.

"I guess," Uncle Aubrey said. "But that's because I'm different. Those men we just left in the bar are also different. But we're still the same as any other human being. What we do, and how we live our lives, is not shameful. We have feelings like anybody else and we take pride in our difference. You may not understand now. But I'd be very pleased if you remember what I've said . . ."

POST-NUCLEAR SLUT (1993)

Cary Alan Johnson

Tony says they don't make a limbo pole
low enough for him
whore at a jerk-off party
he was ejected by the safe-sex gestapo
for opening his thighs to probes.

Boy had a body like America
bi-coastal and symbolic.
He too digested truth in small doses.

He had no problem learning to pray
He would drop to his knees on a dime.
He'd worshipped more men than icons
More johns than Jesus
Genuflection was a familiar point-of-view.

To him Black men were a treasure map
the desert of their underarms
the forest of their lower backs
the tundra of their bellies.
Ah . . . the geography of it!

He complained to friends
that being a butch bottom
was a tough row to hoe
always getting the shitty end
of the stick.

Oh there were the nights
of doing nothing
and nothing doing
and channeling and channeling
and still nothing

But then there were the nights
of three a.m.
fear burning like a rock
in his stomach
and he hurried to haunted mansions
with sticky floors
where even the ghosts
trembled.

THIS CITY OF MEN (1994)

Darieck Scott

Dear Danielle,

Kansas City International Airport. Return of the Native—of a sort, for I was (am) no native really, only a past sojourner in these parts, returned after an absence of twelve years for reasons of irony more than anything else. As the automated door slid open and I glanced around for the shuttle to take me to the rental car, I thought the slant of the horizon looked familiar. And though I had forgotten that this part of Missouri is rather hilly, my body did seem to recall the dip down toward the traffic light as I drove through Platte City (a town, actually, very small, and devolved from beige to sullen gray) on the way to the state line, and to Leavenworth.

Except for these physical recollections—which, because they stood in the here and now, made my remembered images even more dim—I could recall little that was specific. The name, the sights of Leavenworth, such as they were and are, had become in my absence mere proxies for misery: two miserable high school years of friendlessness and quiet, nameless dread. But perhaps the problem was that the town itself has changed not at all in the years since I graduated and my family left, that it is a mausoleum, requiring no independent memory to preserve its past. Everything is the same. The army base. The prison.

Eric

But everything has changed about him.
Or has it?

209

But just one more gate to traverse, before I get to Eric, just to set the tone (it tantalizes me, too, to procrastinate this way, but you know me, and, hopefully, have learned to be patient):

The Missouri River travels along the border of Kansas and Missouri proper, rounding a bend and rolling serenely through a wide ravine just outside the town's eastern limits. Nothing stands along the banks here, only the bridge, the dirt, and the trees. One imagines, looking down upon the water, European explorers in small boats, peering up into the dark and dangerous woods with little spyglasses held to their eyes, while the people for whom Kansas and its many towns would later be named followed along under tree cover, themselves pondering danger and impending darkness. But the river must have been higher, faster—bolder—then. Now, in this season at least, it is slow and sedate, and from a modest height looks like a long shallow pond in movement.

This is where my thoughts wandered as I drove toward the bridge along the ponderous arc of an empty two-lane highway. And then I felt, just as I reached the bridge and saw clearly the scattered, dark-windowed homes uphill from the river's edge, a small flutter. A twitch. It was—do not recoil—my (the language is best at conveying its meaning in these matters when at its most stark, so:) cock. I didn't—*wouldn't*—acknowledge it then, though I will now. I can't remember now what I told myself; I likely ascribed the movement to a contraction of abdominal muscles engaged in digestion, perhaps, like Ebenezer Scrooge proposing the undigested-food hypothesis to Jacob Marley's ghost. But that was I-then, and this is I-now.

Now I know better.

There: Now, it's not my intention to confuse you, Danielle, though I know I have. But remember that evening, at Green's on the Marina, when you said (quoting Joan Didion, I believe) that we tell ourselves stories in order to live? I'm trying to make what's happened one of mine. And I'm hoping that you'll bear with me, and understand.

I am a homosexual. Surely you guessed it, when you read Eric's name? Even if you did, the shock is probably no less; I'm saying it now because I don't want you to dread it as my story unfolds, to know it without consenting to know. I would apologize, but I can't. I didn't choose it. I knew about it (*it*; already I cannot bear to name it, and must rub it away, elide it beneath the most impersonal of pronouns)—I knew when I met you, yes. When I proposed to you, surely. You, no less than I, can now thank the gods that you turned me down, but did you *know*, the way you knew when you read Eric's name? I don't expect you to write back, but I wonder.

I discovered what I had long refused to know sophomore year in college. My roommate was a football player, a halfback who was never around because he was being courted by professional scouts and preferred the company of his fellow athletes to the rest of us in the dorm. One night I came home late from a screw-your-roommate party and he was there. I think I smelled them before the door was fully open. The light from the hallway fell slantwise across their bodies in the pitch black room. I saw his huge butt, its thick, curly black hair bristling in the crack, wildly bouncing up and down, and heard the two of them breathing like running hogs. His asshole—I do apologize for this, but I want to be clear; I don't want to leave you with any illusions—clenched and unclenched with a mesmerizing power. I couldn't see her at all, but I knew I wanted what she was getting. And just as promptly I shut the door, and left, and decided I wouldn't get what she got, that I wouldn't even seek it. I would be honest with myself, I decided. I would not forget, would not call myself bisexual, would not slip on drunken nights as I happened to go to a gay bar. I would face it. But I wouldn't do it. You understand, I think; you can guess the reasons—your father was as sternly Catholic as my own. And then there are the sexual standards we black men must meet—because we are not permitted to be men anywhere else, we must at least be men in the bedroom, etc.— though I hardly need tell you that.

And Eric.

I write that, knowing that his name, too, at this place in my story, is a trick of reconstructed memory. He is significant, true, but to what extent, then as now, he was (is) only a trigger, perhaps a vessel in which I bottled a part of myself, I cannot say. I do wonder whether and how things would have been different here, had things been different between us then. I wonder what meaning this town, this wretched little patch of earth that I've held tight-fisted in my memory as the quintessence of what is contemptible in my life and in the world—I wonder what meaning it would have had. And I wonder if Andy Brent assigning me to this case merely hastened a transformation that was inevitable, and I would have had to return here eventually, anyway.

But Eric: It's an effort, I find, to describe him. My words are so spare when I try to *think* of Eric—embellishment, nuance, metaphor, eloquence, disappear as into a hungry black vacuum, and my voice becomes as laconic and laden as the air on an August Sunday afternoon. I can describe only what it means not to be able to describe; I describe only the difference between the me without him, and the me that is now. Oh, he takes me, Eric does. He takes me and I am left dry, bland, malleable, like sand on an exile's desert isle. He takes me and I am left: Wanting.

No, this is not a love story. It is a story of evil.

Eric is in prison.

I picked up the phone book in the hotel room the second night that I was in town. I had to send out for it because, as the pale and hopelessly adolescent bellhop explained, the previous occupant (I surveyed the dust on the table rammed into the corner against the shabby window, when had *he* been here? five years ago?) must have made off with the room's copy. He handed me the slim volume, white and yellow pages combined, revealing a spray of red acne blotches on the underside of his arm as he did so. His was not the sort of presence in which I usually become flustered, but I felt the blood rise in my face as the boy smiled apologetically and backed out of the room. I was embarrassed, you see.

I had felt no sense of urgency when I first contemplated returning to Leavenworth, about Eric or anyone. I had no wish to contact any of my former classmates (nor, I am sure, would they have any desire to come into contact with me). Indeed, driving to the offices of White & Weinberg to meet with opposing counsel that very morning, I saw someone on the sidewalk I'd run track with; he looked my way and I glared in the opposite direction. But when the bellhop handed me the phone book, it became clear what I was doing—frighteningly clear, like the sudden resolution of a shapeless shadow into the distinct features of a malformed brute raising a butcher knife above your head. (Melodrama, you'll say. Yet I swear to you that this whole matter has played in precisely that fashion.) I was lonely, I said aloud; there was nothing playing at the town's one movie theater but something I had seen weeks ago; I had finished preparing for the next day's depositions—those were my excuses.

I was calling Eric.

Or his father, rather, who has the same name. The phone book says Eric Reede without a senior or a junior, so the man who answered when I called thought I wanted to speak to him. I told him that I was a friend from high school, that we had been in Spanish class together junior year. I said, "Do you remember me, Haze?" using his nickname. I spoke with a presumptuousness that, as I think of it now, must have been my way of flirting.

"Oh, you mean my son," Eric Sr. said. I was embarrassed, and fell completely silent.

"He's in prison, you know," he said tentatively.

Again, I said nothing.

"You never heard?"

"No"—I tried now to speak in a professional, detached manner—"no, I haven't been in contact since we graduated high school. I live in San Francisco now." As if that explained anything.

"Oh," he said. Evidently it didn't. "Well, you wanna talk to him, you gotta call his lawyer. He don't see nobody but his lawyer these days. Jeff Weinberg, you can look it up. Eric won't see you, though. Just wants to see his lawyer."

"I am a lawyer," I said.

"Oh!" this evidently did explain something. I imagined that he sighed—it seemed that his silence became less wary, anyway—and so I asked, "I hope you don't mind my asking, but—where is Eric in prison, and what for?"

"Right here, in the Leavenworth federal pen," he said. "And *why,* well, if you ain't heard, they say he *raped* a boy—I don't like to say *boy;* Eric wasn't but two years older—but they say he did that to a young man on the army post, on federal property, see what I'm sayin', which is why he's in the Leavenworth pen. But you know that, you're a lawyer."

It will be odd to you—it is odd to me—but the moment (I describe this conversation to you because of the moment)—it lived in me, Danielle. I felt a pulsing, breathing, kicking space explode into being inside me as Eric Sr. spoke. I didn't reply, or gasp, or tremble. But I twitched; I twitched again, down there.

"Course, I don't believe it," Eric Sr. said.

I did.

That's what I mean, when I say this is a story of evil.

NOTES ON ERIC:

As I said, we were in Spanish class together, junior year. We sat at tables rather than in rows—Mrs. Astorbrook maintained the view that students learn languages best in conversation with one another rather than with the teacher. Eric sat next to me. He missed the first two days of class, and arrived late on the third, smelling as if he had just come from gym class without showering. (This was my story for him. He didn't explain, so I didn't find out, nor did he ever return to class in such a deliciously fulsome state. It's likely that I was titillated, rather than revolted as I pretended to be; the girl on my right and I traded wrinkled-nose faces when Eric sat down.) We didn't talk at first. Mostly we listened to Mrs. Astorbrook. But Eric smiled at me when the bell rang, and asked me for the missed assignments. Something about his smile—I ascribe lasciviousness to it now, but surely it was something different. I gave him the assignments, in any case, and was rather happy to do so, and then forgot about him, until that night at the football game.

I had left the bleachers and passed back through the ticket gate on the way to the parking lot. It was halftime, and colder than I'd expected. And since I was new to town, I didn't know anyone, so I was likely despondent, fearing that I would never make friends, never belong—the all too common run of nightmarish insecurities that comprise the cultural bludgeoning we conceal behind that clinician's term *adolescence*.

Eric came up to me, and he didn't seem to be feeling any of that. He was walking in my direction, smiling again, if not lasciviously, then conspiratorially at least, exuding an ease and familiarity with which I would not have been able to greet my best friend, if I had had one. He wore a long-sleeved thermal T-shirt under an open checkered shirt (a look I associated with white boys—and they excited me, too, I must say now), tucked into the town's one pair of button-fly Levi's 501s (everyone else—I swear—wore boot-cut zip-ups or Wranglers). The billowing shirt gave him a broad-shouldered, narrow-waist look. There was a bulge in his right pocket.

"Hey, Jules! You leavin'?" He punch-touched my shoulder, as men and boys do.

"Well, yeah," I said—or something in a casual tone, grateful to be swept into his conviviality. "It's cold. And we're losing anyway."

"Don't go away yet, man. Stay with me and hang out. I'll warm you up."

He reached into his pocket and drew out a small copper pipe, short-stemmed and wide-cupped, with a fine wire grating in its mouth. "Why 'on't you come and help me fire this up?" His eyes were seductively hooded.

We got stoned that night, and infrequently over the rest of the year. I never proposed these assignations; I lacked all confidence that anyone would want to spend time with me unless as a last resort, and so waited, impatiently, the junior high school girl with ugly knees and braces in her mouth, for occasions of last resort. For reasons at which I might guess (or, truth be told, which I might wish), Eric kept coming back, and during and after stoned stupor he would talk to me, almost confessionally, about matters that concerned him. I was privileged to be only the second person he told about his first experience of sexual intercourse, for example. I remember that my head rolled slowly forward from the soporific cushion of a beaten faded blue couch in his basement bedroom when he told me. I couldn't speak, as hashish rendered me dumb rather than chatty like Eric, but my face tried to register the surprise I felt. Eric smiled. "She's a white girl," he told me, and watched with satisfaction as my mouth opened. "She was crazy, she wanted it so bad," he whispered. Several days later I stood in the cafeteria lunch line behind him and her. She remarked that whatever was passing for meat that day didn't look very tasty, to which Eric loudly replied, "Want me to put some sperm on it?" The white guys behind us (not to mention the girl, whose name and face I cannot recall) were, as you might imagine, less than amused. But I relished the moment—for reasons that require very little speculation now, but then were cloaked behind Eldridge Cleaver–like exultation about one of *us* having taken one of *their* women.

I saw Eric less frequently senior year. He didn't take Spanish II, or any of the other precollegiate track courses where I was often one of two, at most three, black faces. I saw him in the hallway, lined up against the walls with his fellow athletes, and nodded, as men and boys do. He and his new girlfriend had become very close, I was told.

I've said nothing about his looks, in part because I believe it is their meaning rather than their actuality that's important to the story. Yet again, however, in searching for meaning I am reduced to the kinds of breathless description one might easily find in a teenage girl's love novel—or in pornography. Eric had a farm boy's lanky physique, I would say, the deceptive power of its modest musculature honed by sweaty tussles on wrestling mats after school. I think you can imagine the rest—how his legs and buttocks looked in his worn 501s, and other such salacious trivia.

About his color I can say more, I fear. His skin was (and is) very dark, poised just at the edge of ebony, finely dusky and suede-smooth even to the eye. You understand, Danielle, don't you? His skin was the kind of skin we say we most admire in our people— though, as we've rather guiltily discussed, we rarely date anyone of that complexion. There is a compelling sensuality to the color, a physicality. A sexual potency. I know where such descriptions originate, of course. Remember what you once said, that sometimes you think that the way you're attracted to black men like that is through the worst of racist stereotypes, of you and of them? You as the wanton woman of color who wants it all night, and he as the big, mean, monstrously endowed and insatiable, slavering buck? Eric isn't big, but he's six feet or so, with broad, powerful shoulders.

So you understand, I think, part of the (perniciously conceived and guiltily repressed) meaning Eric has for me.

Eric Reede is in prison for sexually assaulting a male minor, two years his junior, at the boy's home, which was on federal property. So Jeff Weinberg, Esquire, echoed Eric Sr. as we drove from the courthouse downtown to the prison on the town's outskirts. Weinberg, founding partner of White & Weinberg—coincidentally the very firm that represents the plaintiffs suing the corporation my firm is defending—agreed to help me see Eric without further question once I told him that the two of us were old friends. "It's important that Eric not become a one-man freak show," he told me, by way of apology for his initial suspicion. He said that he was Eric's friend, too, though he had only come to know him during the trial, and related to me the tale of Eric's unspeakable deeds with blunt stoicism and occasional unblinking eye-to-eye contact, as if to say, *Man to man, between friends, we both understand how to speak about and react to these untidy matters, right?* He intended quite the opposite, but his presence and comfortable *male* demeanor shamed me.

Eric may have been drunk, Weinberg said, but then again he may not have been. The "boy"—Todd Stoffen, a name that, when Weinberg said it, I felt some dim connection to—was probably a homosexual, but as there was no evidence of prior acts, and laws prevented Weinberg from probing the matter too vigorously, and the prosecution managed to present over objection testimony that Todd had dated several girls and had a wonderful time at his junior high prom, etc.—that may not have been true, either. It is undeniable, however, that at approximately four in the afternoon of a Tuesday in July, Eric entered the Stoffen home, apparently at Todd's behest, and, for whatever reason—Weinberg used precisely that phrase and shrugged: "for whatever reason"—punched and kicked and wrestled Todd "into submission," and then "literally" dragged him up the stairway and into Mr. and Mrs. Stoffen's bedroom, where he lashed him with twine to the posts of the Stoffens' Victorian antique bed, and anally and orally "sodomized" him.

"The whole thing must have taken about thirty-five, forty minutes," Weinberg said, and stopped.

Weinberg drives a sleek red European convertible, a diamond among the Leavenworth rough of Trans Ams and Firebirds and Ford trucks. A short, Superman curl of brown hair blew back from the top of his forehead in the wind as he talked to me, and I chose to focus upon it, in an effort to appear wholly unconcerned with the rest of the story. The clarity of my memory of his curl—I can see its individual strands, the minuscule S-tail at its end—suggests something of my state: I was experiencing a kind of tunnel vision, like an accident victim's disoriented focus upon the sight of fuzzy dice, dangling behind the windshield of the approaching car just before it strikes her. I was breathless.

Weinberg made no effort to rescue me. "He brought the twine with him," he continued. "So evidence of premeditation was there. The worst part was the, the *ejaculate*," he stumbled, staring up into a green traffic light. "When the general's wife came home—must've been as short as five minutes after Eric left—she found it smeared all over Stoffen's forehead, cheeks, and lips." He shook his head. "Eric must've had a lot to blow!"

I fear this tale must now become truly lurid and macabre, because Weinberg, quite uproariously, in fact, laughed. I didn't—but I laugh now, as I write this to you—I twitched.

(There is a scene from an all-male pornographic video I've just received in the mail—its name escapes me; I ordered several—in which the star makes his penis "speak" by contracting his well-exercised abdominal muscles so that it lifts and bounces, in a way that calls to mind the *boiinnnng!* sound that would spring from the panels of Archie comics when Archie or Reggie saw Veronica. This repulses you, I know. But I can't restrain myself now. You have become my mother confessor, distasteful though it may be to both of us. I am taking you, one step by one and later three by three and then over tall buildings in single bounds into what you might call my particular hell. I don't know if *I* call it hell, or whether one day I will feel justified in doing so. It is, I confess, a place where magazines torn from plastic bags scatter the dust of the hotel room floor beneath my bed. It is, if you will, a place of sin.

And I must walk you there with me now, my dear. You must follow as I recount, because I must, the labor and birth of—*this*, whatever we choose to call it. There are two metaphors here, you see: one of journey, one of birth. The journey is for you, a narrative straight-line path with signposts and sights and historical trivia. The birth is mine, the Rosemary's Baby metaphor for what I feel: a deep and terrifying physical evolution.)

The Fort Leavenworth prison is massive and imposing, as one expects (though I did not remember) a federal prison to be. With its rotunda dome and gleaming white paint, and its position atop a low hill overlooking the ripple of valleys that house the greater part of the town, it looks like a state capitol rather than a penitentiary, or like a patrician palace of ancient Rome, towering above the hovels of the plebeians. Indeed, the only other building of such majesty is the courthouse, which pales in comparison. To complete this law-and-order trinity there is, of course, the army base itself, Fort Leavenworth, a green and sprawling country club miniature town that is the site for the War College, and where, every year, officers the rank of major arrive to be schooled in Clausewitz and other masters of the art. The open gates of the fort are a two-minute drive, west to east, from the gates of the prison. Together, the War College and the penitentiary are the town's distinguishing features (the courthouse fades, like the Holy Ghost), colossi of federal power bestriding the supine and meek local body. No doubt they provide the greater part of local jobs, as well—twin patriarchs, one might say, tall, grim, strong and solidly male. Women here disappear into their vital and invisible helpmeet roles: wife, mother, teacher, nurse, secretary.

It is in this city of men that Eric grew to what we may charitably call his adulthood.

(I have enclosed for your perusal a few copies, randomly selected, of homosexual pornographic magazines. They're the kind with fantasy experiences detailed in letters, so you needn't worry about offensive photographs. Just note one thing: the frequent reoccurrence of military and prison themes.)

"It's racism that put me in here, man," was the first thing he said to me. The necessary fiction Weinberg concocted to persuade him to see me was that I was a criminal lawyer, looking for grounds on which to reopen the appeal of his conviction—preposterous, of course, and I felt guilty about it. Perhaps I mumbled something or other about constitutional reversible errors and racial selection of jurors, etc. He was sitting down behind a glass partition when we arrived, so that I couldn't see his lower body. His shirt, long-sleeved, hung loosely on him, but his pectoral muscles had a more powerful presence than I remembered.

I interrupted him. "Are you saying that you're innocent?" I asked. "I have to know," I added quickly, like a television lawyer.

"I fucked him, but I didn't rape him." He was blunt. I caught the faint whiff of musk in the slot at the bottom of the glass.

"Lotta people, lotta guys, get real nervous when I say that shit.

But I fucked him. I was curious. Lotta guys are curious but don't say nothin'. You, too, probably."

He spoke as if in challenge to a duel. I said nothing. I felt heat, though it wasn't hot.

"You, too," he said again. He hadn't recognized me, it seemed. "But I did what other guys've done. I'm not worried about it. I'm not a faggot." This cheerfully enough, but with a force that made the teeth in his smile look feral. "It wouldna mattered if he'd been black, that's what I'm trying to say. It doesn't matter! But he's a white boy and a general's son and was goin' to college, so some shit had to happen behind it. He asked for it. And if he'd been black, who cares? Nobody gives a shit about a black faggot."

He paused while I nodded in grave assent. He looked at me more closely. "So what else do you need to know? I went and read that jury selection case. I don't think it can help me."

I groped for a lie. "Well, there's a Ninth Circuit decision with some language about how a federal statute about rape doesn't extend to violations of the anatomy of the sort suffered by a male victim," I burbled. It was all rather comic, as I look back on it now. The room was intolerably, stiflingly hot, I remember that. Rivulets of sweat ran down from my underarms along my stomach, which, incongruously, made me shiver. "But you say—he asked for it?" (You will note again the devolution of my language as well as my capacity for subtlety: he asked for *it*, I said.)

His eyes flickered upward, toward Weinberg, who stood many feet back, behind me. I was suddenly struck by his eyes—their size and roundness, the soft brown color like a child's eyes. His lashes were long and curved.

"I know you," he said.

I introduced myself then, crafting a smile of some kind, and jokingly invoked the memory of Mrs. Astorbrook. His eyes widened. "We were friends," he said, with, perhaps, a measure of incredulity.

"We were," I replied. And then, of course, I pounced. "And I'll need to know everything in order to help you. From you, not Jeff. As a friend," I said, and swallowed, because I had become thirsty beyond reason. "But . . . I have to go now." It made no sense even to me. But I had to leave. It was an imperative. It had to be different from this, I thought. The setting had to be different, and it couldn't happen now, so quickly.

"We'll schedule it," he said, official but gruff.

He stood then. Eric stood, and Danielle, I've said that I would take you through this by steps, but this moment was not a step; it cannot be imagined or understood as part of a path *to*, as a paving stone in the grass of a park winding toward a garden. It *was*, Danielle. He rose: I watched and felt his torso, the dark valley between his legs, rise, slowly, above the horizon of the table, and, to employ the metaphor of the journey, I was *there*. I didn't have to go anywhere, I was there, *it* was there, and *it* was me. Did it puzzle you when I began to describe our conversation, that my story lacked a moment of recognition, a catch in the throat when I first beheld him again, a misty-eyed locking of gazes, a surge of excitement and fear? Perhaps not; this is, of course, not a romance. It is perversion, pure—unspeakably pure—and simple. In the vacuum created by that lack, by the absence of an acknowledged or acknowledgeable link, romantic or otherwise (this was a meeting of shames, after all: his shameful deed to my shameful desire for him—shame deflects; it does not bond)—in this vacuum I sat at the partition without actually sitting there. I looked through the glass without seeing him, listened without listening. But when he rose.

I beheld him. And he was firm, and full, and strong.

Outside the prison, Weinberg asked me what he had said. He was uneasy with the idea of another attorney talking to his client. I thought of Eric's eyes, and asked Weinberg whether Eric was separated from his fellow prisoners. "He wasn't segregated at first,"

Weinberg said, seeming to catch my meaning. "But he is now." He said no more, choosing for the first time to be mysterious.

In the convertible, I said that I would be returning to speak to Eric again, and wondered aloud whether there might be some way to see him next time without the glass partition.

That night was the first night I didn't call you. I looked at your number in my address book, because I was unable to remember it, but I didn't call. I sat on the bed instead, held there without will to move. To explain why, or how I felt, I have to tell another story, one that took place twelve years ago, the summer after I graduated from high school. It may not do the trick, but the memory of it moved through my mind that night, and it seems appropriate to tell it now: Two fellow track team members and I had planned to drive up to Chicago for a few days—ostensibly for some concert or another where Stevie Wonder headlined a string of performers like Sister Sledge and Ashford and Simpson. I had dreamt of this trip as others dream of a weekend in Paris. I relished the anticipation of laughing in the car with my teammates, of hearing about their scandalous sexual escapades with girls, of—so I hoped—picking up women under their tutelage (or perhaps the same woman, a fantasy towards which my thoughts often tilted in those days, for reasons that now seem more clear). But one of them, the younger one, Kelvin, who was still a junior, backed out at the last moment. Kelvin was a small, svelte boy, but abundantly hairy, with sideburns and five-o'clock shadow and a mass of fine, curly black hair on his trim, chestnut-brown chest. I waited all afternoon by the phone in my mother's house for him to call and tell me whether his parents would let him go on the trip.

A slight and paltry memory, this: But it was with precisely that unnameable longing and unbearable fear that I sat up that night, held upon the bed, poised to make a phone call I never made, until at last I collapsed and slept.

I saw Eric again, two days later. It was relatively easy then, and most times afterward, to be granted an audience, since Eric—quite without my asking—had informed the prison officials that I and Weinberg both were his attorneys.

Each time I visit him I walk through four gates: The first is not a physical construct but an imagined one. The prison building's doors stand atop a wide white stairway that travels up from an innocuous parking lot and a capacious green lawn seemingly open to all. The appearance is almost suburban, as of a great grand house across the street from mother, apple pie, and the two-car garage, though I cannot shake the feeling—prisons being prisons, or what we *think* prisons are—of being within a tale more gothic than fifties sitcom. Behind the doors is a rotunda hall with polished floors and large, grim paintings; from that reception I am ushered through the first of several metal detectors into a carpeted rectangle that has the ominous air of an interrogation chamber, complete with an impossibly high desk shielded by bulletproof plastic, and stark gray walls bearing a lone square placard that details do's and don'ts in red letters (DO follow the instructions of the corrections officers/DON'T smoke); and from there past another gate into a long, empty hallway with a low ceiling (no paintings or placards, just glowing EXIT signs pointing the opposite direction); then finally outside the building and into a gravelly courtyard, and through a final gate to a row of dilapidated barracks. At the door to the especially forlorn one where I usually meet Eric one might expect to read *Abandon hope*—or, perhaps, *Arbeit macht frei*. On the other hand—to balance fantasized horror with absurdity—I feel like Don Adams at the beginning of *Get Smart*. The second or third time I saw him he was waiting for me, sitting with his hands quietly clasped on a bare table. Always when I first see him there is a moment of disjunction. He is not towering or imposing or *meaty* there as in my fantasies, but a slight, human figure in gray coveralls—grainy almost, colorless like a figure in a videotaped seventies TV movie. It is when he speaks that he ascends to his full power.

That day I sat at the opposite end of the table, and laid a brief-case between us. The guard left us alone, without explanation.

"I'll tell ya something else," Eric said. "Todd was always hinting. At first he was subtle, right, like asking me shit about my girlfriends. Stupid shit, you don't really ask like I bet you and her have a good time, tell me the dirty details an' shit. And then laugh like it was a joke. I wouldn't answer. But he'd always find a way to bring it up: I saw Angel today and she was walking funny, so I knew you'd busted her stuff good last night an' shit. Right? After a while I just started waiting, you know, waiting to see how he'd do it. And I thought maybe, you know, he's inexperienced and he's two years younger and he wants to live vicariously 'cause he doesn't get any an' shit. But something didn't feel right. I mean he didn't *touch* me or look at me weird, but I knew something even though I didn't think about it. Maybe it was the way *I* felt around him when he asked that shit. *My* body felt different. And it had to be *him.* You understand that, am I making sense?"

"Yes," I said.

"And that feeling, Jules—you *know* this feeling, man—it got to be *exciting* and shit, right? Yeah." He paused, looked down. I remember clearly, because we both had time to readjust our breathing. "Yeah, sometimes that summer I was so bored I looked *forward* to him coming by. I looked forward to him asking, right, and feelin' what was happening when he asked it. I think—well, yeah, that was when I first let him come down to my room."

Something in me wanted to prolong it. "How did you ever start hanging out with Todd?" I asked. "I didn't even know you knew him in school."

Eric laughed, which he doesn't often do. His mouth was enormous. "He was fuckin' *weird*, man!" he shouted. His demeanor seemed to me outrageous, distorted and lurid like eerie reflections in an amusement park house of mirrors. I twitched again, but by then, sad to say, that had become a frequent occurrence.

"He was *strange!* I mean, an officer's kid an' shit, a *general's* kid, lookin' for jobs doing menial shit off post, in town? He was lookin' for trouble, I think. Nobody even knew who he was. He came up to our house in some Japanese truck and asked my dad if he wanted somebody to mow the grass every week, and Dad said what the hell, I was workin' in Western Sizzlin' full-time, my brother was too lazy. Dad said he'd get a kick out of having a white boy mow his grass, so. Then he started cuttin', started showin' up more than once a week to do the hedges and pull weeds an' shit, for free, he said, but Dad paid him anyway. They got to start talkin' a lot, and I was there, and so we talked, about school at first, and how he wanted to go out for the wrestling team next year and shit. I guess he was about to be a senior then. We *talked*, like I said. I got used to havin' him around, like rich white folks get used to havin' the maid around, right?" He stopped and looked at me suspiciously, as if he expected me to think this a lie.

"So you took him down to your room?" I asked.

Eric smirked—wild again, outrageous. "I had a bench and some weights down there. We went down and lifted. He kept askin' questions that I didn't really answer. I tried to ask him some shit about his girlfriends—I didn't care, but I just wanted to see what he would say. He just smiled, real stupid, and made some bullshit noise about some girl he liked and he was gonna ask her out and he was a one-woman man. Just shit like that. Pretty soon we'd work out together every other day. He liked comin' by, he was always cheerful." He spread his hands on the table and shrugged.

I fumbled, looking at his dark eyes. "But you—did anything unusual happen? You said he *asked*. . ." I couldn't complete the sentence.

He didn't smirk this time, as I expected he might, but he leaned forward. His words and manner, his voice and hands (despite a certain studied dispassion that was his version of the requisite masculine cool), were always intense, taut the way a prisoner needing to do whatever, say whatever, in order to achieve freedom likely must be. But below the neck, other than the hands—I rarely saw him below the waist, you recall—his body was generally relaxed, at indolent rest. He leaned forward then and changed that. I confess I very much wished, suddenly, that the guard had not left us.

"One time," he said in a lower voice, his gaze focused away from my face, "he fucked up and put too much weight on the barbell. He was too weak and couldn't handle it. I'd already warned him, but he was too busy tryin' to be like me an' shit. So the barbell got unbalanced when he was doin' a press and one whole side of it crashed down on the floor. I got real pissed. My dad was right upstairs in the living room tryin' to sleep, and here he was making all this noise, right? I was pissed. I got up in his face. What the fuck, mothafuck, I told your skinny ass not to do that shit. Shit like that. He got scared. White boys like him get scared when you go off on 'em. So you know this little son of a bitch started to *cry?* Not hollerin' and shit, but his eyes got wet, and he was holdin' his stomach in like he wasn't gon' breathe. I was about to just throw his ass outta my house. But somethin'—I mean it was a turning point. Curiosity took over me, like I told you. He had his back to me and I grabbed up under his arms like I was doin' a nelson on him, and just started wrestling him. At first he was scared, saying don't hurt me and whiney shit, but then he figured it out and started wrestling back. I played cat and mouse with him till I got tired—'cause he couldn't even *think* about whippin' *my* ass—but then finally I pinned him down. On the floor. We were both real funky. I held him down on his back, both shoulders down, you know, for a pin, and my face was right over his. He just laid there, pantin' hard an' shit. He looked up at me, right? It was like—when you wrestle, and you pin somebody, they don't look at you like that, most people don't look at you, period. He looked, and it was like, like *total fuckin' submission*. Which is a fuckin' weird feelin', man."

He looked sharply at me. "But he liked that shit."

I was by this time insatiable, Danielle, insatiable.

"So you took this to be—an invitation?" Laughable, but I actually said it, and with a straight face. I often found myself, in conversations with Eric, saying such things, playing an odd and utterly fallacious part: my detachment to his passion, my subtlety to his melodrama, psychiatrist to patient, lawyer to criminal. It was, as you can see, quite a farce.

Eric, as he occasionally did, usually at precisely such moments, put on the air of one entirely unimpressed—of someone with power. "What's all this got to do with that Ninth Circuit decision—which I looked up and read?"

"I need to know everything, every detail," I snapped, slipping easily into the television lawyer role.

He stared for a moment, grim, then rose and walked to the door. I looked straight ahead as he passed out of my peripheral vision. My flesh felt horrifyingly—but titillatingly, Danielle—exposed. There was a knock, and the guard entered.

"See you in a couple of days?" he said, turning his head back over his shoulder as I turned mine. He smiled.

Back in the hotel room I cried, and then masturbated until my sweat spread out in a dark pool on the white, pressed sheets.
Later I remembered Todd. I remembered the thick, pale blond hair on top of his head. I remembered this because sometimes he rode

the school bus from post with me, and he always looked down, reading, maybe, so that you would see the top of his head if you sat in front of him and looked back. I hated him then—a casual hate, without fire, as one hates the fat kid in third grade who smells like spoiled milk. No one paid attention to Todd, which seemed to me quite proper, since no one paid much attention to me, either. But occasionally when some of the others were laughing and clowning and I, aloof and excluded, was watching them, I saw Todd watching them, too. The expression on his pasty, plain freckled face was ingenuous, and dumb with terrible, terrible need.

I tormented myself, Danielle, as I now no doubt torment you. You know this in me—the compulsion to hold satisfaction at bay, to dangle it out of reach, and suffer trials to reach the place where I myself have set the prize. I visited Eric, many times. The depositions that I had originally been sent to conduct were concluded. You phoned, and I left oblique messages on your machine when I knew you would be out. Weinberg grew testy, but could do nothing. Eric insisted that he would continue to see me. Whether he knows my purpose, my passion, he has not said. But he must. I daresay he may know better than I.

What follows, then, is the climax, as it were, the journey's end. That is for you. For me there is no climax, no end. Perhaps I do not seek one. My obsession is in the details, in the slow, exquisite nursing and labor of this birth that has already occurred, and will never be complete. Eric understands this. But he has given you, Danielle, something as well: an explanation. I do not subscribe to it, but neither do I deny its power.

"It's about power, man," Eric said. He turned his head and blew smoke from his mouth. I brought him, with official permission, a package of cigarettes. We sat at a table again, but two guards stood in the room's far corners. "I thought a lot about this. Read some of that New Wave, New Age shit. Everybody's got power. Everybody. Some got more, some got less, but they got it. And some—*most, prob'ly*—are afraid of it, see what I'm sayin.' They want somebody else to do it for them. Nothin' new about that, right? I mean that's like Nietzsche an' shit—oh yeah, I read some of that, I read some of everything. It's just plain psychology. Passive-aggressive, puttin' themselves someplace where somebody else can accomplish for 'em what they want. It can be extreme, or not extreme. Todd, he was extreme. Little white soldier boy—he was in ROTC, did I say that? He wanted authority in his life. Liked to bend over, right. That day—I don't remember what day, you have to look it up—somethin' made me think about him. I meditated on him. I don't remember exactly—but about his little body, little weak ass, half-flabby body, and that goofy golly-gee-you-my-big-brother shit. And then he called me at work. Right when I thought about it. And he said come over, I got a new weight set. And I got mad, man. He was so fuckin' goofy, just thinking about him *wantin'* me, you know, but he couldn't say it because he was so *weak*. So I said yeah I'll be over. I had some rope in the car, so I could move a bookshelf and tie down the hatch. And when I got to his house I'd brought the rope up from the back to the front seat."

He stopped and calmly tapped cigarette ashes into a tray. This was the kind of detail that, evidently, I had somehow communicated to him that I wished to hear. Patiently he allowed me to contemplate the movement of the twine, while he tranquilly blew smoke into the air above our heads.

"And then?" I said thickly.

He nodded, satisfied. "Todd answered the door and looked real proud of himself. Because he got the weight set, I guess. Which made me a little more mad, kinda. I grabbed him from behind after he shut the door, in a full nelson, as he was walkin' up the stairs, and he laughed an' shit, said let's wait until we get upstairs, we'll fuck up my mom's shit. I said yeah we'll go upstairs, all right, and dragged him up, hard, right, with his face down, over the steps. The steps weren't carpeted, they were just bare wood. He was gigglin', though, like a little kid. He kept laughin' and jokin' around an' shit till I tied one of his wrists up. He started squirming then. Which I have to admit was kinda nice. I was gettin' into it. Made me even more curious. But mad, too, a good kind of mad. That energy, that power, right. He still didn't know what was up. All right, that's enough, let's stop, he said. I tied up his last ankle and he said, stop, Eric! Which was funny. That was his moment of power. Stop! Like he was a general. I ripped his pants down to his spread-out ankles and his breath caught. I heard it. He didn't say anything, which was very nice. I got hard, man, real hard. You ever feel a boner like that and you'll know how it makes you feel. I pulled it out and it never felt bigger. He said he was gon' scream, so I slapped him and said if you do, I'll kill you. Which he should've known was a lie! But he shut up! Abandoned his power, just like that. He coulda stopped it then, but he wanted it, Jules. He wanted it bad. I dipped my dick in his mouth to get it wet. He slurped it good when I pushed his head down on it. Then I went around and porked him. You ever see that movie Deliverance? I almost laughed when I remembered that. Blood got all over his ass and I had him lick everything off my dick before I fucked him again. I did it as hard or as soft as it felt good, but I tried to do it hard mostly, because that's what he wanted.

"You know that whole time he breathed hard and whimpered an' shit, but he didn't cry out? What a little wimp. I bent over close to him and held his shoulders down while I screwed him, because I wanted to keep my face right in front of his and look at him, eye to eye. He couldn't hold it, though. After a while he looked away. He closed his eyes. I felt sorry for him. I guess it'd started to hurt by then. And see, he didn't expect that."

He grinned, with frightening and hypnotic charm.

I slumped in my hard chair. I must say—and this will be the last of these perversities—that my bottom felt tinglingly raw as it slid forward in the smooth depression of the chair. And I had gone quite beyond twitching. I couldn't bring myself to speak.

Finally, Eric did.

I could do it to you, too. Would you like that?

They grabbed him then—I suppose they had heard him—a veined, straining hand laid hold of his arm just below the shoulder and pulled at him, like the crook of a cane from offstage at a burlesque show. He rose from the chair without resistance. He must have known, as he was pulled away backward, that I would follow his eyes.

I did. They were gentle.

I have been told that he is in "isolation," and that I won't be able to see him for some time.

I am sitting now, at a little round table, writing in dim light. The view from the window of my hotel room is of a dirty, empty street, parking meters unattended except by a few lone, dusty cars. It is early evening in August, twilight.

I wish that I had an ending for you. I've been writing for hours. At the very least, it seems, I should leave you with some image—something metaphoric, something haunting, if possible. Something poignant or lyrical, some fantasy construct by which we—we, as in you and I, separately—might assimilate changes, by which we might pretend to conclude one way of living or thinking or loving for another, or reverence that we have known as if it had truly passed, when, in truth, everything continues even as everything disintegrates. The obvious symbols of descent and ascent and gates, of heaven and hell, of prisons both physical and psychological; the unrelenting frenzy and insatiable appetite of desire deferred—these, perhaps, will have occurred to you. They have, no doubt, inspired images of your own, stronger and more true for you than any I might devise.

But you will ignore such considerations. You will want an image. To have communicated the matter to you as a story, with plot and quotes, demands it.

A note, then:

The Leavenworth streets at night are caliginous passageways, as dark as a backwoods country road. Barely illuminated by feeble streetlamps, they meander away into the distance under droopy tree branches to become tunnels of gloom, a habitat for skulkers and prowlers, for ghosts, perhaps, and presences.

I have begun to drive these dark ways, with the windows up and the radio off. So far I've seen only potbellied white men in baseball caps, staggering over rocky driveways toward their trucks. But a thrill, fierce and expectant, returns me to the streets, night after night . . .

I will disclaim this image, whether adequate for your purposes or not. I have no need of images or metaphor, having lived, in this instance, what they purport to represent. But if I chose an image for myself, it would be starker. Like, perhaps, the card I hold in my hand now. I purchased it along with the magazines. On its face is a white man—I could not find many cards of this variety that boast black men, which is both an outrage and a blessing (the latter because I frankly think I would be a bit undone if I encountered a menagerie of Erics, parading themselves in row upon row of porno- graphic splendor on card shelves).

But the card: The model is white, rather slight and not particu- larly well built, moderately hairy, with large hands. His undistin- guished morphology serves to accentuate a single feature: He has no face, you see; the picture cuts off above his bare shoulders. What he does have, what he sports, is a thick and prominent erection, clad— if that is the word—in damp white bikini briefs. At a rightward lean, it laughably resembles a Coke bottle with a ballooned cap, nes- tled in a man's crotch.

I say laughable. I'm not laughing at it. I fear—I know; I don't fear—that this is the image that adorns the altar at which I shall be worshipping for some time.

That is, if one needs images—or stories, for that matter.

Yours,
Julius

A COURTESY, A TRENCHANT GRACE (1994)

Cyrus Cassells

for Jim Giumentaro (1959–1992) and for Terry Pitzner

Leaving you,
Knowing you would likely die
While I was away,
Made me recall
The photographer's tale,
How he ventured into a realm
Of monkey temples, rickshaws,
River-pilgrims, ghats,
The numerous cities of Benares,
And discovered an urchin
Toppled in a clamorous street:
No one would touch him;
Not one among the merchants
Or mendicants.
He lifted the dust-checkered child,
Swabbed his hands, the russet
Planet of his face.
You understand,
The photographer was a man
Annealed by war,
Inured to suffering,
Yet at having to leave
The frayed child
Only rupees, a little food,
He felt his surgeon's soul unclappered.

But on his return
The following day, he found
The boy of the holy, moribund flesh,
The threadbare boy,
Upright;
The city of ash and fervent pilgrim's prayer
Seemed unstainable then,
The yogi's poise by the river
More radiant—

Jim, once we lay in the lee
Of the plague's unblooming
Gusts and battleground,
On a calm bed,
The gift which at the very last
Had to stand for
All my allegiance,
My living arms' goodwill:
I cradled you,
Mindful of your shingles,
Let you doze
For an unhaggard hour:
I was giving you my bed
To die in.
And in my grief and will
To absolution for what seemed
My gargantuan failure
To keep you alive,
It was as if I was fashioning
An inmost shrine,
An evensong to be stationed
Wherever on this earth

A courtesy, a trenchant grace
Is enacted
In the smallest gesture:
Soup spoon tucked
Under a lesioned lip,
Palm-and-lotion laving
A wand-lean leg;
Above the intravenous tube,
Or through a martyrdom of flies,
A true and level gaze
Is manna,
In laboring hospices,
In compassionless, dusty streets,

In the sacred city of Benares.

WHERE WE LIVE: A CONVERSATION WITH ESSEX HEMPHILL AND ISAAC JULIEN (1994)

Don Belton

A t the twentieth century's close, independent filmmakers Marlon Riggs, Isaac Julien, and poet Essex Hemphill are likely the artists/activists whose work most richly articulates and extends the represented range of black gay men's identity. Their daring interventions advance the project of healing the whole of black masculinity by celebrating acts of dialogue, compassion, and love between black men across the spectrum of sexual orientation, as well as between black men and black women.

Riggs's landmark documentary *Tongues Untied*, along with Julien's *Looking for Langston*, a cinematic meditation on the life and legacy of the closeted Harlem Renaissance writer Langston Hughes, served stunning notice that black gay male silence and invisibility had ended. For two decades, Hemphill has crafted elegant poems that illuminate the life-giving geography of black men's love and grief.

Riggs died on April 5, 1994, of complications due to AIDS. In December of 1994, I brought Julien and Hemphill together for a conversation around the completion of Riggs's film *Black Is . . . Black Ain't*, which explores the nexus of black identity and masculinity. Hemphill appears in the film, along with cultural activists bell hooks, Michelle Wallace, Cornel West, and Angela Davis. I met with Julien and Hemphill at Hemphill's apartment in West Philadelphia. Hemphill showed an advance cassette copy of the film. The following is excerpted from conversation between Julien and Hemphill that afternoon.

HEMPHILL: I find myself resisting popular notions of black masculinity while at the same time being attracted to them. Early on, I learned ways to protect my masculinity or, I guess I should say, my homo-masculinity. I wasn't inclined to be athletic. In the black neighborhood I came from, there was an emphasis on being able to play basketball or football. I, instead, was attracted to gymnastics because of the way the body looked. But I knew instinctively that if I had said, "I want to be a gymnast," among the fellas I ran with I would have been labeled a sissy. As an adult, I've had to resist the idea that I'm not a man because I don't have children or a woman.

JULIEN: I think this is a good place to start. Initially, masculinity was about living up to the fiction of normative hetereosexual masculinity. Growing up, I remember men in the community who were a part of my parents' circle commenting in Creole about how I was such a *petit macqot,* which is a small boy, *un petit garçon.* It was also a way of calling a young boy a sissy. A means of saying he's already displaying feminine traits. Maybe I wasn't interested in trying to conceal that part of my identity. So, in a way, it began a war early in my life, but not a bloody war. It was a war of positions in the sense I did not want to totally participate in being a straight black male in the conventional framework. My feelings for boys my age happened very early on—I must have been eight years old. In the playground, I saw the shorts fall off the goalkeeper's waist during a sports match. I remember feeling very erotically charged by the image. There was already in circulation the idea of black men having this hypermasculinity that was tough and resilient. It was tough growing up in London in the 1970s. You had to be tough to physically contest the everyday racist treatment by the police, by various authority figures and institutions. Therefore, you understood that this toughness was a mask and a defense. Questions around being black and male came to the forefront for me when I began to pursue my education and most of the other young men around me were being arrested.

HEMPHILL: We're faced with redefining what masculinity is. We're faced with constructing a masculinity for all of us, one that will be useful as opposed to disempowering. I think that, given issues like economic oppression, we feel safe holding on to the model constructed out of athletics, around street toughness and other conventional models of masculinity. You know, "My gun's bigger . . ." The gun is supposed to be an extension of you or your anger, and it's the bullet that strikes, not the fist. I can't think when I last saw two black men physically fighting. And not that I'm endorsing fighting, but I think the gun has become an apt metaphor for our isolation from our own rage and frustration. Our increasing isolation from one another's humanity. Then there's the masculinity that we're getting via television, film, and magazines. We need a masculinity that brings us more into contact with one another. A masculinity that is intimate and humane. A masculinity that allows if I feel like being soft my softness won't mean I'm a sissy or a punk.

JULIEN: In *Black Is . . . Black Ain't*, bell hooks and Michelle Wallace talk about the language of sexism and the presumptions around gender. That's really where everything begins to shut down. We both grew up experiencing scenes in which black men could not cry or express fear. Growing up, I very much identified with trying not to reproduce the dominant ideas of being a man. There's an overvaluation of strict gender codes in the black community. "Only sissies cry." When that was told to me, I said, "Fuck this. I'm not going to live like this." Those stories or fictions of "real" masculinity are learned early in life and then become ways of toughening young boys. That sort of information isn't useful to our community. I think there should be more of an investment in unlearning those codes, because they end breeding a certain inhumanity. Our redemption as a people is *not* a "dick thing," as bell hooks points out in the film.

HEMPHILL: I believe that many of the destructive lessons taught in our childhood homes is the result of the desperation of our parents. They were children at one point and were made to learn those same lessons. I don't know how we begin to unlearn that behavior.

JULIEN: Well, it's true that the codes we're meant to adhere to—masculine and feminine—are prescribed in childhood. As black boys and girls growing up in families attacked by racism from the outside, we are made to feel a kind of double restriction on the expression of ourselves in any way that might go against the grain of dominant ideas. We, as black men especially, are supposed to instill and police these codes within ourselves. But where are these codes coming from? I think that in America, but not only in America, there is this obsessive concentration on the family—the notion that everything can be resolved within the family. But this middle-class notion of "family" seems to me the space where we first learned how to fear one another and to fear the free expression of ourselves. As a result, the debate around black masculinity in the U.S. has become so topical with films like *Jungle Fever* and *Boyz in the Hood*. One of the problems with the *New York Times* article/symposium on black men [*Who Will Help the Black Man? New York Times*, 4 December 1994, v. i, 74:1] is that it is exclusively a discussion by and about black middle-class, presumably heterosexual men. The question at the center of that discussion is really, How can we get black people, black men in particular, to get over in the American Dream? It should be obvious by now that's just a poor question. I also think the street tough machismo identity is bankrupt. It's just producing a competitive, nihilistic environment for black men to destroy themselves and each other. It's difficult to have a position on this without talking about the disappearance of real economic opportunity for the black working poor and the infiltration of drugs in our communities in both the U.S. and London. Marlon's film carries an important critique of black manhood along these lines.

HEMPHILL: Yes, and the critique bell hooks provides [in the film] of the black macho pose of the 60s and 70s is so powerful because if the sum of black political struggle is about empowering the black phallus at the expense of all other cultural issues, we cannot succeed. Or else that success will have no meaning. Our masculinity must encompass diversity and nuance. There should never be a question about whether Sally can drive a rig or whether Tommy can raise the children. There are also important class issues. The *Times* piece represented the black male middle class. I'd like to see that [discussion] take place with representatives from a broader range of possible black male identity. I'd have loved to have heard someone who flips hamburgers for minimum wage talk about how he views himself as a man. A construction worker. An emergency room doctor. I had problems with one of the participants in that article referring to working-class blacks as "black trash." Its a simple-minded analogy he was trying to draw—that you have white trash and you have black trash. Well, come on, baby [laughs], . . . who says any group of society is to be regarded as trash? So for me the *Times* piece was not a broad enough conversation. It was a safe conversation for the *New York Times.* Safe for the particular men who were included. And self-serving.

JULIEN: It became a spectacle, a symbolic discussion of black masculinity in a white newspaper, a discussion where very little was actually said. The patronizing and vindictive tone toward black working-class people, even by the one speaker who actually does work with young black men from impoverished backgrounds. . . .

HEMPHILL: The absence of debate on gender issues. . . . The absence of any gay voice. . . .

JULIEN: It's a question of power. Black men have been rendered powerless by the dominant society, and it's that drive to have power at any cost, no matter what is silenced or dismissed. It isn't very different from ways in which blacks are excluded from the representation of "true" American masculinity.

HEMPHILL: Yes. It's important to realize it isn't black women who are gunning down one another. Black women are not gunning *us* down and beating us to death. *We* are doing this.

JULIEN: We won't be able to abate this hatred and annihilation of self by flattening out and silencing differences within our community. These differences are vital to our mutual survival.

HEMPHILL: In a recent issue of the Nation of Islam's newspaper, *The Final Call*, Louis Farrakhan called for a "million-man march" on Washington, D.C. A march of one million black men on the nation's capital. The call itself is historic, though I've heard nothing about it in the mainstream press. But who's going to be on the stage when those one million black men assemble in Washington? You? Me? Would Marlon have been invited to speak? Hardly. It will be men who are considered safe. Safe for me equals ineffective—men who will not take risks in their intellect and who will not take risks in their compassion. I think of the ending of *Black Is . . . Black Ain't*, where bell hooks speaks about replacing the notion of black unity with the notion of communion. The root meaning of communion suggests that our union is based on a willingness to communicate with one another. It's a beautiful idea to pursue. [In the film] Michelle Wallace says, "I always get the feeling that when black people talk about unity and community that it's a turf war thing, you know—we're gonna get together and this is gonna be our block, and if you come on our block, you know, we're gonna kick your ass." Michelle says, "I always think I'm gonna be the one whose ass is gonna get kicked." I've always felt like that as well. I'm as black as anyone, but not by the criteria the nationalists construct.

JULIEN: It's about wanting attention and power in the system. Farrakhan demands this march on Washington. It's about another spectacle of middle-class black straight men claiming ownership of blackness. It's just another bankrupt political discourse.

HEMPHILL: But if this march happens, it will have historic ramifications. A new kind of power will be unleashed—a power that shows us the possibility of unity among black men. I think black gay men need to at least bring the issue of our participation to the table. We should press to have gay voices at the podium.

JULIEN: I think that within a Farrakhan march of black men on Washington, anyone attempting to read its meaning in any way that could be considered homoerotic would be dealt with. I don't see where the intervention can be made there.

HEMPHILL: Given some of the dangerous places gay men are often willing to go in the name of love or desire, why would intervening at the Farrakhan march be any less dangerous?

JULIEN: I say just the opposite. I would say we should be going back to the communities we are a part of and working on a grassroots level to get the black community to challenge hetero-normative assumptions. I think that would be the way from a grassroots level to change destructive assumptions about blackness, gender, and sexual identity. Otherwise, we just become a part of Farrakhan's spectacle.

HEMPHILL: I still think we need to bear witness in the representation of black male identity. Those black men who will march will largely be lower- and working-class men—your grassroots level. The march may not be framed around their identities, but they have always been the essential part of the Nation of Islam's political base. Of any black political base. For that reason, I believe we ought to try to participate. So at least, for the record, there is the fact that we were there to claim our membership in our communities.

JULIEN: Why should we try to claim membership in black masculinity through the Nation of Islam?

HEMPHILL: Big spectacle-oriented groups like the Nation of Islam are winning minds and support among everyday black people. Either we are a part of black communities or we aren't. Our presence has always been crucial to our communities, yet within those communities and the larger society we're still rendered as nonexistent. We're still considered to be not interested in something like this. There is a danger in that. As black gay men we need a politic that touches the vast majority of our brothers where they're at. Otherwise as gay men we only represent a breakdown. . . .

JULIEN: I think failure is something that should be celebrated. I don't want to be in a formation of black male identity where one has to hold oneself in a rigid way—as in a march—even against how we might feel about ourselves in terms of our pain, our skepticism, lack and self-doubt. All these things are as much a part of black male identity as the things we might want to parade, like toughness and unity. We have to be willing to engage in a process of thinking through our failure as black men in this society. Black masculinity has always been a "failed masculinity" in relationship to white male colonialism. Black macho discourses of empowerment will never truly reach us where we live. There is something interesting we can learn from our so-called failure, because our failure also contains our resistance. Failure to live "up" to oppressive masculinity is a part of what it means to be queer. That's what my work has been about. What your work is about. Being black itself is seen as a failure in the white world. We want to remember that, and there is a way we can use that failure to critique white supremacy. If you want to be a black version of white supremacy, of course you end up with a Farrakhan.

HEMPHILL: So where do we intervene?

JULIEN: Use the media. If you're going to make the intervention it would be, "This is a problem, and you know . . ." If, when they march, you have an interview on CNN, and CNN runs it only five times that day, then you'd have a larger audience than their march on Washington.

HEMPHILL: Definitely, yes. But I still come back to the power of the possibility of black men coming together. I'm not being romantic here. When Marlon was working on *Black Is . . . Black Ain't*, I went with him to a theater in South Central Los Angeles to film a meeting between the Bloods and the Crips gang members. It was historic. Some of that is in the film. I will never forget stepping out of the van when we arrived at the theater and looking up, and along the rooftops of the theater and the houses on the block were these SWAT teams of uniformed policemen holding guns. There were at least one hundred men, most of them white, which underscores this nation's real terror of black men cutting back on the violence against one another and creating a space to come together.

JULIEN: But what are these black men coming together to do?

HEMPHILL: Don't quash it yet, Isaac, [Isaac laughs] without taking into account that an agenda would have to be defined. Maybe it's desperation that draws me to the march despite my aversion to Farrakhan. We can't just attack his ideology. What good is that? I can't look at television without seeing negative representations of a black male. He's either in handcuffs or he's been shot by one of his brothers over whatever foolishness is out there.

JULIEN: I don't think it's a matter of desperation. The desperation is that people are looking for black straight men to provide political leadership against white patriarchy. The problem is with these very selective representations. We're dealing here with white society's own anxiety and fear about black men and about the black underclass, the working-class populace.

HEMPHILL: How can we control it?

JULIEN: That question is part and parcel of the postslavery experience. I don't know how one negotiates oneself out of it.

HEMPHILL: I don't think you addressed my concern [about] whether or not there's a necessity for black men to assemble anywhere in this country.

JULIEN: I just question the whole premise. I can see a homoeroticism in it, perhaps, but I have to see it for what it is—a fantasy.

HEMPHILL: You're not in any way interested in a million black men assembling?

JULIEN: No.

HEMPHILL: Okay. I guess that's our first point of contention. [Both laugh.] So what is the perfect site for our resistance?

JULIEN: An intervention like *Black Is . . . Black Ain't.*

HEMPHILL: What about the troublesome issues of Marlon's dying of AIDS and his sexuality? There are public television stations and schools that won't run it because of Marlon's candor.

JULIEN: You have this distribution out of, say, Sony Classics. That film can be seen in twenty cinemas in New York alone. That sort of intervention would be profound, and it could be marketed toward black people.

HEMPHILL: This isn't about art cinema. I'm talking about addressing raw black life.

JULIEN: Yes, and that's what I'm addressing as well. I'm talking about the apparatus of mass culture. Which is Sony. Miramax. We don't own the means of production. Even certain aspects of our blackness are being experienced through what comes through the marketplace.

HEMPHILL: I see your point, and I respect that. But, I guess, with your hypothetical way for intervening . . . what comes to mind is that I come to the table with an idea and you come with an idea, but now we have to take our ideas to something that doesn't come from us, the media, corporate distribution. . . . For me, the way I live, my blackness is the priority. Period. Be it my identity as a gay person or as a person with AIDS or my identity as a writer . . . I'm still dealt with as black, first and foremost.

JULIEN: I think it's a product of segregationist thinking about sexuality and gender that we have to prioritize our identities.

HEMPHILL: I don't want you to misunderstand me. In 1991 or '92, when I was on tour in England, I had trouble with customs, and the trouble I had had everything to do with me being a black man in bomber jacket, in jeans and construction boots. All these other people are flowing by me in customs with no problem, but they stopped me every time, because I fit a certain profile. That's why my blackness has to be there first for me. It's a battle around that place where I am desperate and wanting to see some of the dying stop.

JULIEN: But a march won't stop that. Anyway, I think the image of one million black men marching on Washington is phallocentric and misogynist. I don't know. Maybe I'm just cynical.

HEMPHILL: I don't think it's cynicism. We share a similar concern and pessimism. I think we articulate it differently. I agree with you about the phallocentrism and misogyny. . . . I stopped three or four young brothers on my street last spring, and they were bigger than me. It was after school, after business hours. These young fellas had taken Magic Markers and written all over the storefront windows. And something in me just snapped. I'm sick of there being no intervention. I told them, "Don't do that. That's a black business. You're destroying property." I was scared to death, but I wasn't going to my apartment and locking my door. The truth is I might not be sitting here now because of that act. Even a simple intervention could cost our lives.

JULIEN: Generally, there's a breakdown of the civil society in America.

HEMPHILL: Various horrifying themes occur in all our communities. Why is there such tremendous disrespect among black men towards women, regardless of our sexual orientation? Even a statement like, "Miss Thing is gonna take me to a new level of sensuality." I was wondering why it's never "*Mr.* Thing." Why is it "*Thing*"?

JULIEN: I thought "Miss Thing" was about a parody of a sexist comment.

HEMPHILL: Think about the things you've heard among gay brothers about women. How much different are some of those statements from the ones by some heterosexual brothers? There hasn't been much discourse among black gay men about that. But I know sisters are anxious for that. Not just conversation, but deliberate work. I don't think current notions of masculinity work for any male. I don't think they work for anyone.

JULIEN: I think the social complexities around contemporary male identity are just deepened by issues of blackness and gayness.

HEMPHILL: This is why, for various reasons, including expediency, I've elected not to take a white lover when that option has been there. I feel like this is the worst country to try to love outside the race. I can't imagine what you deal with in your relationship [Mark Nash, Julien's life-partner of seven years, is white].

JULIEN: My experience being in America with Mark has not been one where I've been rejected. If blacks or whites want to reject me, they're not my friends and I don't feel I've lost anything.

HEMPHILL: It seems so incredibly important, the way that Marlon's use of the slogan "Black men loving black men is *the* revolutionary act" in *Tongues Untied* has been so fucked by so many people [because Marlon's partner, Jack Vincent, is white].

JULIEN: I just don't agree with a slogan like that. Who's to say what *the* revolutionary act is, anyway? Who can prescribe that? If I'd grown up in America, I don't know what I would be like. The positioning of a slogan like that—the way it is positioned in the film—is fine, I suppose, but when it's used as some kind of moral code to police interracial desire, then I think it's really about our shame about the range of our own desires.

HEMPHILL: The act of black men loving black men isn't only about our sexual expression. It means everything, including intervening downstairs when those young black men were defacing their neighborhood. That was about my love for them. If I didn't love us, I wouldn't care. You know—"Just go ahead. Get your Magic Markers and do the block. Do the block!"

JULIEN: I think it's very complicated, the discourse of love in relationship to yourself. Unlearning self-hatred and fear is hard work. I've had to be in America to really begin to understand that, being so marginalized here.

HEMPHILL: In some ways, I think we *have* failed.

JULIEN: We have to be willing not to reject that failure out of hand. That's essential to experiencing humanity.

Vital Signs (1995)

Assotto Saint

for David Frechette

medical absurdities multiply in necessity
stripping all dignity
low rate

there is this masked ball
nurses waltz out their delirium of blood
cold black hands; this hour, friends are few
how could six months elapse without a vanity mirror
our brother, our brother: how it was
to be alive

unearth
from a pillow of sorrow
the logic of illusions—just that, only that—
wrapped with fungi, your tongue sprouts no more
metaphors
but the will endures like eucalyptus
oasis of fear

every minute or so
your red traffic-light eyes glare
& ward off the ghost who like a crow
looms to swallow your guts

numb your body into
a corpse

A Boy Doesn't Know (1995)

Forrest Hamer

A boy does not know these things.
He plays with himself, engages
others,
    but he doesn't understand
why lying on his stomach
    or on his back with raised legs
and having the man edge himself past
    and then inside
is what the man really wants him to do.
A boy doesn't know

    and so   he leaves himself
lying on a bed or on a floor or up against a wall;
he watches and he waits,
pulls up his pants and wonders what to do
    with the stickiness on his fingers, how to take
himself
        from that place to another.

After the semen dries and the clothes from that day
have been buried, he spends forever
trying to remember if the numbness that flared
in his nostrils and consumed all air

distracted him from noticing the yank and tug
there *must* have been when something in his middle
not yet named, yet missed,
was taken easily as breath.

UPRISING (1995)

G. Winston James

I want to start a campaign
One that gets homosexuals
To recall
What it means to be gay
A campaign that will scrape away
At millennias' worth of stone
To unearth the legions
Of sissified warriors
Who lived, died,
And worked their magic
In, on, and about
This world.

I want to ignite a protest
To gather all the mystics
In one place,
That we might speak that one truth
Which will suck the moisture
From the air
And create oceans at our feet
That truth that will
Snuff out the light
And remind the Children

That we have been here
Since creation.

I want also to invoke the Bible
To say that in the beginning
Was the word
And that word shaped the Universe
Into a thing of so many wonders
That mortal man
Can only fail to see
Unless he admits that
He is as blind as the stars
And far less significant
Than the trees that have survived
Far longer than he.

I want to summon
The truth of names
And the defining energy
That dwells within them
To let the mouths of our enemies
Show us that
They have always known
That we were defined by power
As the fairy's magic lives
The flame of the faggot burns
The strength of the dyke holds
And the gaiety of the queer endures.

I want to ignite a blaze,

A conflagration of lesbians who remember
What it was like to watch
Their sisters burn in the night
Struggling against the fetters
That bound them
To the witching posts
And to the lies
And to the angry penises
Jealous of feminine power
So softly displayed like iron
At the hot core of the earth.

I want us to shatter the windows of heaven
With diamonds
To assemble before the throne of God
Dressed in the stars
And holding the planets in our hands,
Asking the angels simply:
Are we not beautiful
That the rivers and the wind
Sing our names in the gloaming?
If we are not, then destroy the world
For you have put nothing marvelous
In it.

FROM 2ND TIME AROUND (1996)

James Earl Hardy

I never thought I would be at a weddin and there ain't no bride. When Little Bit first told me that B.D. 'n' Babyface was gettin married, I laughed. I mean, I just knew he was jokin. I ain't never heard of no men gettin married. Well, I had read stories about two men and two women *wantin* ta do it, but none about 'em doin it. But then I knew it wasn't no joke when . . .

"Hello? Raheim?"

"Yeah . . . who this?"

"Well, how soon they forget. . . . It's B.D."

"Oh. What's up?"

"So much is up that I wouldn't want to bore you with it all, darling."

"Little Bit ain't here. You want me ta—"

"I didn't call to speak to him. I called to speak to you."

"Me?"

"Yes, you. I was wondering if you would be free on Valentine's Day."

I laughed. "Yo, what's up, G, you tryin ta step ta me?"

"As *lovely* as that idea sounds, no. I want you to be an usher at our wedding."

"Yo' *weddin*? Who you marryin?"

"Silly, who do you think? Babyface."

When he said it, it just hit me like a brick.

"Hello? Hello?" He tapped tha phone. "Is this thing on? Raheim?"

"Yeah, yeah, I'm here."

"So, can I count on you to bless us with your magnificent presence? I'm sure the Children will *love* having you greeting them and escorting them to their seats."

"Uh, uh . . . I don't know."

"Well, what's wrong? Oh, I'm sorry. Do you have plans that evening?"

I didn't, but he gave me an easy out. "Uh . . . uh . . . yeah . . . yeah, I do. Me 'n' my Li'l Brotha Man. We got somethin really, uh, special planned . . . a surprise fuh Little Bit."

"Oh, how nice. A *family* outing. . . . OK, Raheim, tell me why you don't want to come to my wedding."

Uh-oh.

"You can tell me. Don't worry. I may be a little bit fragile, but I won't break. You won't hurt my feelings."

"Uh . . ." *Get it tagetha, mutha-fucka.* "B.D., it's just that I . . . I don't think I would be comf'table, that's all."

"May I ask why? I mean, it's not like I'm asking *you* to marry *me*— even though, if the truth be known, I would if Little Bit and Baby-face weren't in the picture."

I blushed.

"Uh-huh, go on ahead and blush."

Day-am, how he know?

I was drownin, so I tried ta save myself. "B.D., it's all just . . . new ta me. I mean, I ain't never gone ta no weddin where . . . you know. . . ."

"Believe me, darling, the only difference will be that *this* bride will not wear a veil or train—and that's because my soon-to-be husband won't allow me to—and almost all of the guests will be fine Black men on the arms of *other* fine Black men. So you will be *very* comfortable. You will be amongst your peers. You'll be in, to borrow a phrase, *jood* company."

"I . . . I don't know."

"Listen, I don't want to push you to do anything, and I don't want you to do anything you don't want to. But I would love for you to come. And I'm sure Little Bit would too."

Yeah . . . I know he would.

"Will you at least think about it?"

"Uh . . . uh, a'ight . . . I don't know if I'll change my mind, but I'll think about it"

Well, I thought about it, and I still ain't wanna go. Tha whole thing was just rubbin me tha wrong way. I mean, I don't really believe in no God; you know, all that Adam and Eve not Adam and Steve shit. But tha whole thing felt . . . I don't know . . . funny. Just what tha fuck is gonna happen? How they gonna do it? B.D. said he was the "bride," which means Babyface must be the "groom," right? Is B.D. gonna walk down tha aisle on his daddy's arm? Is he gonna throw a bouquet? Are they gonna have a best man and a bridesmaid and all that other traditional shit? Are they gonna say some kinda vows? And *who* is gonna perform tha ceremony? I ain't never heard of no preacher joinin two men tagetha in holy matrimony. I ain't wanna ask B.D. or Babyface about it cuz I ain't wanna seem dumb. I also ain't wanna seem curious. I mean, we know what that shit did ta tha fuckin cat, ya know?

Yeah, I just knew I couldn't go. I also knew Little Bit would want me ta. But thinkin it's all about me and believin that he'd do anything fuh his Pooquie, I did a real *stoopid* thing: I asked him not ta go.

"Pooquie, you should know better than to even ask me that."

"Why? I'm yo' man."

"*And?* What does that have to do with anything?"

"I don't feel right wit' it, so I don't want ya ta go."

"Uh-huh."

"I mean, *we* should be spendin that day tagetha, Baby. Just us. It's gonna be our first Heart Day."

"Uh-huh, we *can* spend it together . . . at the wedding."

"C'mon, Baby—"

"C'mon, *nothin*. Not wanting to be an usher is one thing, but asking me not to go just because you think you won't be comfortable is another."

'Yo, ain't I important ta you?"

"Yes, you are, Pooquie. But two of my very best friends plan to embark on a new life together, and I plan to be there when they do it—with or without you."

'You mean . . . you go wit'out me?"

He ain't miss a beat. *"Yes, I would."*

"Why?"

"*Why?* Why not? I'll be damned if I'm going to miss one of the happiest days of their lives just because *you* don't want to go."

"Whatcha sayin? You love them mo' than me?"

"Raheim, don't even try that. This has nothing to do with my love for *them*; this has to do with your love for *me*."

"Fuh *you?*"

That's right, for *me*. Did it ever occur to you that I might want you to go with me because this will be one of the happiest days of *my* life?"

"What tha fuck you talkin about?"

"I'm *talkin* about sharing a very special experience, a very important moment with you, the man I love. This whole day, this whole event is about love. But all you can talk about is you, you, you."

I ain't know what ta say, cuz he was tellin tha truth.

He sighed. "I should've known this was coming."

"Pardon me?"

"First, we had to take down your drawing of me and put away the photo of us in the Village because of Junior. Then it was the movie poster in the bedroom. Then you decide to sleep on the floor in the living room with him sometimes, for appearance's sake. Then you refuse to go with me to any Brotherhood meetings. Now, this. I'm sorry: I will work with you on being, as you say, more comfortable about yourself, about us, but that doesn't mean I'm gonna live in *your* shadow."

"*My shadow?*"

"Yes. I know you want to be careful because you are not ready to tell Junior, your mother, or Crystal—even though they already know. . . ."

"Yeah, we already been over that, a'ight?"

"Yeah, I know. Junior is too young to think that, and your mother and Crystal would never think a man like *you* could be *that* way, right? Well, fine. I can handle that because that is where you are right now. But as you trip over stuff like that, you also have to be careful of how you treat my love, how you treat us. You can't let your fear come between us."

"I ain't."

"Yes, you are. What if it were us, Raheim?"

"Hunh?"

"What if *we* were getting married? Would you leave me at the altar because the whole thing makes you uncomfortable? Or would we never even get to that point?"

Jood questions. I ain't really know.

He gave me his bottom line. "If you don't want to go, fine. But if you don't, you'll be spending Heart Day alone."

I still ain't wanna go but did any-ol'-way cuz if I didn't, he was gonna go wit'out me. In a way, he was forcin me, cuz he knew I wanted ta spend tha day wit' him. I musta gave him that impression, cuz he said straight up, "Don't go because I want you to or because you feel you have to." But I ain't want him fallin up in there by himself. All them folks knew we was tagetha, and they would just know that somethin was up if I ain't show. Gene would get so much mutha-fuckin satisfaction out of me not bein there, mo' proof fuh him that we ain't s'pose ta be tagetha. I know it's fucked up and that once again it comes down ta me, but I was goin ta show that I could stand by Little Bit.

Uh-huh, I was standin by my man.

I don't know what I expected ta find when I got there, but one thing was fuh sure—I wasn't uncomf'table. There was like fifty people there. Just about ev'rybody was in a suit and tie, but most of 'em looked like brothas from around tha way. And they all had it *seriously* goin on. B.D. wasn't lyin. There was brothas who were little like Little Bit, and tall, dark, and lovely like Tha Kid. If I wasn't wit' Little Bit, I woulda been clockin me a few numbers—or at least tryin ta. Just about ev'rybody was wit' someone. Tha wild thing is, some of 'em had already gotten hitched like Babyface 'n' B.D. was gonna do, and they had been tagetha fuh like years. After tha ceremony, Babyface 'n' B.D. had three couples take a bow cuz they all had tied tha knot on Heart Day too. One couple, Jameson 'n' Devon (he was gettin everything on videotape), been tagetha fuh fifteen years. *Day-am!* I can't even imagine bein wit' anybody, even Little Bit, that long. Now, you *know* there's gotta be a whole lota love there. . . .

Anyway, tha ceremony was really cool. Ta my surprise, it was held in a church called Unity Fellowship, not far from Little Bit's crib. Tha program said Unity was "a place of worship for same gender loving people of African descent, but its doors are opened to people of all colors, persuasions, and orientations." (Hmmm . . . "same gender loving?" I'm gonna leave *that* alone.) B.D. ain't walk down no aisle, and ain't nobody give him away. Both "bride" and "groom" was sittin in tha front row, Babyface wit' us, B.D. wit' his moms (who came all tha way from down South) in tha row across. They was both dressed in matchin black tuxedos. B.D. had on a long red silk scarf, and Babyface, a green one. Tha music started, and they grabbed hands, got up, and stood in front of one of tha few sistas there, who turned out ta be tha preacher. She said a few words about love bein love, no matter what form it comes in (there wasn't no "Dearly beloved . . . "). Then Babyface 'n' B.D. said they vows—I guess that's whatcha call 'em—tellin each other how they felt and why they was takin this pledge, makin it official by exchangin rings. Babyface even got on one knee when he said his. Little Bit, B.D., B.D.'s moms, and a few other folks started pullin out Kleenex and shit. Yeah, it was touchin.

Tha best part, tho', was when Little Bit sang. He ain't even tell me he was gonna be singin. I woulda been so fuckin angry if I had stayed home and then found out I missed him. I had heard him a few times hummin and singin "You & I" by Stevie Wonder in tha house but ain't think nuthin about it. I'd tell him, "That sounds jood, Baby," and he'd thank me. But when he rose outa his seat and took his place by tha piano, tha cat was outa tha bag. I was shocked but so fuckin proud. When he sat back down, I grabbed his hand and gave him a kiss, knowin folks was lookin. Yeah, he was surprised by it. And then it hit me: I just kissed him in front of ev'rybody *in a church!* Yeah, I started ta shrink in my seat. . . .

Tha preacher went on about commitment, blessed them, had us all pray, and then two sistas came up ta tha front carryin a broom. I was like, *What tha fuck they gonna do wit' that?* And then it clicked: like they did in *Roots*, they was gonna jump tha broom. And whatcha know, I was right: after tha preacher pronounced them "soul mates," they took that leap. Then B.D. leaped inta Babyface's arms, and they kissed. Little Bit, who was snappin shots of tha whole thing, really started lettin them tears flow. I ain't never seen him so worked up about somethin befo'. It was then that I understood. . . .

Ev'rybody congratulated them, and tha festivities continued a block away at this brotha's house named Godfrey. (I stayed outa his way—turned out we had gotten busy a coupla years back. Uh-huh, he was another one I couldn't remember, but fuh a jood reason: tha sex was *wrecked.*) On one flo' they had small black tables wit' red tablecloths on 'em and green chairs (nobody but Babyface) and one big table wit' a weddin cake (no, it wasn't white; it was chocolate) that was three stories and—I ain't lyin—had two little Black men holdin and kissin each other instead of a man and a woman on tha top. Its base said, BABY-FACE & B.D.—LOVE IS FOREVER—FEBRUARY 14, 1994.

They thanked ev'rybody fuh comin; B.D. looked straight at me when he said, "And thanks to those for not *depriving* us of their esteemed company" (yeah, I blushed), and introduced his moms, who was *still* cryin. She said she was "so, so, so happy" ta see her son "settle down," and that she "couldn't have asked for a better son-in-law." Babyface ain't had nobody on his side of tha family givin testimony, Little Bit told me his parents ain't wanna have nuthin ta do wit' it. His only brother, Tracey, was there, but he ain't say a word. He left when they started cuttin tha cake.

After they fed each other cake (they was really eatin it off and out of each other's mouth) and opened their gifts (they cleaned up—a weddin album; bottles of bubbly; gift certificates galore, dumb dollars, and *stoo*pid checks; a trip ta Jamaica from B.D.'s moms; lingerie fuh B.D. and silk pajamas fuh Babyface; and, of course, HIS & HIS matchin towel sets and robes from me 'n' Little Bit)—they had us go upstairs. It was time fuh their first dance, and "Always & Forever" was their song (I think that must still be *the* slow jam folks play at a weddin). When L.V.'s "Here & Now" came on (prob'ly number two on that playlist), Babyface stepped aside fuh B.D.'s moms, and other folks started dancin. Little Bit looked at me.

"Come on, Pooquie."

"Baby, I don't wanna dance."

"Since when *you* don't wanna dance?"

"I ain't up ta it."

"Well, would you mind if I danced with somebody else?"

I wanted ta say "Yeah," but I decided ta play it cool. "Nah, Baby, I don't mind."

Yeah, he was gaggin. "You . . . you don't?"

"Nah. Why should I? I mean, just be-cuz I don't wanna dance don't mean you don't hafta."

He just looked at me; I know he thought he was dreamin. "Uh . . . are you sure, Pooquie?"

"Yeah. Go on ahead. Have fun, Baby."

"OK." He smiled. He gave me a kiss on my cheek. "I'll be back in a bit."

It looked like he was gonna ask Jameson ta dance when Babyface swept him up. I know you ain't gonna believe me, but I wasn't jealous. I knew that Little Bit was dancin wit' somebody who had a special place in his heart, but it wasn't like what he felt fuh me. And wasn't nobody in tha room—not Babyface, not Gene, not B.D.— and there ain't nobody in tha world could love Little Bit tha way I do. He mine, so what I gotta worry about?

So I stood there by myself, against tha wall, just watchin them dance when . . .

"Excuse me?"

I turned ta my right ta see these two queens, Mutt 'n' Jeff, who had been scopin me out. They was just waitin fuh Little Bit ta leave my side, schemin. I just knew they was prob'ly tha only two brothas up in tha place that wasn't wit' somebody. I mean, who would want 'em? They looked and acted so fuckin desperate. When I smiled at them, they was just too thru. Yo, if I had just nodded in *that* direction, both of 'em woulda been on they knees befo' I could say, "Wanna taste?"

"Yeah?" I asked.

"Uh, I'm Eric," said tha tall one, "and this is Julius." Julius nodded at me—or, should I say, my piece. His eyes ain't move from below my waist.

"Raheim," I said. I wasn't about ta hold out my hand, since my hand wasn't tha thing they wanted ta shake. Besides, Eric was busy talkin wit' his hands and Julius was afraid ta show his—he was hidin them behind his back.

Eric giggled. "Uh, this is going to sound crazy, but . . . could you be that guy in the All-American ad?"

Befo' I had tha chance ta answer, Julius gave me what he was hidin: a copy of *YSB*. Yup, that was me. I had seen tha photos they had decided ta use but only mock-ups of tha ads. This was the Real mutha-fuckin McCoy. There I was, wit' nuthin but tha American flag wrapped around my waist, lookin straight at tha camera wit' that devilish smirk, my arms folded across my waist, my body just arched a little ta tha left. Tha background was white, and tha tag line read, THE RED, THE WHITE, THE BLUE, & THE BEAUTIFUL; ALL-AMERICAN 4 ALL TIMES. THE JEANZ 'N' THANGZ COMPANY (I came up wit' that last line, and it got me an extra thou). Tommy Boy said I wouldn't be seein myself till March, but I guess they was able ta squeeze inta this issue.

I was kinda miffed—not only cuz it was tha first time I was seein it. I wanted Little Bit ta be tha second person ta see it.

"Yeah, that's me," I said, tryin ta smile about it.

"*I told you, I told you, I told you it was him!*" screamed Julius, who pushed a pen in my face. "Would you please, please, *please* sign it? 'To Julius, Love, Raheim.' "

"Sure . . ." And I did. And then Julius went around ta almost ev'rybody at tha party ta tell 'em we had "a star in the house" (yo, those was his words, not mine, a'ight?). You think I was Denzel Washington and shit.

Now, I said he went up ta *almost* ev'rybody. Tha one person he ain't show 'n' tell was Little Bit, who, even tho' he was happy tha ad was out and that it looked jood, was not happy I signed Julius's magazine wit' "love."

"Baby, it's what he wanted me ta say," I argued as we came inta tha house. "What tha fuck was I s'pose ta do, say no?"

He looked up and turned ta me. "Yes."

I followed him inta tha bedroom. "Now, how that sound? We talkin about my fans. I gotta keep 'em smilin."

"Uh-huh, and what else were you plannin on doin to keep that tired child smilin?"

"Whatcha talkin about?" I said, takin off my clothes.

"You know what I'm talkin about, Pooquie," he said, doin tha same. "All you had to do was drop your pants right there, and he would've swallowed you whole. And what fans do you have to keep smiling? We're talking about *one* person."

"Yo, ev'rybody wanted ta talk ta me about it."

"Maybe so, but they all weren't askin you for your autograph. Anyway, that is not the point. I don't think it is necessary to sign your name with 'love.' I mean, it may give some of these children the wrong idea. And I hope you're not going to let this go to your head."

I grinned. "Which one?"

"Funny, very funny."

"Baby, don't be so serious."

"Well, you *have* to take it seriously, Pooquie. You are a spokesperson for a corporation now; you represent them. So every time you are in public, you have to be mindful of that. And people can be funny. You write 'love' on their picture, and they think that means you *do* love them."

"But I wrote '*Peace* and love,' so why would he think that way? That's cray-zee, Baby."

"I know, but it happens. Ask all those stars who are stalked by fans who mistake their being gracious and friendly for something else. I just want you to be careful, that's all."

He kept takin off his clothes wit' that low face.

"Little Bit?"

He sighed. 'Yeah?"

"You ain't gotta worry about nuthin, Baby. You ain't gonna lose me."

"What are you talkin about, Pooquie? Why would I think that?"

I took him in my arms. "Cuz just like me, you just saw this whole thing as being fun. But now that it's out there fuh ev'rybody ta see . . . I ain't gonna change, Baby. I ain't goin nowhere."

He looked at me; he sighed. "I guess . . . it's a little scary."

"But it's a'ight ta be. And it's a'ight fuh you ta be jealous."

He pushed me away. "*Jealous?* Now, why would I be jealous?"

"Cuz of tha attention I get. Like tanite. I mean, it's only natural."

"Uh-huh. And I guess that would be the way you feel about B.D., Babyface, and Gene, hunh?"

"Huh?"

"Admit it. You are jealous of what I have with them."

"Baby, you cray-zee. Why would I be jealous of them?"

"Because, Pooquie, it is a part of my life that exists apart from you. And even though you know you can be a part of that, it's hard for you to because it's all new."

Day-am . . . he just read me like a book.

His clothes all off, he got in bed, pullin tha blanket back and settlin under them on his right side. "Am I right?"

I eased in too, restin on my left side. "Yeah . . . I guess."

"It's OK . . . You know, I'm sorry if I sounded so demanding about you going. But I really wanted us to share this day together. I knew you would have a jood time . . . didn't you?"

I shrugged, "Yeah, I did. I mean, it did feel a little weird. But I'm really happy fuh Babyface 'n' B.D. And I *did* enjoy bein crowned a star."

He sucked his teeth. "Uh-huh, by that no-class queen."

I chuckled. "Ha, yeah . . ." I held his hand.

"Pooquie?"

'Yeah?"

"I'm proud of you."

'Yeah?"

"Yeah. I know how much it took for you to go tonight. And Gene, Babyface, and B.D. were really happy about you coming."

"I know. They told me. But I'm surprised Gene ain't faint or somethin."

"What do you mean?"

"I mean, as many times they said tha word *love?*"

He laughed. "Well, I guess Carl has something to do with that. They look jood together."

"Uh-huh. And you *sounded* jood, Baby."

"Thank you, Pooquie. I was singin it for them, but I was really singin it to you."

"I know. That's why I kissed ya."

And I kissed him again.

"Baby, I'm sorry."

"Sorry? About what?"

"About bein so . . . so . . ."

"Pig-headed? Domineering? Overcautious and overprotective?"

"No."

He giggled. He pecked me on my nose.

I frowned. "I couldn't give ya ev'rything ya wanted."

"What do you mean?"

"You know . . . not dancin wit' ya tanite."

He rubbed my head. "You gave me what I wanted, Pooquie. I loved my card. And the candy. And the flowers. And the BE MY VALENTINE balloon. *And* Pooquie Jr.!" He smiled at tha small black teddy bear I gave him; it was sittin on tha windowsill wit' tha other Pooquie. "And I *love* the way your gift looks on you." He gave me five pairs of bikini briefs in diff'rent colors. They all had red hearts on 'em. I wore tha blue ones tanite.

"Ya want me ta put 'em back on?" I asked.

He pulled me on top of him. "No. I'll only want you to take them back off anyway." He frowned. "But—you wanna know something?"

"What?"

"*I* wanted to get your first autograph."

"Don't worry about it, Baby. Julius mighta got tha first autograph, but you can always get somethin better."

"Hmmm. Now, *that* sounds better than an autograph." He squeezed my ass. "It *feels* better than one, too. And I *know* it's gonna taste better than one. With a giant chocolate kiss like you, *every day* is Heart Day."

I blushed.

"So, can I have some now?"

I licked them honeysuckle lips. "Baby, you ain't even gotta ask."

FANTASY (1996)

Cy K. Jones

When next you bed
a lying piece of shit
—of course
you've made him shower first
and hidden little valuables;
when next you bring
the asshole home
to wine
and feed and fuck;
when next you lend an ear
for half-sobbed tales
on bridges burned behind
while squelching your
I-told-you-so's
and what-did-you-expect's;
when next you cum
or, no, he cums
you erupt with fantasy;
when next you think
you can help
this cute deadbeat
if he'd only clip his toenails
lose his wife

and maybe, one day
rise above parole;
when next he claims
he's coming by tomorrow
his treat to a movie
and you, idiot
contemplate that date—
get with this:
eat a bitter apple
before you play yourself,
take a chill pill, honey
and look for love in poetry.

ARABESQUE (1996)

Gary Fisher

Tied up.

"Can you get your hand in there? Three fingers?"

He was pushing my hand, bending my wrist this funny way, telling me to bunch up my fingers—three, no, four—into a tube, "loosen yourself up for my cock." I told him it wasn't possible, that I didn't get fucked anyway, but he kept pushing my own hand into me, making the grunts of enjoyment that perhaps he thought I should be making. Reminding me that I belonged to him—exclusively to him—even more than I belonged to myself, and that I would enjoy this whether I wanted to or not.

"Four, try four."

My nails hurt. I wasn't as moist as I should have been. He slapped me for hesitating and wrapped my head tightly in the red and white gafiya he'd made me buy. "Do you know there's a war going on," he asked while knotting the scarf, "and that hundreds—thousands of little Arab boys are being killed—blown to bits, shot, crushed in their bunkers, starved? Aren't you glad that I captured you and made you my slave, my toy?" We'd had dinner at Square One, delicate portions, but I wouldn't starve. He'd paid with a credit card.

I didn't speak, couldn't really, but I didn't nod either. He'd wrapped me so tightly I had trouble breathing, the pressure on my ears made them sing and shards of light erupted behind my bound eyes. "What if I sent you back?"—he seemed to want an answer and struck me a hard, glancing blow to the head—"back to the front lines, back to the trenches?" Couldn't I hear the bombs falling all around me, curled up in my fear, my desperation at the dark bottom of that hole? It was only a matter of time before death took me— or some other master. Did I want that?

"You want to kill me, don't you?"

He curled me more tightly. "You know, you're my first Arab?" My wrist ached. I mumbled ineffectively that he might be breaking my wrist and he swatted me hard across the back. "My first Arab slave." The wrapping and now the full weight of this man bore down on my breathing. The shards of light leapt more violently against this constriction, and the singing seemed to be completely outside of me. I felt the man's rough hair against my back and my butt, his hand suddenly fumbling with my mouth. Wasn't it better to be safe here, half a world away, in this slavery? "Arabs," he explained, "can die or they can serve." Couldn't I see how simple it all was?

The hand fumbled around my lips, like a blind thing discovering them. Then I heard the scissors—snap! snap!—brandished above me. I tried to move away but he was big and strong and held me still, curled neatly beneath him. I felt the cloth pulling forward, felt it intensely around my ears and the back of my head, until the scissors whacked out a two-inch plug. I touched the metal, thought I could taste it, but it was the air filling me so sharply.

"Lick them."

Now I did taste the cold metal, then the salt and warmth of his hand, then the metal again. "Grateful?" He could have suffocated me, could still cut out my tongue, he said. I heard the scissors again, felt them cold on my shoulder, my back. "Who would care? Who could you tell—especially if I—?" He laughed, there were Arab boys dying by the thousands, the tens of thousands—"who would care?" He was in my face, breathing near my mouth—explaining, "life has dealt Arabs a bunch of bad cards." Did I understand Israel? He struck me two disorienting blows and punched open my mouth so he could spit in it.

"Do you understand it as a concept?"

Stupid of me to think he cared about my breathing—"don't you know what that hole is for?" He turned himself around me, tightly, like a ratchet wheel around its pawl. "Of course you know, of course you do, don't you." It was a physical law, he informed me, "just the way God intended it." I sucked in a lot of air, knowing that he'd take it from me again.

"You do understand, don't you?" he laughed—

Said I engaged this thing in him, this need to refill me with all the dangers he'd just saved me from. I'd been a soldier on the front lines about to die—did I understand why he'd saved me? "It sure as hell wasn't charity." I felt him fumbling around my mouth, but more bluntly now, and more urgently. He slammed my head with some part of his body, said I wanted to kill him—"You have to want to"—then slammed my head several times more and begged me not to resist, but begged me to want to kill him. He didn't want to hurt me too much, but he would, he said, he wouldn't even hesitate, because that gave him pleasure too. He didn't want to give over to that sort of pleasure, but he would, if I resisted, even a little bit. He said he was looking for the smallest reason to give over to it. My submission must be unconditional or else—but even that might not matter. Could I imagine what it was like to suffocate?

"I'm going to choke you to death, and you're going to love it."

Didn't I want to die a hundred times this way? Wouldn't I be happier? I hadn't seen his cock, didn't know it would be so big, so unmanageable—hadn't I always wanted to die this way? He pushed toward my throat, curled me still tighter, and drove my head down on it, still talking about death like it was our only alternative. Maybe I understood this mechanism I'd become the middle of, understood its strength, its unrelenting, its selfishness and selflessness. I tasted his salt, his ooze, and my throat jumped but I couldn't dislodge him.

"It's okay if you choke, Arab."

I shook to dislodge him. Of course he knew I wasn't Arab. He didn't know any Arabs. Could I please humor him and choke? I did this.

He rubbed my wrapped head like I'd done a good thing, said it was my duty to make him feel strong, that nothing short of my choking would make him feel strong, and he drove my head onto his cock even past the possibility of choking. If it crossed my mind to bite him I don't remember. I did try to struggle—he told me to—but it seemed to make so little difference that I immediately wished I hadn't. Now hopelessness closed on me and suffocation seemed too easy but also the chill sensation of sexual release, waves and waves of this threat—

"Choke! Choke!"

He drove with a desperation that actually amused me more than it frightened me, but then I was outside of myself and somewhat embarrassed with myself and needed to laugh at it all to keep from blacking out. I'd laugh for a moment more, then politely register my need to breathe—didn't know how I would do either, but at the time this didn't seem to bother me—it all seemed so funny, my fucked-up priorities, especially the need to laugh at this man's desperation before I took another breath.

"Choke! Choke, you Arab bastard!"

The need to swallow was now a long time gone, and that felt funny—felt strangely new to me, like the first time I came myself and thought I would die; or perhaps long before that, like my first sip of mother's milk—it felt foreign to me or a very long time removed, but something I had to get used to. I felt myself falling toward a womblike coziness, despite my amusement and the violent buffeting my body took.

"Goddamn-you-to-hell, choke on it, you piece of Arab shit!"

I felt myself falling even as his thick, insistent ropes of cum jumped past my need to swallow them. "Damn—goddamn—blow your fucking head off!" Even as he fumbled to unsnap his leather cock ring to release the second great dam of his pleasure, "—oh, goddamn—god-damn—got-tamm—blow your fucking brains out!"

And all the while he fucked himself relentlessly against the calm walls of my throat, milking out himself with friction and brutish thuds what I could no longer coax from him with swallowing—

"—"

—and seeming to enjoy my acquiescence most of all—pleasures that rekindled themselves against the fullness of his bladder, the crashing of his heart, the quickness of his breath, perhaps even against sensitivity itself. He was tortured to a new pitch, driven past pain and into a sweet delirium where he might just forget to ever let me breathe.

"—"

When I awoke he said he was sorry. He grinned a great deal while patting my cheeks and forehead with a cold cloth. My mouth tasted like piss. "Didn't I tell you it would be intense?" He rubbed my wrists, almost gently, one in each of his big hands. "Didn't I tell you?" He licked his lips and slid off the bed beside me. "Next time—" he began. I sat up as he hobbled on his knees to the foot of the bed. Suppliant and dreadfully handsome he began to rub my ankles where the ropes had reddened them. "Next time we can play Intifada."

His eyes got big as he imagined it for me. Would I like to stone him? he invited.

YOUR MOTHER FROM CLEVELAND (1996)

Bil Wright

H ad to sign my Black self the hell out!"
Your Mother from Cleveland came at me from up the
block and across the street, bellowing. I didn't have a chance to get
any further than the top step of the stoop.

I hadn't seen her for weeks, it was true, but twenty minutes before
I was due at my desk forty blocks away was not an ideal time for an
explanation. We weren't friends. We were neighbors. Still, it wasn't
the first time she'd made me late. Your Mother from Cleveland
dropped a shopping bag directly in front of me as a roadblock.
Plastic bottles, sample cards of yellow pills and a pair of savagely
soiled size fifty-two pajamas spilled out of the bag.

"Got a show on the twenty-fifth at The Red Rug. That's this
coming Monday. You better write it down, Baby Louise. I want your
face close enough to sit on. Doing my special tribute to Josephine
Baker in the first act. Big Maybelle's Big Band Classics in the second.
Intern was fightin' me to stay, but a week's worth of bedpans is all
Your Mother from Cleveland could bear. Besides, I figured if they
could still pick up a pulse after a week, I was pretty convinced I
could do my show.

"You know anything about pneumonia? They sure don't tell you
anything you could get a hold on. Like how do you get pneumonia
in the middle of July? They just kept talkin' about 'bacteria.' I think
that's why I didn't listen so good. Even 'pneumonia' don't sound as
deadly as 'bacteria.' That's a ugly ass word. Now, you think about a

word like 'BACTERIA'—makes your damn skin crawl. Then you think about a word like—'SEQUINS'! Imagine a good-lookin' intern strolling up to the side of your hospital bed, takin' your fleshy black palm in his, leanin' over close enough for you to smell his shower soap an sayin', 'You got Sequins. Too many Sequins. They're all over everything. It's probably the worst case I've seen.' Now how bad could you feel? Even if you thought it was incurable, it couldn't be but so bad to go out from too many Sequins, could it?

"But they weren't sayin' anything that encouraging across town at St. Helena's, up on sixteen, Coleman ward, bed B. They weren't saying anything that made me wanna do a thing but get the hell outta there and get ready for my show. That's all I could think about, baby. Monday night. Your Mother from Cleveland is gonna give the children Festival of Lights. Carnival in Rio and Aida's Fourth Act Finale. All in twenty-two minutes. On a four-by-four platform in the Bronx. If they like this one, they're gonna give me Monday nights for the next couple of months. I'm gonna do what I do better than anybody, an' it sure as hell ain't layin' up on a bed of concrete in St. Helena's.

"We will not do anymore masks and plastic gloves. No more bad hairdos in nylon dresses masquerading as professional nurses telling me, 'Don't get your hopes up, Bed B. No tellin' how long you'll be in here.' No! No more four syllable pneumonias, and I'll be damned if I'll listen to one more announcement that evil 'bacteria' is storm-trooping through my damn lungs. Not while Your Mother from Cleveland still has it in her to give you a show. Don't you even think about not being there, Baby Louise." I winced. I'd only been 'Louis' once, the first time I'd introduced myself to Your Mother. After that, it seemed as if she'd made a point of letting the entire neighborhood hear her calling me "Baby Louise."

Your Mother from Cleveland approached the steps of the

crumbling east-side tenement we both called home. Except that she was Leontyne Price laying claim to Egypt at the Met. The only thing louder than her wheezing was the mint jelly green of her raincoat as Your Mother carefully negotiated her way through the front door and down the hall.

I missed Your Mother from Cleveland's show in the Bronx. I'd only seen her perform once, and although I'd made countless promises since then, with all the best intentions, I'd never made good on any of them. The one time I'd traipsed out to Brooklyn Heights on a Wednesday night, Your Mother hadn't gone on until two o'clock in the morning. Despite a tour de force performance from Your Mother, the evening yielded *tres, tres* bitter regrets. The next day, two other night birds in my department called in sick, leaving me to lay out over two hundred display ads single-handedly with a Budweiser hangover and an hour and a half of sleep.

As usual after not going to one of Your Mother's shows, I started tiptoeing past her apartment, hoping I wouldn't run into her. A month later, on my way to work, I noticed a yellow flyer taped to her door. I glanced at it on my way out, sure it was a promotion for yet another performance. And in a way, I suppose it was.

YOUR MOTHER FROM CLEVELAND
(1961–1994)
WILL BE GIVEN A LEGEND'S FAREWELL
AT GRAPPLER'S MEMORIAL CHAPEL
337 WEST 23RD STREET, N.Y.
SATURDAY 8/31/94 1:00 P.M.

I peeled the tape slowly from the door, careful not to rip the flyer. I had a vague thought that I'd make a copy at the office and replace it. I knew I wanted one for myself, though. Leaving the building, I tripped down the stairs I'd been climbing for two years and looked back in that ridiculous, automatic way, as though the stairs had somehow repositioned themselves since I'd last used them. I stood whimpering like a toddler abandoned in the middle of a department store on Red Tag Day. Then I headed for the subway.

Work was hellish. I spent most of the morning shuffling ads randomly and rolling dust from my desk between my fingers. By afternoon, I'd taken the flyer out of my desk to stare at the picture of Your Mother from Cleveland. Somebody'd spent money on a color Xerox, and it was worth every penny. Your Mother was wearing a gold halter gown that looked like Eartha Kitt in her I Want to Be Evil days. But even Eartha could not possibly have managed the box-hedge Afro with the greased and straightened bangs and Scotch-taped spit curls. "It's my Odetta meets Tammi Terrell sixties tribute," Your Mother had once informed me, and I wondered if she'd stipulated somewhere that she be laid out in it.

The following Saturday morning I took a cross-town bus that let me off about a half block from Grappler's Memorial Chapel. Grappler's had the pulse-quickening distinction of preparing more gay men for burial in the last ten years than any other funeral home in Manhattan. I'm not quite sure what I expected, but it turned out to be as anonymous looking as any other funeral home I'd been in, although there hadn't, thank God, been that many. Sitting at the entrance was a relic who looked like a waxed extra from a B movie about organized crime. He pointed over his shoulder to a staircase.

The room at the top of the stairs was very dark with a soft pink glow. In the center of the room was a sand-colored casket which I assumed held Your Mother, although I couldn't see her very well from the doorway. There were only two other people, grey-haired women in simple black dresses sitting silently in front of the coffin. I wondered if one of them might be Your Mother's mother.

It was a quarter after one already, and I'd cursed myself coming across town for probably getting to Grappler's too late to get a seat. Because of the flyer, I expected that there would be quite a turnout of Your Mother's friends and family. I was so shocked that these two women were the only ones in the room that I stood in the doorway, feeling uneasy about going in at all. I must have stood there for almost ten minutes before a stampede came up the stairs behind me. I cleared the entrance to the room for at least a dozen drag queens of varying shades and sizes, mostly large, wearing every variation of day drag imaginable, from Geoffrey Beene to Buffy's Budget Basement. As the new mourners filled the room, the two older women got up, stood together for a moment at the coffin, then passed me on their way down the stairs. I went in and found a seat over to the side and towards the back.

I couldn't bring myself to go up very close to Your Mother. I've only been to a couple of these things, ever—and I never get up very close. But what I could see from where I was sitting startled me—a big, bald, cocoa-colored man in a navy blue suit, wrinkled, yellowed white shirt and a hopelessly off-center salmon print bow tie. He looked like a high school science teacher or a midtown accountant; some bifocaled Mr. Brown or Mr. Jackson who'd disappeared into an office building one day and been trapped irrevocably inside—until now.

Eerily, the navy blue suit could easily have been the one hanging in the back of my own closet, the uniform I'd worn from one side of the city to the other trying to find work when I first moved to New York from Chicago. I'd considered wearing it to pay my respects to Your Mother, but it was unmistakably her voice behind me at the door of my closet laughing, "Relax, Baby Louise. The suit's going too damn far." Now I knew I'd heard wrong. Or maybe I hadn't. Either the two women who were there when I first arrived were responsible for how Your Mother was dressed or maybe she'd talked me out of wearing my own suit, knowing she'd already decided on one for herself. In a room full of "Des Sisters De La Drag," as Your Mother called them, all giving you designer mourning cum Auntie Mame cocktail ensembles, Your Mother from Cleveland was serving up tailored and tasteful burial attire— conservative, male drag.

I'd assumed because of the flyer that someone had organized the service, but after almost an hour, nobody seemed to be taking charge. There wasn't a moment's silence in the room, though, as entrances were dished ("Oooh, Miss Sissy, if you're not throwing us Supreme Jackie Kennedy! The veil is on fire, darling, on *fire!*") and exits observed ("You got an appointment, bitch? Is he paying?")

As the din peaked to a shrill cacophony of laughter and pump heels beating the floor for emphasis, I realized that what was going on around me *was* the service. This *was* the Legend's Farewell the flyer had promised. All of the ceremony that I expected, and per- haps thought only appropriate for a presence as large as Your Mother's, didn't seem to be on anyone else's agenda. I was disap- pointed, but I definitely didn't have the guts to pay her any kind of tribute myself. And after all, I reminded myself, she wasn't really a friend, she was my neighbor. I barely knew her. I waited a few min- utes more and started over to Your Mother to say good-bye.

An elfin-looking man who appeared to be in his early sixties, with a face so deeply flushed it looked more eggplant than red, weaved over to where I was standing. He hung perilously over Your Mother's open coffin toward me.

"This one," he rasped, "was a survivor. This one had a helluva lot of balls. I knew it when I first seen him do a show out at Coney Island. Club called the Plucked Pigeon. I said when I seen what he did, I said, 'Balls.' " He leaned across Your Mother at me. "You know Coney Island?"

"No. No, I don't."

"Clubs out there, ya don't see hardly any coloreds at all. Not without a whole lotta trouble. Whoever booked this kid wasn't doin' him no damn favors. Coney Island ain't no Greenwich Village. It's da last friggin' stop on the line. It's more like the rest of the friggin' world. I thought there'd be hell to pay for a while, that night! But he gave 'em a show an' a half, all right. Colored or no colored.

"Kid reminded me of myself back when I still had it in me to do what I done that night o' Stonewall in sixty-nine. I know you know about Stonewall, don't ya, kid?"

"Well . . . I mean I'm not an expert or anything. But I know about it."

"Well, I am. I am a friggin' expert on it. I'm as much of an expert as you're gonna get." The elf was pretty loud by now, but no louder than the queens around us. I think it was that he was yelling over Your Mother that bothered me. I kept watching the spit fly out of his mouth and into the coffin.

" 'You can kiss our sissy asses!' That's what we told the world in sixty-nine. And this kid right here had the same kinda moxie. No matter what you see in front of ya, he was a survivor."

I looked from the diminutive man with the liver spots freckling his pale, rubbery scalp to Your Mother from Cleveland barely contained by his coffin. I resisted even imagining any kinship between them. Why? The man was earnest enough. Sloppy, repulsive even, but earnest. He'd paid the tribute to Your Mother I didn't have the nerve to. Hadn't I wanted there to be some kind of eulogy? Wasn't the purpose of a eulogy to tie, however clumsily, all of our lives together in some comforting daisy chain of commonality? Hadn't that been what the drunken elf had attempted to do?

The one time I'd seen Your Mother from Cleveland perform, this queen, Demeana Divina from Brooklyn Heights who did Barbra

Streisand and Maria Callas, was the headliner. Your Mother from Cleveland was one of seven Guest Stars.

Apparently Demeana had come up with this gospel finale to be performed (read lip-synched) to "Oh Happy Day," originally recorded by The Edwin Hawkins Singers and covered by The Staples Singers with Mavis Staples steam-piping out the lead. The very blonde Demeana, of course, was doing Mavis's voice, and the Guest Stars had been assigned the chorus. After all, they were performing on her turf, *n'est-ce pas?*

As drag divas are wont to do, I suppose, Your Mother missed her chorus cue and entered from the wings directly on Demeana's (i.e., Mavis's) opening solo line. She had forgone a finale evening gown like the others and was wearing a white choir robe with a red sequined stole and matching pumps (also sequined). Her wig was a towering Mahalia-meets-Clara-Ward with sausage curls big enough to hide money in. Demeana, in a pink cotton shift, close-cropped yellow Afro wig and checkered bandanna, was beginning to resemble a spastic albino sharecropper mutely mouthing prayers for rain.

Now, Your Mother wasn't lip-synching at all. Your Mother was wailing live harmony off Mavis in a gospel tenor that took me back twenty years to a sissy in the church I grew up in, who would make old people jump over pews when he sang. The crowd rushed Your Mother with dollar bills. In my delirium, I forgot that the only bill I had left was a twenty, which I'd vowed not to spend and should have left at home. I thrust my last twenty into Your Mother's hand and then kissed it passionately, honored that she'd allowed me to do so.

The climax of the number, as if it needed one, was when Your Mother jumped out of her sequined pumps, presumably taken over by "the spirit" in a brilliantly choreographed strut from one end of the stage to the other. Yes, *c'est vrai, c'est vrai.* The evening's curtain calls were fraught with high tension, but Your Mother was glowing unmistakably triumphant, having further established herself in the Firmament of Legendary Drag Artistes.

I wanted to share my memory of that night with the rest of the people in the room with me and Your Mother at Grappler's Memorial Chapel. I wanted to tell them Your Mother from Cleveland's "Oh Happy Day" was as much a moment of theatrical genius as any I'd seen on Broadway in the last five years. I turned to the Stonewall Survivor, but he'd retreated to a darkened corner where he was nursing a small flask. The others were cataloging Your Mother's repertoire, a drag queen's legacy they were greedily dividing up amongst themselves.

I thought about Your Mother's apartment and all of the costumes, makeup and wigs that she must have left. Who'd get the gold halter gown on the memorial flyer, for example, a number that could have supplied the power for the state of Texas?

Hell, Your Mother liked me. I'd bet she'd want me to have something to remember her by. Like the choir robe with the red sequined stole. I supposed the pumps would be too much to hope for. Besides, what would I do with them? You couldn't sit around eating takeout in red sequined pumps, could you? Shit, if they were mine, I could do anything I damn well pleased with them, couldn't I?

I didn't have the nerve, though, to go up to any of the others and stake any kind of claim. I turned back to Your Mother. This time it would really be good-bye. I stared at her smooth, dramatically chiseled face. My eyes traveled down to her hands folded over each other and I remembered how she waved them about as she carried on about any and everything. It was the navy suit that still seemed so odd and uncharacteristic. It was I, I thought, who'd someday be buried in a suit, and no one would think it was strange at all. But Your Mother, I was sure, had changed out of this straightjacket as soon as her soul had taken flight from her body and changed into something . . . well, something *tres, tres* Your Mother.

I tried to imagine what someone like Your Mother would wear in the Great Hereafter as I headed for the staircase. I got halfway down before she stopped me. I could feel her standing behind me, although I didn't dare turn around. I wasn't afraid, but I did get goose bumps on the back of my neck when she spoke. "You better go back up there and get what you want, Baby Louise. Ask and ye shall receive."

Actually, I was no more surprised by Your Mother than I'd ever been. I suppose I was more impressed with how well she seemed to know me and grateful that she didn't hold it against me for missing that last show. I did as I was instructed, thinking that if I was going to ask anything of these queens, though, I'd better be specific. I might have to be tough, maybe even a little ruthless. I might have to do my best Your Mother from Cleveland right there in front of her. I had to have a first, second, and maybe even a third choice. I'd ask for the sequined pumps. And the choir robe with the stole that matched them. If I couldn't have another chance to see Your Mother give the children Festival of Lights, Carnival in Rio, and Aida's Fourth Act Finale all in twenty-two minutes, I'd be grateful as hell to have whatever The Legend, Your Mother from Cleveland had left behind.

Damn it, I wanted to slap myself. I was shocked and embarrassed at how badly I wanted the wig. The Mahalia-meets-Clara with the curls big enough to hide dollar bills in. But I'd ask the queens anyway, and I knew Your Mother from Cleveland would make sure I received.

THE LETTER (1999)

Donald Keith Jackson

"Part of my soul went with him."
　　　　　　　—Winnie Mandela

Dear Joe,

Your mother asked me, "Did you know that my son was special?"
When I told her, "Yes, yes, I knew your son was special," my answer
brought back those wonderful days we spent together while serving
in Uncle Sam's military. Both of us were young and vulnerable. I was
stationed at Cherry Point Marine Corps Air Station. You, a navy
hospitalman, were attached to a marine corps unit at Camp Lejeune
Marine Corps Base.

I remember the day that I received orders to report to the 3rd
Marine Division, Okinawa, Japan. My heart was broken thinking of
how I was going to live so far away from you. You were so reassuring
to me. You told me that oceans and mountains could never come
between us. You told me that we will always be together " 'til death
do us part." Joe, do you remember how much we laughed until we
cried when only one week after my news of leaving, you said that
your unit, the 2nd Marine Amphibious Unit, was to leave for six
months' duty as a peacekeeping force in Beirut?

We spent our remaining days preparing to say good-bye. This was
going to be the first time that we would be so far apart from each
other. I was trying to be a brave marine, but baby, my heart was

breaking inside. We laughed a lot and talked a lot, sharing the things we feared. I remember your face when you asked me if I really loved you. No, I said, I'm very much "in love" with you. I knew at that moment our dream of building our lives together would come true. We gave each other an early Happy Birthday. I was to soon turn twenty-one. We took great pleasure in preparing our last dinner together. That night we had veal parmigiana with linguine, a salad, and red wine. So many times while we ate, I would stop to watch you twirling the noodles on your plate. It was then I realized that our stomachs were full of butterflies, not food. So powerful were your touch, your smell. Your soft lips gave passionate kisses. And those beautiful "life-giving" eyes, all played a part in the intense lovemaking rituals we shared before we said our good-byes.

Arriving in Okinawa was an exciting and very lonely experience, especially today, my birthday. Twenty-one is the age when one becomes an adult, but today I feel like a little boy. I wish that you were here with me to tell me that everything will be all right.

Many letters and cards have been exchanged between us. Today I felt a strong need to pull out the first letter you sent to me, telling me of your arrival in Beirut. You said that this is not a place to spend a vacation! It's the kind of place that could drive you to extreme boredom. I do not want you to be bored, my love, so I will be sending you plenty of letters and cards with goodies to keep you going on and going strong. We continue to tell each other of our lives in foreign lands. The one thing that keeps my sanity is the thought that our eyes will soon meet again; to hold you and to be held by you. I always think of your beautiful smile, the smile that could always penetrate me and give me a warm and secure feeling.

Another letter arrived today from you to tell me that the weather is "hot as hell!" and that you have been stuck with "duty" again. It was food for my soul to read that you miss me and you "love (me) so much." You tell that you received my cards and that it brightened up your day very much. Each day I live, I am living for you and me.

As the months pass, time is growing closer to when we return to the States. The letter that I received today brings me the news that during the middle of a volleyball game, your unit was hit real bad by incoming mortar rounds from the Drews and that you were forced to stay in the bunkers until morning. "Don, two marines were killed, seven marines were seriously injured." I hear the fear and hurt in the words. "It's so hard to believe it happened," you tell me. "Muffled and confused" were the words you used to tell me of how your days have become. "I wonder if it will end soon?" I begin to feel the tears rolling down my cheeks. Joe, I am afraid for you. As I begin to fold the letter to put back into the envelope, I say to myself that this madness will end soon.

Each night, I pray to God, asking Him to protect you from all harm and to give you enough peace of mind to maintain your sanity. I always end my prayer by saying, "God, I love him so much, please bring him back to me safely."

Tonight, I am going to take a break from writing and go into town with a few fellow marines. I feel justified in getting drunk. Even when I was in town hanging out, I longed for you to be beside me. How much I would give to hear you laughing with me right now.

When we returned back to our barracks, I reached over the lamp to turn on the television in my room, not to watch it but to have some noise as a distraction. There was a news announcement that flashed over the TV screen, saying that there had been a bombing at the marine barracks in Beirut. As I was trying to make sense of the message in my drunkenness, I heard a marine shout in the background, "Oh hell, we finally going to go to war now! Better get your M-16s ready!" Honey, it did not dawn on me in that moment that it could have been your unit that had been bombed. I went to sleep.

After a long day at the office, I walked over to the Post Exchange to buy you a card. As soon as I left the post office, I walked over to the chow hall to grab a bite to eat. On the way, I picked up a copy of the base newspaper to read while I ate. Flipping through the paper in a very nonchalant manner, I came upon an article on the marine unit bombing. A strange feeling came over me as I continued to read this article. Something sounded familiar, but I didn't know what. That's it! It finally hit me—this was Joe's unit. I almost lost every bite of food I had consumed. My heart pounded like a hammer. I rushed to my room to get a letter to match the address. I was hoping and praying that I was wrong. I stood in the middle of the room, trembling with fear because the letter in my hand matched the unit identification in the newspaper.

Before the sun had set that day, I had placed at least ten pieces of mail in the mailbox, each addressed to you. Words full of support and deep concern. Things were not moving fast enough. The mail is just sitting there in the bottom of the mailbox. Doesn't the postman know that I need to get these letters to the man I love without delay? Before I go to sleep I will write to you once more and say a special prayer for you, for us. I will have to be patient. I know that I must stay strong in order to survive, but I am getting depressed. Please, Joe, hurry and send me a reply, just to let me know that you are all right.

Weeks have passed, and it is now November. It's a Saturday and the mailroom is open. I remember very clearly the three pieces of mail I received: a renewal notice from *Ebony* magazine (I have never been a subscriber to it), a letter from my mother (I know that she is going to lay me out for not writing to her in such a long time. She would not want to understand that I have been a mess worrying about the man I love), and the last envelope, which had my address on the front. My heart skipped a thousand beats when I realized that the handwriting on the letter was yours! Quickly I went to my room to read the letter. Thank you, dear Lord, for not letting me down. You really heard my prayers. As I read each line of your letter, I could hear the sound of your voice. In its pages, you congratulated me on becoming a noncommissioned officer and told me that you enjoyed the Halloween card I sent you. Finally, I can sleep knowing that you are all right.

I don't remember how many times I read the letter. It did not matter, you were fine and that was everything to me. As I was beginning to put your letter away, a voice inside my head said, "Look at the postmark on the letter." At first I resisted; then I turned the envelope over. The postmark said October 20, 1983. My heart sank deep within me. That was the moment I knew you had died in that bombing. I knew that I did not have anything to give me a sense of hope that you were alive. I remembered that the bombing took place on October 23, 1983.

I was so empty inside, I could not shed another tear. All I could do was moan. Grieving widows and fellow marines got sympathy, grieving homosexuals like me get interrogated by the Naval Investigative Services and discharged. I told my fellow marines, mainly those who could tell that I had been shaken up, that my girlfriend had just been killed in a car accident. You better believe that when I told my story, I would be monitoring every word that comes from my mouth, making sure I used the "proper" pronouns.

How can I ever know what happened to you on that horrible night when the angels of death came knocking on your door? Sometimes when I think about your dying in those barracks, so far away from home, family, and me, another part of my spirit died. Joe, were you sleeping when that bomb exploded? Were you having a late-night conversation with another service member about coming home? Were you writing those wonderful words of love to me? My prayer will always be that you were in a deep sleep and felt nothing. I will always believe that.

They say that time heals all wounds. This is not a wound, this is my heart, a heart that was so full of young, passionate, and innocent love, now shattered. I feel so alone in my darkness; not enough light to guide me through this maze of misery. It has been so hard for me to come to terms with your untimely death. You were my first love. I felt that I could face anything the world put before me. Your love gave me courage. Only you and the Lord above knew the depths of my love for you.

So when your mother asked me if I knew you were special, I could emphatically say yes, because your presence gave joy to those around you and most of all, brought to me the gift of love.

Love always,
Don

LIVING AS A LESBIAN (2001)

Robert Reid-Pharr

I n 1985 Barbara Smith came like a fresh wind to Chapel Hill. She brought with her a vision of home unlike anything I had imagined. Home held out promises of redemption and nurturance, acceptance and love. Home was populated with brothers and sisters so unlike my own "natural" family in their politics, their progressiveness, their passion. At home we would recreate ourselves and our world, fashion a new mode of being, map a way for living in which the vision of the black freedom struggle would be realized in the daily interaction of black lesbians and gays. In coming home, I told myself, I would finally be able to articulate that which I had known all along, the centrality of the black woman, the black faggot, the so-called black underclass, and especially the black lesbian to the project of redeeming America. Armed with strong doses of Audre Lorde, Pat Parker, Cheryl Clarke, and Donna Kate Rushin, I felt, for a brief moment in my life, as if I knew in which direction to place my feet, saw clearly the road before us.

The most general statement of our politics at the present time would be that we are actively committed to struggling against racial, sexual, heterosexual, and class oppression, and see as our particular task the development of integrated analysis and practice based upon the fact that the major systems of oppression are interlocking.[1]

My sister had been in early life the quintessential daddy's girl. To him she was "his heart," the proof of his own self-worth, his princess to be protected from boys, men, and the great unfriendly world. It seemed to all of us that only a moment had passed before her long hair, fancy dresses, and sassy little-girl style gave way to cigarettes, a Jheri curl, unquestioned prowess on the basketball court, and then eventually to her first woman lover, Rose. News of the passionate love affair between seventeen-year-old bulldaggers hit my family like the news of death or war. After months of histrionics and therapy, my parents packed first my sister and then me off to live with our aunt in Brooklyn for a boring summer of softball and Coney Island. When we returned, our parents announced their divorce, or, rather, our mother announced that she would be leaving our father.

My sister's lesbianism had by all indications been cured. She started a tempestuous relationship with Darryl, another impressive basketball player and the father of her child. She suffered through years of drug and alcohol abuse and raised her son, in working poverty, always stuck in the shadow of my parents' smugly secure comfortableness and my own unquenchable thirst for success. She pushed forward, however unfruitfully, into the mystique of heterosexual acceptability until unexpectedly Rose, her ex-high school lover, suddenly reappeared, moved in, and began receiving well-chosen gifts from my parents during the holidays.

> Afraid, jealous, or stuck in some foaming
> funk I learned from her in the circumstances
> of her loneliness, I push away from my lover.
> This hotness, this coldness still
> in her aging she tricks me.[2]

My students and I have been discussing Audre Lorde's *Zami* in a monstrously large Harlem building with few windows. We keep the door to the classroom open to save ourselves from roasting inside the six-inch-thick cement walls. I present the text to them like a scarce and delicious morsel. They snatch it up, hungrily consuming what they like, leaving the rest to scavengers.

"I'm not a lesbian, still I can relate."

"I'm Caribbean and these Caribbean writers just get under my skin."

"Was she abused as a child?"

"Was she afraid of black people?"

"I didn't read the whole book, but. . . ."

Audre Lorde, Audre: Poet, Mother, Sister, Lesbian, Warrior, Cancer Survivor, was for them—and for me—just the third assignment in a fourteen-week syllabus, sandwiched in between a collection of Lower East Side writers and Alfred Kazin's *Walker in the City*. They liked her, they said. I talked about her being the poet laureate of New York, one of the great prophets of multiculturalism and the concept of overlapping identities. They blinked back at me and argued among themselves about whether lesbians could walk the streets of Harlem holding hands.

To whom do I owe the power behind my voice, what strength I have become, yeasting up like sudden blood from under the bruised skin's blister?[23]

"He looks just like a girl," well-meaning ladies would giggle as they passed by me, sitting on the front steps, my Afro braided down into neat cornrows. Other children would respond cruelly that indeed I was a boy, that it was only my fat body and long hair that so obfuscated my sex. And yet even they could not resist taking me around by the hand on Halloween nights, when dressed in a skirt and stockings, I would present myself as a rather delectable treat on neighbors' doorsteps.

"Stop acting like a sissy," my father would bark at me, his eyes fixated on my limp wrist as I crossed the street from the school bus.

"Mira Loca!" my Dominican neighbors would yell years later as I issued forth, in full butch queen regalia, from my newly rented Washington Heights apartment.

I have acquired this ill-fitting masculinity at considerable cost. There were years during my adolescence when men would start to scream at me as I walked out of public restrooms, assuming that I was some crazy or radical woman breaking into their most sacred domain. In graduate school I became the first male T.A. for the "Introduction to Women's Studies" lecture. My sections filled up with the few men taking the course. One of them would eventually break down in class as he recounted the details of his having been sexually abused. Another wrote to me privately that I was the only thing standing in the way of his acting on unspecified rape fantasies. I assigned him the grade check, as opposed to check minus or check plus, and told him that this was one of the most interesting things he had written.

> *This anger so visceral I could shit it*
> *and still be constipated.*
> *My ass is sore with the politics*
> *of understanding the best given the circumstances.*
> *I could spit this anger*
> *and still choke on the phlegm.*[4]

My lesbianism takes me to dyke parties in Brooklyn, small clubs hidden away among the West Side warehouses, the odd women's gathering, and a wealth of impromptu therapy sessions. I know all the young black female film and video makers: Cheryl, Shari, Dawn, Vejan, Yvonne, and even Michelle, not to mention Jackie W., the children's writer; Pamela, the performance artist; Cathy, the Ivy league professor and AIDS activist; bald Jackie B., the erotic poet; Jewelle who needs no introduction; and, of course, Barbara, the mother of us all. I am asked with a regularity that never ceases to surprise me for my sperm and then asked, ever so gingerly, to step quietly aside.

My files are packed with back copies of *Sinister Wisdom, Off Our Backs, On Our Backs,* and *Conditions.* I have recently removed my copy of J. R. Roberts's bibliography, *Black Lesbians,* from my bookcase, afraid that this most precious piece of lesbian ephemera might be damaged on my crowded shelves. I continue to keep my three issues of *Stallion, Male Pictorial,* and *Honcho,* my two issues of *Drummer* and *Mandate,* my four issues of *Advocate Men,* and my single issues of *Inches* and *Torso* in a box under my bed.

The book you are holding in your hands is a kind of miracle. The fact that hundreds of Black lesbians have found the courage to commit their lives and words to paper is miraculous.[5]

To become myself I have become a lesbian, or at least that's what I have been told. I have found my way into dozens of women's beds, been thoroughly schooled in the intricacies of women's relationships, learned to sit quietly and listen as the many vulgarities of "The Man" are rehearsed:

> *how like a man*
> *is the ku klux klan*
> *it comes in the night*
> *to wag its ugly shaft*
> *to laugh at the final climax of its rape*
> *as rope chokes out the final cry of "why?"*
> *blood blurring sight of a naked cross.*[6]

And yet. And still. Even as I stand before the bathroom mirror, my dick tucked between my legs so that only the bushy triangle of pubic hair is showing, I continue to smell my own heavy man's smell, a scent not very different from the musky sweetness my father left behind in my childhood memories. Of late I have taken to rubbing my face along the cocks and balls and inside the buttocks of my lovers, hoping that in their scent I might find something of my own, or my father's, or his own unknown father's. I lick the sweat off bellies spilling over too-tight jeans, suck gobs of chest hair, and underarm hair, and scrotum hair into my mouth, gorging on the rough texture, begging to be pinned down to the bed, to be penetrated by a vigorous and vibrant masculinity. My lovers whisper, "Whose pussy is this?" as they struggle to slip their cocks into my ass. I haven't the heart to answer simply that it is my own.

> *Adrift on this windless sea*
> *this independence*
> *we have brushed and skirted*
> *shells*
> *compelled by current.*[7]

In 1985 Barbara Smith came like a fresh wind to Chapel Hill. She brought with her a vision of home unlike anything I had imagined. It would be years before I would look up to find that as I searched for home I continued in my isolation. It was the death of Pat Parker that first alerted me to the fragility of both our dreams and our community. First her then Joe Beam then Donald Woods then David Frechette then Rory Buchanan then James Baldwin and Roy Gonsalves then Audre Lorde herself. In response I wrote:

> *I could have fucked him*
> *Head on rumpled pillow*
> *Ass lifted towards heaven*

Like she cat
In season
In heat

I might have cut into flesh
Leeched out blood
Bitten into gristle
And Swallowed

    And yet
    And Still

I tried saving him long distance
Tied up phone lines preaching brotherhood
Wrote treatises on community
Debated love and metaphysics at the institute
Took clever men to bed

Shall I scratch his name onto parchment
Press it to my lips
Arrange it among the relics on my altar?

Shall I build a memorial
Great Edifice Reaching forth to God
Higher than misery?

I showed this, my only attempt at poetry as an adult, to my boyfriend at the time, who told me that the "She Cat" line made him uncomfortable. We broke up. I left for the comfort of my girlfriends. He started dating women. We both resisted the somewhat

Afrocentric, Brooklyn-centered black lesbian and gay community, finding that our own deepest desires had turned back in on themselves.

> *I'm a queer lesbian.*
> *Please don't go down on me yet.*
> *I do not prefer cunnilingus.*
> *(There's room for me in the movement.)*[8]

Cheryl phones on an early weekday morning looking for $100 and advice. I write a check for fifty and remain on the telephone for hours debating the relative merits of worry versus denial. She complains that too many of the wrong kind of women love her. I answer that that's my problem exactly. We laugh, make plans to see each other, and hang up. The two of us maintain a type of charming delicacy with each other. I respect her boyishness as she cherishes my effeminacy. We are a couple, mentioned in one breath as dinner parties are planned, given to public quarrels over the minutiae of everyday life, constantly aware of each other's steps and jealous of the intrusion of outsiders. Our lesbianism runs deep. We are drawn together because of our profound love of women, our unquenchable thirst for companionship, our hot blooded sexual passion, and our constant struggle to find and create home. She chides me to help her write her story. I respond by looking hard at her small breasts, pulling from her the details of her menstruation and resisting the urge to cover my penis, floating in the bath water, as she passes by the tub.

> *Sweet words and warm this time—*
> *not like the last time salty and frigid*
> *over some money I owed her*[9]

Living as a lesbian continues for me to be a process in which I am constantly brought back, in my search for spiritual perfection, for transcendence, to my body, to the luscious beauty of my heavy thighs and hairy chest, my fleshy ass and strong hands. And still I continue to love and desire "her" body, Cheryl's body, Yevette's body, Joanna's, Daphne's, Pat's, Sabhia's, and Nicki's bodies, not simply the image or the promise, but the texture of their hair, the color of their skin, the smell of their sweat.

In 1985 Barbara Smith came like a fresh wind into Chapel Hill. She brought with her a vision of home unlike anything I ever had imagined. It was then that I began the process of becoming a lesbian. It is only recently that I began to understand lesbianism as a state of being that few of us ever achieve. To become lesbian one has to first be committed to the process of constantly becoming, of creatively refashioning one's humanity as a matter of course.

CODA

By becoming lesbian then I have done nothing more nor less than become myself.

I had expected to end this piece with these words, forcing all of us, myself included, to reevaluate what it means to be labeled lesbian, gay, straight, bi, transgendered, asexual. And yet this is not enough. For, even as I recognize the difficulty of giving definition and meaning to our various identities, I also realize that as I struggle to lay claim to my lesbianism I am always confronted with the reality of my own masculinity, this strange and complex identity that I continue to have difficulty recognizing as privilege.

It was a Friday afternoon in September when I had my first bathhouse experience. I'm not sure what I expected, or wanted. In truth, I was compelled more than anything else by Samuel Delany's description in *The Motion of Light in Water* of his visit to the Saint

Marks Baths in the early sixties. I thought that it would be exciting, that perhaps within this outlaws' territory I could throw off the stifling fears and anxieties that shape and constrain our lives, sexual and otherwise. I even felt that, given the name of the enterprise I was about to visit, "baths," there had to be something intrinsically cleansing and healing about them.

Now I find myself asking whether in the bathhouse, the most sacred of male enclaves, where my masculine body and affected macho style increase my worth in the sexual economy, I am still lesbian. Is it lesbianism that spills out of the end of my cock as baldheaded men with grizzled beards and homemade tattoos slap my buttocks and laugh triumphantly? Is it lesbianism that allows me to walk these difficult streets alone, afraid only that I will *not* be seen, accosted, "forced" into sexual adventure?

All my bravado, my will to adventure is caught up, strangely enough, with the great confidence I have gained from "The Lesbian." And yet, this confidence, this awareness of my own body, of my own independence, takes me to places where she dares not go. Perhaps then I am not a lesbian at all, but rather like a drag queen: by day a more or less effeminate, woman-loving gay man, by night a pussy, a buck, the despoiler of young men recently arrived from the provinces and the careful tutelage of their loving mothers. What I know for certain is that this self, this lesbian-identified gay man, is in constant flux. I live like a lesbian, as a lesbian because I know no better way of life. Still, I live beyond her in a province that continues to be reserved exclusively for men, all the while reaping the many fruits of sexual apartheid.

Me, I want to escape . . . this dirty world, this dirty body. I never wish to make love again with anything more than the body.[10]

Perhaps in my next life I will be done with these questions of identity altogether, will cherish fully the body that I am given, begin to see it neither as burden or weapon but only as the vessel of my existence. Perhaps in my next life I will have given up finally this constant struggle to explain who I am not: not woman, not white, not straight, not you and start to revel in the limitlessness of my boundaries. Perhaps each one of us will recapture that which has been lost, start again to accept and acknowledge the profound ambiguity and uncertainty of this existence. It is then and only then that we will find home.

In 1985 Barbara Smith came like a fresh wind to Chapel Hill.

Notes

1. Combahee River Collective, "The Combahee River Collective Statement," in Barbara Smith, ed., *Home Girls: A Black Feminist Anthology* (New York: Kitchen Table Women of Color Press, 1983) 272.

2. Taken from Cheryl Clarke, "No More Encomiums," in Cheryl Clarke, *Living as a Lesbian* (Ithaca, NY: Firebrand, 1986) 40.

3. Audre Lord, *Zami: A New Spelling of My Name* (Freedom, CA: Crossing Press, 1982) 3.

4. Clarke, "No More Encomiums."

5. Barbara Smith, Foreword to J. R. Roberts, comp., *Black Lesbians* (Tallahassee, FL: Naiad Press, 1981) ix.

6. Cheryl Clarke, "How Like a Man," in Clarke, *Living as a Lesbian* 13.

7. Michelle Parkerson, "Refugees," in Michelle Parkerson, *Waiting Rooms* (Washington, D.C.: Common Ground Press, 1993) 4.

8. Cheryl Clarke, "Sexual Preference," in Clarke, *Living as a Lesbian* 68.

9. Clarke, "No More Encomiums."

10. James Baldwin, *Giovanni's Room* (New York: Laurel, 1956) 35.

HOW TO HANDLE A BOY IN WOMEN'S SHOES (2001)

Brian Keith Jackson

N ellie.
   That's my nickname.

The kids gave me that name when I was in second grade. I don't think they knew exactly what it was they were saying. God knows *I* didn't. But the name stuck, and to this day people call me Nellie.

I'm what some would refer to as a "Nellie-would-be-drag-queen." I'm a "queer-boy-sugar-in-my-tank-take-it-up-the-ass sort of guy" they call Nellie.

It was Christmas vacation. The family had come in from all over to meet at my grandmother's place as we did each year.

I was seven.

I sat in the room with the women; not at all interested in the Bowl game, which is what the men and the television had to offer. All the mothers of the family sat and chattered about how fast I was growing and how big my feet were. They went on and on, until finally my Aunt Sue tried on my shoes.

They fit.

She marveled about this discovery and pranced around, feeling that sense of youth while dancing to the giggles of all the mothers. When she returned, I was in a corner trying on her shoes. I got up, tipped around, full of aplomb. Needless to say—she didn't handle it well. No giggled notes sprang from pursed lips.

"What are you doing?" had asked his Aunt Sue.

"Trying on your shoes," he said.

"You shouldn't do that."

"But why?"

"Because these are women's shoes and you're a little boy."

Chile, I thought Aunt Sue was losing it.

You know, it wasn't so much the words behind this exchange that triggered something in me, but the tension that padded the room, bouncing off the walls from every possible angle, ricocheting swiftly back to her mouth.

"These are women's shoes and you're a little boy."

They call me Nellie. That's with an "ie," not "y," for any of you that may be confused. Nobody knows my real name, at least nobody here in Harlem. I just don't use it anymore. Everyone just calls me Nellie. I rarely even think about my real name. Why bother? But I do recall it was one of those with three first names, just like most names given to people in the South.

"Hey, y'all. I'm Marybeth Ann, and we're gonna do this cheer for y'all and we want y'all to yell with us, awright?" had screamed the blonde, enviable popular cheerleader at the pep rally in his high school.

*   *   *

People, here, in the city, are intrigued by me. To them, I'm so free. They like that. It adds levity to the day. It doesn't threaten them and I suppose it shouldn't. There are far too many other pressing issues to concern themselves with than little ol' me. They pass by and speak.

"'How are you, Nellie?'"

"'Fair. And you?'" I say. I always return the greeting, whether they stop to hear it or not; being from the South, they teach us that.

"Boy, if'n you don't take yo hand down from yo mouf and speak to people, you

betta. We taught you bet'tin 'at," had said his rump-round mother with heavy hand, and as heavy heart.

Okay. Yes. I'm a bit effeminate. So what? Men might talk about me by light of day, but at night they're always knocking on my door, calling on Nellie. One man from Jersey would come every Thursday, tapping on my door. The man from Jersey is what I called him, and he called me Nellie.

He had family out there, but worked in the city. That's really all I knew. All I cared to know. I didn't want to see any pictures or think about them, because if I did, that would mean I was a homewrecker, and I had been taught, in the South, that homewreckers were evil. I soon learned a homewrecker's only worth was for that of idle chatter over teacakes and lemonade on a hot summer's evening.

"Did you hear 'bout what happened to Clariece?" had said one woman to another, sitting on the porch, Bible perched on her lap, one Sunday evening when he was just a boy.

"Lawd bless huh soul. I tol'd huh he was up to no good," said the other woman.

"Po. Po. Clariece. I knew it. You just can't trust dem dere menfolk when it come to dem no-'count homewreckers."

At present, I work as a barkeep at this dive bar on the corner of, what I like to call, Patience and Understanding. I'm a horrible bartender. I give more away than I sell. Why should people have to pay to drink when they are evidently already miserable?

I'm writing a book about all the stories I've been told and my advice that accompanies the stories I've been told. I must say, I'm pretty good at handling stressful situations. At least better than my Aunt Sue.

"J&B on the rocks?" I'd heard him say to a new, unfamiliar face at the bar. "No. No. Keep your money, honey. It's on me. What? Nellie. Just call me Nellie."

* * *

After work, heels dangling in hand at my side, I come home; a lovely home, smartly designed, but of course. In my hallway—yes, hallway, not vestibule, my name's Nellie, not Hope—I have a Rockwell original. It's the one with the little boy in the barber's chair. The loss of something old, the onset of something new. In rough times, and there have been many, I think of selling it. But it was a gift, and to sell a gift is tacky. That's what they teach in the South.

"Socks! Gee. Thanks," he'd said to Joey Peterson, who in third grade had pulled his name for the Christmas gift exchange. "No. No, really. Thanks."

Sometimes the knocks at my door just don't appease me. I don't answer even when they know I'm here. "Nellie. Nellie," they cry. But I'm not to be bothered. I'm listening to the patter of rain hitting the window, thinking of the South and how I'd fall asleep as the rain danced on roofs of tin. Music too beautiful to be recorded, for you see, real beauty isn't for sale.

I miss the thunder. As a child I was horrified of it. Its loudness. Its strength. The way it shook the walls that surrounded me. When I got older I realized that it wasn't the thunder I should be afraid of, the lightning is the dangerous thing.

"No need'n bein' 'fraid. Count seven, sweetheart. If'n you can count seven before you hear thunder, then ever'thang gonna be awright. I promise. Just count seven," had said his grandmother on one of the days when the sky grew dark long before night.

* * *

My true love doesn't like Nellie. I give him drinks at the bar. He doesn't like Nellie. He smiles at me, but he doesn't like Nellie. My true love says, "If I wanted a woman, I could have one. I want a man. A man."

And, of course, I'm nothing more than a little boy in women's shoes.

"These are women's shoes and you're a little boy."

One.

Two.

Three.

Four.

Five.

Six.

Seven. No thunder.

Yes, the silence is piercing, but I'll be all right.

MINOTAUR (2002)

Carl Phillips

What stalked the room was never envy.
Is not regret, anymore,

nor fail. We are
—discovered:

we resemble hardly
ever those birds now, noising but
not showing from their double
cloisters—
leaves,
fog.

I miss them.

I forget what I wanted to
mean to you.
        I forget what I
meant to give to you, that I haven't.

Ménage.
You, in sleep still,
the dog restless, wanting

out, like a dream of the body caught
shining inside a struggling whose
end it cannot know will be
no good one.

Outside, the basil shoots to flower; the neighbors'
burro, loose, astray, has
found the flowers, his

head enters and tilts
up from the angle confusable with
sorrow,
adoration. His hooves pass

—like God doing, for now,
no damage to them—

the heirloom tomatoes: Beam's Yellow Pear,
Russian Black,
Golden Sunray, what sweetness once
looked like, how it tasted
commonly.

All that time.

I have held faces lovelier—lovelier, or
as fair.
        They make sense
eventually. Your own begins to:

fervor of a man
cornered; unuseful tenderness with which,

to the wound it won't survive, the animal
puts its tongue.

FROM A LONG AND LIBERATING MOAN
(2002)

L. M. Ross

I 've been called a romantic. But that's not entirely true. Hey, man . . . like most anyone, there are times when all I really want or need is some head. You know? You meet someone. You click. It's purely animal. You're not even checking each other's credentials. Somehow, you just click, and before you know it, you're rubbing genitals inside the risky hole of night. The sex, it's so hot, it's like it almost has meaning. You shiver that shiver of absolute satisfaction.

"And then, it's over. He looks at you. You look at him. And all you've really shared is sweat and cum and this pregnant pause that never gives birth to anything real.

"Just once, I wanna feel something real. I want to shudder in the cool blue hue of the moment. Just breathe and rest in it, and not worry or wonder, or stress my impending mortality.

"See, my truth is: I do not identify with 'The Life' out there. Would you mind getting to *know me* before you suck my dick? Wanna know what kind of freak I am? I actually wanna talk to people, see them in the broad daylight. I wanna see every beautiful flaw. I wanna know who they are, who they wanna be. That's the kind of freak, I be. Is it not considered *fabulous* to be kissed by somebody who knows how, and who means it?

"But nothing is that deep or spiritual anymore. Hell, maybe it never was. These days, you front and pose and maybe you'll get blown, or you fuck and pray 'please don't let this freakin' condom break, in the middle of all this meaningless shit!'

"In 1980, I was still shell-shocked. See, my best friend had just been stolen from me. But before I knew it, it was time for college, when I wasn't even ready for the fuckin' world. I was eighteen, and a fuckin' closet widow. Wasn't I supposed to be young, full of dreams, semen, and good cock-strong intentions?

"In late '81, every now and then, I'd hear whispers about a 'gay cancer.' Queer little oxymoron, don't you think?

"In '82, while at school, I had everyone using that old motto: 'No fools, no fun.' I was young, fairly cool, somewhat hung. But I didn't suffer fools, and never gave myself permission to have big fun.

"1983 was the season for young white men in the Village to wear the latest in new purple sores. They were sweating, losing weight, and falling by the wayside of an urban wasteland. By then, they'd given the 'cancer' a proper name.

"By 1984, I was one of the walking petrified. People I knew, people with whom I'd been very intimate with, had died from an Intimacy Disease. At first, I freaked. Then, I grieved, and I've never stopped grieving. Suddenly into the cage of my skull came that shrill and urgent voice, and I could not seem to turn it off. That voice told me: Get your ass to a clinic!

"So I tested. For two weeks, I did nothing but sweat. I prayed, made promises to God, on my knees pleading, crying—for myself, and for all the unlucky rest. Thanks to the Grace of God, and providence, I tested negative.

"By 1987, I spent most of my time reflecting upon a choir of my new and tragic friends. Some screamed and some roared, others moaned that their songs were unfinished. Each of them vocalized now, in purgatory.

"These days I'm too afraid to fuck without meaning or rubbers or prayers. I've been celibate. There's no shame in surviving, is there? My friends are *missing* my life. Hell! *I'm missing my life!* I need to *know* the reason why I'm still here and they're not. I have to believe they were just unlucky. I do know this: They never got their rightful chance to feel *realized*. Now, they're gone.

"But some things you hold on to, like *him*. I wear his tattoo where no one can see it. And the one you can see, I reserve for an intimate few. See this? This blue stain inside my bottom lip? It's really a tattoo of a name. The asshole artist fucked up and etched the word 'Tick.' My lover's nickname was 'Trick.' This stain is *supposed* to read 'Trick,' damn it! But sometimes I wonder if it *really* was a mistake, because maybe it signifies *tick, tock, tick tock*.

"God! Am I crying? Do you have a fear of gay African American men with chests full of rage, and eyes full of tears? Shit! Better tell me now, if you do. You. You sit there in that cool strong face, like no one and nothing can break you. Just wait. It *will* happen. If it doesn't, or worse, if you don't let it, then wherever you are, I'll feel sorry for you. The last thing you want to be is one of those solitary old queens, alone by a fence on the playground. Alone in the park, or alone in the streets, just always alone, with your overcoat hanging 'round you like a death shroud.

"It doesn't pay to affect the cool desperado. You have to love and let someone love you. That's it. That's all, man. See, just when I thought two people together, two men together was some kind of miracle, I found him. My big black, thick-skinned, crotch-grabbing miracle!

"Well, he's gone now, and maybe I've already had my quota of miracles. But you have to go on, right? I mean, don't you? That's why I'm here tonight, trying to go on. I just wanted you to know besides these tight jeans, my eight-inch erection, and the cock-ring that glows in the dark . . . I'm more than this.

"What am I, you ask? I'm a designated war correspondent, because this is a war, you know? I guess it took Death to get me off my pacifistic ass. But I'm finally fighting now, because I have to, even with a pen full of bullets."

And after Tyrone Hunter's endless riff, his first date of that New Year asked,

"Yo, man. It's gettin' late. So, you still wanna fuck, or what?"

MAGNETIX (2002)

Tim'm West

for dad and Joseph

I have loved black men
agitated by the thick of it . . .
guarded like when they anticipate
the sting of a racial slur,
or a gender reprimand
for not being a manly enough boy.
I have caressed the tight in their backs
still longing for fathers to come back
with explanations for absence.

I have encountered baby daddies
oblivious to the souls that haunt them
Daily
In order to stay sane—
mandingo sons, weakened by their own
sense of potentiality
and too many deferred dreams.

I have forgiven men who have
inherited cycles that return
deadly as a boomerang
I have kissed them
before they could speak sharp words,

like what they silence say.
I have held their hand for dear life
before they could strike me
with they fists,
or pull a gat on me
for reflecting they black back to them:
beautiful
in ways that would bring them to tears
if they accepted it.

And I have been a man
terrified of being loved by these men,
preferring lonely corners or playboy paraphernalia
to being cradled
and feeling safe enough to cry.
I have been a man
who has witnessed my brother fall
just as his fingertips admit vulnerability
outstretched and longing for connection
and falling
like rainbows
foreshadow a smile.

I have been a man
who smiles when I want most
not to
show
that side of myself—
trusting and delighted
like a lil nappyheadedblakkboy

unafraid of afro picks,
or being found hiding
by another blakk boy
behind a lil' tree
half my size.

I have been a reflection of myself
in the morning
eyes blushing or troubled or smiling
and wondering
what kind of man I will be
today, tomorrow
And shedding yesterday's illusion of failure
for a better man
standing strong
open to loving real good
especially
myself.

FROM BEYOND THE DOWN LOW: SEX AND DENIAL IN BLACK AMERICA (2004)

Keith Boykin

A THOUSAND DIFFERENT MEANINGS

T he down low is a story about lies. Actually, these days, anytime you read almost anything about the down low, you may already know it involves lies. But this is a different story. It is not just about the lies that men on the down low tell. It is a story about the lies that men and women tell themselves about their relationships. It is a story about the lies we tell the media, which the media in turn tell us back about who we are. Yes, it is a story about lies in black America, but it is also a story about lies in white America. It is a story about men lying, but it is also a story about women lying. It is a story about the way in which lies become mistaken for truth when repeated often enough and about how we use those lies to deny our personal responsibility to find the truth.

America's recent obsession with the down low is not about the truth. It is about avoiding the truth. The truth is, more than a generation after the so-called sexual revolution and decades after the beginning of the AIDS epidemic, we are still a nation in deep denial about sex, race, and relationships. In black America, with the all-too-willing assistance of white America, we are still afraid to hear, understand, and process the truth. As a nation, we would rather talk about "the down low" than to talk candidly about sex, homosexuality, bisexuality, masculinity, racism, homophobia, and AIDS—and about our collective responsibility to find solutions for these problems. Of course, it is easier to believe the hype than to engage in a sensible dialogue based on real information, but we cannot find solutions in a sensationalist conversation based on fear and blame. The solutions lie in a conversation about love and personal responsibility. So it's time to get past the fear and the blame. It's time to go beyond the down low.

We begin in February 2001. George W. Bush has just been inaugurated as president after a controversial election in which he lost the popular vote and won a disputed contest for the electoral ballot in Florida. Former President Bill Clinton has moved to New York with his wife, who has just been elected a U.S. senator from that state. Clinton has been hounded by a "vast right-wing conspiracy" throughout his tenure in office and impeached by a Republican Congress because he lied about a sexual relationship with an intern. I feel the president's pain.

After eight years of living in Washington, I was ready to leave. I moved to Washington to work in the Clinton White House, and suddenly the city felt unwelcoming to an exiled Democrat. Then, one day I was invited to dinner with three friends who were in town for an AIDS conference, and that's where I first heard about "the down low" as a term to describe men who have sex with men but do not identify as gay. As a black gay man, I had known about such men for a decade. Ever since I came out in 1991, I had been working on issues of race and sexuality during most of that time, and I had met or interviewed dozens of men who would qualify as down low. What could possibly be new about such an old occurrence, I wondered. Was it just a new word for an old behavior?

Over the years, I had heard a number of terms to describe these men and their behavior. Some were dismissed as "closeted." Many called themselves "bisexual." Some said they were only "messin' around" while others accused them of "creeping." Most of the supposedly straight men I had met had always seemed resistant to labels. Their interest in me was usually physical, not intellectual, so they were seldom willing to answer probing questions about their lives. Nevertheless, I had interacted with these men for years. There was the police officer I met in Los Angeles, the postal worker in Chicago, the corporate executive in Maryland, the Web designer in North Carolina, and the government official in Washington, D.C. All of them were black, several were married, and a few had young children. Then, there were dozens of men I had met at an infamous gym on L Street in Washington. Many of these guys seemed to be making hookups on a regular basis. It didn't seem very underground to me, but that was because I saw it happen so often. A few of the guys would talk to me on the sly, while others—who had seen me talking about gay issues on television or in the newspaper—would walk a country mile to steer clear of me. In fact, I could almost identify who was in the closet based on how much effort he put into avoiding me.

In 2001, the down low was old news to me, but for the mass media it was the beginning of a profitable period of exploitation of black grief. To some in the media, the down low seemed the missing link to explain the AIDS epidemic in the black community: HIV was spreading more rapidly among black women than in almost any other demographic group, and if these women were unknowingly having sex with black men on the down low, that could explain the problem. The overwhelming majority of black women with HIV contracted the virus from heterosexual sex, and some black men who call themselves heterosexual also had sex with men. So these black men could have been responsible for spreading the virus to unsuspecting women. It all seemed to make sense.

Others were a bit more skeptical. There was no research to prove the down low was responsible for the spread of AIDS in the black community, and no one knew how to study a population that was unwilling to be identified. These skeptics feared that focusing on the down low would distract public attention and public resources from what they perceived were the real needs of the community. Focusing on the down low would mislead people into thinking that AIDS was spread by men on the DL rather than by HIV. And instead of encouraging individuals to focus on their own safe sex behavior, we would encourage them to focus on the behavior of their partners. Even worse, public policy decisions would have to rely on anecdotal evidence from those who had once been on the down low, a group that was admittedly notorious for its untruthfulness. In other words, we would have to trust the liars to tell the truth about their lies.

Despite the uncertainty about the issue, just mention the words "down low" to someone in the know, and you're likely to hear remarkable tales of sex, lies, and deception—all supposedly brought on by a small, dangerous and influential fraternity of black men leading double lives.

Since the down low story broke, many journalists have been convinced that men on the down low are responsible for the spread of AIDS in the black community. Books have been published that claim to teach women "the signs" to tell if a man is on the down low. Black women have been deputized as down low detectives and told to watch to see if their male partners stare too long at other men. The media and the public have developed a whole new fascination with all things down low.

But is all this hype really necessary? Is the information even true?

We should start with a basic question that needs to be asked at the beginning of any serious discussion about this issue: What is the down low? Before you answer, here are a few examples to help us understand the question. Try to figure out which of these people are on the down low.

Raheem is a twenty-four-year-old black man in northeast Washington,

D.C. He looks just like any other young man on the street on a hot summer afternoon. He is wearing a XXXL-size plain white T-shirt, oversized baseball cap, droopy jeans, and sneakers. But Raheem is different. Raheem says he's "on the DL." He only "messes with" brothas, and he has a computer at home that he uses to find them in chat rooms and Web sites on the Internet. Although he has not been involved with a woman since he graduated from high school six years ago, he still dreams that one day he will settle down with the right woman and get married. Is Raheem on the down low?

David is a thirty-six-year-old black man in Stone Mountain, Georgia. He lives with his wife and two kids in a two-story, three-bedroom house and commutes to work in midtown Atlanta. He wears a business suit to the office but brings his gym clothes to work out at the gym near his job. A few years ago, he started meeting men at the gym and taking them to hotels to have sex with them. Eventually, he worked up the nerve to go home with the men he met. He enjoys his sexual encounters with men, but he has no plans to leave his wife and kids, and they do not know about his homosexual experiences. David has recently heard of the term "down low," but he does not identify with it. He calls himself "straight." David is HIV negative. He doesn't want to run the risk of getting caught, so he always uses a condom with his male sex partners and he only plays the role of a top. Is David on the down low?

Jabbar is a twenty-nine-year-old black man in Dayton, Ohio. He's a shoe salesman for a high-end department store, and he prides himself on the way he dresses. He's fashionably conservative and considers himself very masculine. Jabbar's deep bass voice and tall good looks help make him an effective salesman, but Jabbar has a not-so-secret life away from the department store. Once or twice a month, Jabbar drives his BMW to the gay clubs in Cincinnati. He's very popular with the black men there who see him as a good catch, but he's never allowed himself to be "caught." He loves being single, he loves the attention he gets from men and women, and he loves being so "unclockable" that no one can tell his sexuality. Is Jabbar on the down low?

Joyce is a thirty-eight-year-old black woman in Little Rock, Arkansas. She's the HR director for a major local hospital and has been involved in three long-term relationships in her life: two with men and one with a woman. Joyce's feminine good looks make her very desirable to women and men, but she won't commit to either. She's dating a man right now, but she's also seeing a woman on the side. Her man thinks she's straight. Her woman thinks she's on the DL. Is Joyce on the down low?

Shawn is a twenty-two-year-old white man in Brooklyn. He wants to be an electrical engineer, and he's got a part-time job to help him pay his way through community college. He has a white girlfriend he met at school and a black boyfriend he met in a club one night. Shawn grew up around blacks and Latinos in a racially mixed neighborhood in the Bronx, so he has always been comfortable developing friendships and relationships with people who are different from him. He knows he can never tell his girlfriend about his boyfriend, but he has told his boyfriend about his girlfriend. Shawn considers himself "on the down low." Is Shawn on the down low?

Jerry is a forty-six-year-old black man in Los Angeles. He's a semi-successful visual artist who made a name for himself fifteen years ago and has continued to grow in popularity in local arts circles. Jerry lives with his wife and their twelve-year-old daughter, but Jerry also has a long-term male lover. Years ago, Jerry told his wife that he was bisexual, and after a heartfelt discussion she allowed him to date men outside of their marriage as long as he was safe. Jerry and his wife have made peace with their living situation, but they haven't told anyone else about it. When their daughter found out about the situation recently, she had a name for their relationship. She told her parents that they were a "down low couple." Is Jerry on the down low?

Luis is a nineteen-year-old mixed-race Hispanic man in Chicago. He planned to join the military until he realized the armed forces did not allow gays to serve openly. Almost everyone seems to know or assume that Luis is gay. He says he's very proud of his sexuality, and most of his good friends are gay or transgendered. But his friends don't know the whole truth. Luis has a girlfriend he's been hiding from them. Is Luis on the down low?

Those are the seven people. Now here's the question again. Which of the people mentioned above are on the down low? The question is not as easy as it seems. To answer the question, we have to start with an acceptable definition of what it means to be on the down low in the first place. And that's the problem. In the years since the media began to hype the down low, no one has ever really defined it. You start to realize the problem when you try to pick which of the seven people are on the down low.

Let's start with Raheem. Raheem raises the difficult issue of self-identification. He doesn't fit neatly into a gay stereotype. He doesn't "look gay," and he doesn't call himself gay. He self-identifies as "down low," but he has never had sex with a woman in his entire adult life. So here's the question. Can you be on the down low merely by self-identifying as being on the down low? Most of the recent media definitions of the down low seem to assume that you have to be unfaithful to a woman in order to be on the down low. Raheem, however, doesn't even date women, but he does considers himself on the down low. For Raheem, being on the down low simply means being a man who doesn't look gay and isn't public about being gay.

David raises the other side of self-identification. By most accounts, David fits the classic definition of a man on the down low. He's black, he's married to a woman, and he secretly sleeps with men. But unlike Raheem, David doesn't consider himself to be on the down low. In fact, he's barely even familiar with the term, and he calls himself "straight." If self-identification determines whether you're on the down low, then David is not down low, even though most observers would say he is.

David's story raises another issue as well. Since David is HIV negative and always practices safe sex, David's life challenges the assumption that down low men are spreading HIV to black women. In fact, David's wife is actually safer having sex with him than with an HIV positive man who is exclusively heterosexual.

Next there's Jabbar. On the surface, Jabbar seems to be another candidate for the down low, but beneath the surface he raises troubling questions about looks and behavior. Some would say that you can't be on the down low if you go out to gay bars and nightclubs. For Jabbar, however, being down low simply means being what he considers masculine and discreet. Most people think he looks like he's straight, and since he never hangs out with gay guys in his hometown, he thinks that makes him down low. Is he right?

Then there's Joyce. Joyce's story complicates the simplicity of the down low formula by introducing the issue of gender. Like the men on the down low, she's cheating on her partner with someone of the same sex. What makes her different is that Joyce is a woman and her partner is a man. Most of the public discussion about the down low seems to assume that women don't engage in the same unfaithful behavior that men do. Women are portrayed as the victims, not the perpetrators. Joyce's story forces us to reexamine our simplistic stereotypes about female fidelity and male deceit.

To make matters even more complicated, let's talk about Shawn. If we define a down low man as someone who cheats on his wife or girlfriend with a man, then Shawn perfectly fits the bill. The only issue is that Shawn is white. If white men can be on the down low, why all the fuss over black men on the down low? Is the down low specific to race? There's no evidence to prove that black men are more likely to be on the down low than white men. Maybe we focus on black men because the white men on the down low are not spreading the HIV virus to their female partners? If so, why not? Is it because white men engage in safer sex, and if so, shouldn't our prevention efforts focus on how to get black men on the down low to take the same precautions?

What can we say about Jerry and his wife? If you knew them as a couple and then discovered that Jerry was sleeping with another man, you might think that Jerry was on the down low. He's black, he's married to a woman, and he's secretly sleeping with a man. What else does it take to be on the down low? Well, in this case, Jerry's secret is not a secret from his wife. His wife already knows. The rest of the world doesn't. Does that make Jerry on the down low? Jerry's life raises the issue of disclosure. Once you tell your wife, does it matter that you keep the secret from everyone else?

Finally, let's look at Luis. Luis is a proud Hispanic gay man. He goes to gay bars, he has gay friends, and he calls himself gay. Doesn't sound very down low. But Luis has a secret. He recently started dating a woman, and he doesn't know how to break the news to his gay friends. If being on the down low means lying to the world about your sexuality, then Luis may very well be a member of the group. But if being on the down low only means lying to your opposite-sex partner about your same-sex partner, we've created a very narrow field of concern.

At the end of this exercise, we still don't have a common definition of what it means to be on the down low. So how is the down low defined in the media? To position this story as a cautionary tale about AIDS, the media seem to have accepted a popular definition of the down low that suggests five basic traits for those on the DL. According to the media, those on the down low are:

1. black,
2. male,
3. HIV positive,
4. in relationships with women, and
5. secretly having sex with men.

We've considered seven examples of people who could be on the down low, but each of them challenges the popular definition. Raheem is not in a relationship with a woman. David is not HIV positive. Jabbar is a closeted gay man. Joyce is a woman. Shawn is white. Jerry is out to his wife. And Luis is gay.

Is it possible that none of the seven people mentioned above are on the down low? To resolve this dilemma, I asked several of the most visible black figures who had publicly talked about the down low to answer a simple question: What is the down low?

I began with J.L. King, the author of a book called *On the Down Low: A Journey into the Lives of "Straight" Black Men Who Sleep with Men.* I could not find a definition of the down low in his book, so I decided to ask him myself. He responded to each of my four e-mails but never answered the question, so I went back to his book and tried to piece together a definition from his own words. The subtitle of the book presents one possible definition: "'straight' black men who sleep with men." But that definition doesn't require the men to be involved in relationships with women. The dedication for the book seems to explain more. King dedicates the book, in part, to "all the women whose health has been jeopardized and emotional state compromised by men living on the DL," a dedication that suggests men on the down low are responsible for the spread of AIDS to black women. Should we also be concerned about down low men who are HIV negative and always practice safe sex? King uses other terms such as "double lifestyle" and "duplicitous behavior" to give us more understanding of what the down low means to him. The closest definition he provides, however, is in response to a question from an Ohio health official who asks about the secret lives of bisexual men. "The secret," he writes, "is that men who look like me, talk like me, and think like me are having sex with men but still love and want to be with their women. And they do not believe they're gay." King's definition seems to exclude men who date women just to conceal their homosexuality. In other words, men on the down low would be inherently bisexual. But if they are bisexual and not just in denial about their homosexual desires, then why should we vilify these men who are acting out on their natural desires?

I put the same question to Phill Wilson, the director of the Black AIDS Institute in Los Angeles. "Like many slang terms, 'DL' means different things to different people," he said. "Some DL men identify as straight and have wives or girlfriends but secretly have sex with other men. Others are younger men who are still questioning or exploring their sexuality. Some are closeted gay men. And then there are African American brothers who openly have relationships with other men but reject the label 'gay' or 'bisexual' because they equate those terms with white men."

Many of those black men who do not consider themselves gay would still feel perfectly comfortable cavorting in a predominantly black gay bar. By rejecting the homosexual label, they are not necessarily rejecting the sexual behavior associated with it. Black men often reject the term "gay" to repudiate white social constructs of homosexuality but not to reject their own homosexual sexual behavior. Some black men who openly acknowledge that they have sex with other men have simply found other words to describe themselves, including the term "same-gender-loving." They reject the term "gay" not because of internalized homophobia or because they are on the down low. Instead, they simply want to create their own identities outside of what they perceive to be a racially insensitive white gay world.

Journalist Kai Wright in New York shares Wilson's sense of complexity about the definition. Wright has written extensively about the down low, and he finds the act of defining the term problematic. "It's whatever the person using the phrase wants it to be," he explains.

For black gay men, labeling themselves on the down low is a way to validate their masculinity. Wright mentions an example of a black gay bar in Brooklyn that advertised in a local gay magazine as "Brooklyn's down low choice" or something to that effect. "There couldn't be a less down low place," he says. "It's one of the oldest black gay bars in the city, first off, and it's packed with gay-identified men watching a male strip show!"

For white gay men, "the down low has become the latest way to fetishize the scary, roughneck black men of their porns," says Wright. He fears that "this racist fantasy bleeds into the AIDS activism" of some white gay men as well.

For black women, "the down low has become the classic scapegoat," he says. "It's the reason why HIV is still not their problem, even though infections are skyrocketing among them." By focusing on the DL, black women can point their fingers at "these shady, unidentifiable men who are doing it to us," says Wright, articulating a mind-set that leaves the black women disempowered to protect themselves. Instead, black women "have created a gay monster lurking under the bed," he says.

"That's just the problem with this issue," according to Wright. "It's the perfect boogeyman: a group of shady, dangerous men who are, by definition, hidden and unidentifiable." Kai Wright raises an excellent point. How do you define someone who doesn't want to be defined? How do you identify someone who doesn't want to be identified? And once you identify that person, he is, by definition, no longer on the down low.

Dr. Darrell Wheeler of New York's Hunter College defines the term more broadly than most. The down low is "a term used by some men to describe behaviors that they do not want others to know about," he says. Dr. Wheeler's definition seems to open the door to those who are white, gay, HIV negative, and not in relationships. The "down low" is also a term used to describe men "or women" who are homosexually active but do not identity themselves as lesbian, gay or bisexual, he adds. In other words, almost all people who hide their behaviors from others can be on the down low.

Columnist Alicia Banks in Arkansas says she resents the media characterization of the down low as "an exclusively ethnic moniker to trivialize and exploit a universal issue." Banks also identifies a link between racism and homophobia in the common definition of the down low. All humans cheat, she said, and men of all races creep with women and men. Cheating and lying are both "fatal infections," according to Banks, "whether your partner is creeping with a woman or a man." Her comment implies that the public might not be as concerned about infidelity when practiced in a traditional male-female relationship. But for Banks, the down low is nothing to be proud of. The DL, she says, is both a "damned lie" and a "deceitful life."

Dr. David Malebranche, a professor at Emory University in Atlanta, provides historical perspective in his definition of the down low. "The 'down low' is a phrase that has been part of the black community for ages, and historically meant something that is 'secretive' or 'covert.'" he says. Dr. Malebranche cites several examples where the down low simply means to keep something—a loan, a love affair—a secret. "Only within the past couple of decades has the term become a more specific catch phrase to describe black men who have wives or girlfriends, but also mess around with other men on the side."

Dr. Ron Simmons in Washington, D.C., also associates the term "down low" to its history, describing it as "a hip-hop expression meaning something secret or undercover." Today, however, he says the term "is commonly used to refer to men who have sex with men but self-identify as heterosexual." Simmons runs Us Helping Us, a Washington-based AIDS organization for black gay and bisexual men that provides a down low telephone help line, Internet outreach, and barbershop intervention. "Part of the problem," he finds with the definition of the term "down low" is that "self-identified gay men also refer to themselves as being on the down low." The situation can be confusing to outsiders, and Dr. Simmons recalls an incident when a reporter called him to find men on the down low. "I told her that down low men do not have a physical place or area where they can be found," he said. "She remarked that she had heard that there was a down low party during DC Black Gay Pride. I had to explain to her that this was a party of gay men who were using the term but not the kind of 'down low' men as she was investigating."

The reporter who called Dr. Simmons is not alone. Since the down low story hit the media in 2001, every major newspaper in the country has scrambled to find down low men in their community. Black magazines like *Essence* and gay magazines like *The Advocate* have covered the down low story, while many of their reporters have struggled to find men on the down low and others have stretched to define the community they were covering. An August 2004 article in *The Advocate* starts with a visit to a popular black gay bar called The Study, but for black gay men in Los Angeles the location, situated on a major street in Hollywood, is hardly a secret. Do "real" down low men go to gay bars? The story quotes a young man named Ezel, who declined to give his last name but is described as a volunteer for the Minority AIDS Project and who is distributing condoms at a table in the bar. He's married, bisexual, and in the closet. But is he on the down low? It is hard to imagine that a man on the down low would volunteer for a gay-identified AIDS organization that hands out condoms at gay bars. It's even harder to imagine that such a man would give out his first name to a reporter. It wouldn't take a lot for a curious reader to piece together the details of his life and blow his cover. If someone like Ezel is on the down low, then just about anyone can be on the down low. And that's exactly the problem. Without a uniform definition of the down low, we are left with no clear boundaries in defining this mysterious group of men.

Fortunately, we now have reference books to give us some guidance in defining the terminology. The down low has become so pervasive in the public discourse that the term has even crept its way into Internet encyclopedias, but the definitions employed by these reference materials often simply repeat the popular perceptions. One online encyclopedia explains, "Among some sectors of African-American homosexual sub-culture . . . same-sex sexual behavior is sometimes viewed as solely for physical pleasure. Men on the 'down-low' may engage in regular (though often covert) sex acts with other men while continuing sexual and romantic relationships with unsuspecting women." Another source defines the down low as "men who discreetly have sex with other men while in sexual relationships with women." These are fairly common definitions, but they exclude a large segment of the population who self-identify as "down low" but do not have relationships with women. In addition, the first definition seems to exclude whites and others who are not black, while the second definition excludes women on the down low.

So once again, what is the down low? The answer may challenge everything we think we know about the subject. The only point on which the experts seem to agree is that the down low is about secrecy in our sexual behavior. You don't have to be black, you don't have to be male, you don't have to be HIV positive, and you don't even have to be in a relationship to be on the down low. The down low is everything and nothing. In fact, the down low seems a bit like water. It has no shape, no form, and no color of its own. Like water, it is flexible enough to adapt to the shape and color of any container. It can mean whatever the user wants it to mean.

For closeted black gay and bisexual men, the down low is a way to validate their masculinity. For straight black women, the down low is a way to avoid the difficult issues of personal responsibility. For white America, the down low is a way to pathologize black lives. And for the media, the down low is a great way to sell papers.

For a phrase that is subject to multiple interpretations with no uniform definition, all we can conclude is that the "down low" is a term that is widely used and even more widely misunderstood.

THE DEATH AND LIGHT OF BRIAN WILLIAMSON (2004)

Thomas Glave

Brian, September 4, 1945–June 9, 2004

This much is true: the brave, loving man who was murdered in Kingston last week (on the morning of June 9, exactly) will not be forgotten. His name was Brian Ribton Bernard Williamson. None of us who are gay, lesbian, or bisexual will forget him, and neither will many others.

He was a founding member of the Jamaica Forum for Lesbians, All-Sexuals, and Gay (J-FLAG). I remember him from that time. That was where I first met him—where I first had the privilege of getting to know him. We all were meeting in great trust, hardly sensing at that time, in the latter months of 1998, how daunting and ultimately vital our mission would be. But in 2004, six years later, despite severe challenges to its health, safety, and the morale of its members, J-FLAG still exists—proof of the importance and utter correctness—necessity—of that work. Jamaica's viciousness and hatred, no matter how brutal, could not destroy us then, and will not destroy us now.

I remember Brian as a laughing man: a man with "a head of silver coins," as I sometimes joked with him about his head of curly silver-gray hair. He loved laughing and laughter; though it is often said of the dead even when untrue, he truly did love life, and exemplified that love in his formidable bravery where sexuality matters were concerned. He was not afraid to open and operate, from the late 1990s until only a few years ago, the gay and lesbian dance club Entourage, right in his home at 3A Haughton Avenue, New Kingston.

Entourage was a place where so many of us gays, lesbians, and bisex-uals could go to dance, laugh, flirt, party, and share time with friends and loved ones—a place where we could breathe freely and openly, delivered for a few hours from Jamaica's otherwise repressive, hateful anti-gay environment. At Entourage and in other places, Brian was not afraid to challenge the police, fiercely, when they attempted to harass him. He was not afraid to represent J-FLAG on the radio, using his own name, and to appear on television representing the organization, showing his face. He did it all with great humor and generosity, and lived, until last week, to tell about it. In that regard, he was truly an example to all of us who are gay, lesbian, or bisexual— an example of just what bravery and risk can accomplish.

It remains to be seen whether Brian was murdered specifically because he was gay, although, given the crime's extremely violent nature (numerous stabs with an ice pick to his neck, at least one chop to his forehead with a machete) and his being so widely known as an outspoken gay man—and given Jamaica's unabashed hatred of gay and lesbian people, which hatred gay men and lesbians them-selves, not surprisingly, as social creatures and vulnerable human beings, internalize—one would be a bit naïve not to wonder. These are hard times for all Jamaicans living on the island, but they're espe-cially hard for men who love and are attracted to other men—for any man who either consciously names himself as "gay" or "bisexual" as well as those who—married, otherwise involved with women, or even confirmed men of the cloth—insist that they are not "that way" or "so," yet seek out other men whenever possible, whenever and wherever imaginable. Many men who desire other men in Jamaica continue to live with an enormous amount of anx-iety, shame, and fear. Such is also the case for women who love other women. Those of us who are men, particularly after an inci-dent such as that which took Brian's life, return to that gnawing fear: will someone strike us down anytime soon because we are "battymen"? How will it happen? With fire?—gasoline tossed over us as we sleep, assisted by a well-tossed lit match? The stench of our burning flesh, and the sound of our screams, bringing sleep-smiles to the sleepers and dreamers who, even at rest, continue to hate us? Will it happen with machetes aimed to rip apart our softest parts? Or with pickaxes, hammers, guns? Knives, or simple strangling? Or will it be "just" a beating? Or a good old-fashioned stoning? Will our father do it to us, or a neighbor? A boyfriend of ours, or a co-worker? Will everyone in our community turn on us? Will it happen in the cool, quieter hours of the night, or beneath the sun's blazing afternoon—or just before morning's first shy streaks, on its reliable way in from the east? Will people laugh after our death, as they did after Brian's? Will some cry for us, as many did for Brian? Will people tell each other after our murder that we "deserved" it, or were "asking for" it? Will people in our families be so ashamed of us, and so embarrassed, that they'll refuse to speak about us to anyone, especially when it comes to the men we loved? Will self-hating gay men say vicious things about us—that we were nothing more than a "sketel,"[1] nothing more than a "butu,"[2] so what could anyone expect?

We all have faced discrimination and bigotry from friends, family members, church members, and others; yet many of us somehow manage to survive that bigotry and even triumph. In that regard, we—male and female homosexuals, bisexuals, "queers"—are truly testaments to survival and the human spirit. Jamaica would be much poorer without our talent, hard work, skills, and intelligence, and Jamaica knows it. Jamaica will be much poorer without the light of Brian Williamson, but the gay/lesbian community, and J-FLAG, will continue, and prevail, as Brian himself would have wanted us to.

Make no mistake: years from now, the world will regard Jamaica in this context the way much of the world regards Nazis today. The future world will rightly view Jamaica's hatred of homosexuals as the equivalent of the Nazis' hatred of Jews, as the equal of racist whites' hatred of blacks, as the equal of all hatred everywhere—just as ugly, just as destructive and self-destructive, just as ignorant and narrow. Just as evil. Jamaica's hatred of lesbians and gay men is its own especial Nazism (and most nations have or have always had at least one); Hitler's fury, however, did not obliterate all the Jews, and Jamaica's rage won't kill all of us. It will not even kill those of us who are most vulnerable—those of us who hate ourselves so much precisely because Jamaica has taught us to hate ourselves and other gay people. In our private spaces, we will continue to love and make love to each other. We will continue to tell jokes and drink, play cards and watch TV, nyam[3] our curry goat and brown stew chicken, and drink our rum, Ting and ting. We will live like puss and dog or get on like batty and bench[4], go on bad[5] or act fenke-fenke[6] and tek bad tings mek laugh.[7] We will still dream of love, like everyone else—and, when necessary, we will take care of each other. If anything, Brian's death should teach us all to do all these things even better.

But it should teach us something else, even more important: it should teach us that we, and no one else, will have to make the kind of world we want our children to live in. If one of our children turns out to be gay—and I mean the children of any Jamaican, any person, heterosexual or homosexual, since we, too, produce and care for children—are we prepared to send them out into a world that might chop them up, burn them, dash acid on them, or burn down their house? Or stone them? Or cause them to flee Jamaica, terrorized, into exile? Or cause them to grow up lying about themselves? Lying to their parents, to spouses, children, friends, family—to everyone? What are we all really doing right now, nearly one week after a brave man's death, to protect our children from that world? From that world that is, still, so unfortunately, this one?

Brian featured on the bottom of his outgoing e-mails a quote often attributed to Gandhi: "We must become the change we wish to see in the world." The idea is useful, but the achievement of its sublime essence requires a tremendous amount of human bravery: brave heart, brave mind and soul, and the courage to expand the mind beyond the prejudices that make us feel happy, comfortable, superior. Are we prepared to try to live this way, if only to keep other people from being killed as Brian was killed, and to save ourselves from such a (literal and spiritual) death as well?

Light a candle, then, for this man who was loved. Light many candles, and remember his name. Hear his laughter—recall it, if you knew him—as you envision his head of silver coins. Remember the shine of his eyeglasses and the shape of his everlastingly, incorrigibly round belly. Remember how much he loved other men, and how very much he wanted them—yearned for them—to love him in return. Remember how much he loved his cat, Jonathan, and his dog, Tessa—poor Tessa, who was there, at home, on the morning of his death. Remember how Brian loved his garden, especially the trailing yellow allamanda flowers on his front lawn's overhead trellis. Say a prayer for him, and say another—yes, somehow—for the terribly lost, terribly maimed person or persons who killed him. Remember how much power, love, and life he brought us in Jamaica. Remember how much braver he made so many of us, and how he expanded our entire country. You, dear Brian, whom we will continue to hold right here, deeply in our hearts—yes, closest to our very selves where the earliest breath begins, where memory never ends. Where, amid recurring dreams and sorrow and light, you will be very, very loved.

* * *

NOTES

1. "Sketel": Jamaican Creole for a "trashy," somewhat tawdry person; if used by someone in the middle or upper classes, the insult often makes clear that the "sketel" is not, though might be, of one's own social class. The insult might also be directed toward someone imagined as sexually "loose."

2. "Butu": an "ill-bred" or coarse person; someone who doesn't know how things "ought" to be.

3. "Nyam": eat.

4. "Get on like batty and bench": literally, to get along as well with someone, and/or keep company with someone, as much as a person's backside ("batty") does with a bench.

5. "Go on bad": behave badly, rudely.

6. "Fenke-fenke": highly particular, hard to please, finicky.

7. "Tek bad tings mek laugh": to use unfortunate events for jokes; to use gallows humor.

PALIMPSEST (2004)

John Keene

*The excerpt that follows is an adapted chapter from a novel-in-progress entitled
Palimpsest. Comprising two parallel narrative tracks separated by a span of 200
years (1804 and 2004), this passage explores the shifting relationship between
(John) Estis, a black Revolutionary War hero in his early fifties, who lives in
Boston, and Simeon Walker, the fugitive who arrives one night during a spring
thunderstorm.*

E stis lay quietly in bed beneath his blanket, the evening at the
Abyssinian Society's annual Harvest Dinner still ripe in his
mind. Beside him, Simeon slept swaddled in penumbra, emitting a
soft but steady rasp, as if he were dragging a small, wooden spoon
back and forth across a washboard. Its rhythm, like the conjoined
fragrances of rosewater, sweat, and pomade that rose from Simeon's
covered bulk, captivated Estis, carrying him off from reflection into
reverie.

Less than a half hour before, they had climbed into bed. The
lamp table candle was guttering in its brass holder, the aroma of the
rosemary-scented beeswax slowly diffusing throughout the room. In
the hearth, the remains of a small fire crackled. Estis had closed the
windows facing the street, as well as the door to the bedchamber,
but a chilly draft had found its way in. The cold air, which was
keeping him awake, also aroused a desire for closeness, touch. He
moved under the covers until his foot pressed against the back of
Simeon's heels and his elbow fit into the crook of the younger man's

nightshirted back. Simeon stirred, momentarily growing silent and slinging one of his dark, hairy arms atop the blanket, then resumed his snoring.

Simeon, like many a slave or ex-slave, Estis had observed, could sleep under almost any conditions. Estis also had once been able to close his eyes and plunge into a slumber, whether lamps were burning or not, whether he lay on a frozen shed floor or the ember-strewn straw of a stable. This skill had not only proved useful during the first half of his life, when he worked Lathrop's tobacco fields in Connecticut, but had been an invaluable asset during the Revolutionary War. Once he entered his forties, however, he'd peri-odically struggled to fall asleep without a cup or two of his home-made *Lightning* or a hard day at his used-clothing shop, and if his various ailments were acting up, particularly the pains in his stomach or jaw, he was unable to nod off at all. When these insom-niac nights initially occurred, which was years before Simeon had appeared on his doorstep, he would head to his workroom to recite poems or play his fiddle until he tired himself out. But eventually his memory for lyrics had begun to falter, and then his fingers had started cramping up after several hours of play, after which he suf-fered occasional palsy in his right hand, so he'd decided upon sitting silently in the darkness, allowing it to wash over and fill him until dawn pierced the shutters and it was time to fetch water from the backyard pump, press his clothes for the day, review his personal ledger, and say a prayer, for another day, month, year—at the very least for a night of uninterrupted sleep.

One thing he'd long ago stopped praying for was that his former companion, Amedee, with whom he broken in this bedstead and, indeed, this house, would pine for his old life in the city and divorce his haughty, high-toned wife and fail in his wig-and-dressing business and, in a moment fusing desperation and clarity, see Estis as his sole salvation—but Amedee wasn't coming back, Estis knew, ever, so he no longer sacrificed a breath to what was once his over-riding hope.

Since Simeon had moved from his cot bed in the cellar to Estis's large bed, in late May, however, Estis found it much easier to sleep, even when the younger man accidentally awakened him. For the first few months that they slept together, Simeon's past had continued to roil his dreams. Fear, rage, the memories of what and whom he had left behind and how he had done all lay claim to him, as did the extrasensory vigilance and control that had allowed him to spend days in a sycamore canopy near the boatyards without tumbling out, or remain silent and barely breathing under a tarpaulin until dawn while the pettiauger on which he stowed cut slowly down the Cheseapeake toward the frigate on which he'd sailed north, or to withstand the vicissitudes Estis had either learned or imagined some of the older crew members had subjected to him to, especially when he had first been hired out in his adolescent years to one of the mer-chant boats.

When these emotions and past shadows seized him in his sleep, Simeon would kick away the covers and thrash about the bed. He might hook a leg over Estis's thighs, as if to pin the older man, or seize his shoulders and begin grappling, his snores transforming into broken phrases, shouts, his fingers curling into fists. Estis sup-posed he was fighting past struggles to which the dreams served as direct portals, and held none of these nocturnal battles against him.

Usually Estis wriggled free and shook him until he awoke. Simeon's ready response was to apologize, profusely, in his honeyed bass, and head for the door, as though returning to his basement lodgings. It took only a pat from Estis on the mattress, however, to bring him back. Simeon would slip under the covers, but leave a gulf between them, and forming a cordon of bed linen around himself, attempt to wind his dark heft up so unobstrusively that he might disappear within the sheets' folds. This always made Estis smile, since there was no way that Simeon, who had steadily thickened his short, broad frame since he arrived, was going to vanish into anything.

The night battles had persisted through August, and then, as if he'd finally defeated his oneiric foes, Simeon began to sleep more tranquilly. Estis figured that he was finally growing used to his surroundings, just as he had been growing increasingly accustomed to his new identity, his new self and the life that accompanied it, which Estis had spent the entire spring and summer helping him to create. Around the time that his dreams calmed, he no longer failed to answer when Estis, or anyone else, called him "Simeon," let alone "Mr. Walker"—and Estis strove not to slip up and call him "Scipio," the name he'd shed, he'd told Estis, as soon as he'd set foot on the Boston dock. Simeon, in fact, never referred to himself as Scipio anymore—he cast the name like ashes into the sea and did not mourn it. He also seldom recounted his years under his former master in Maryland, who had "rented" him to those captains whose name he now refused to utter, or his experiences on the Chesapeake, or in Kingstown or Norfolk or New York City. In truth, he no longer was the haggard fugitive who had turned up at Estis's pantry door during the thunderstorm the previous March. He now embodied his new present, as Estis's trainee and friend, and his new past, as the free, itinerant sign painter, with some sea travel under his waistcoat, who had decided to establish himself in the capital. He was so completely Simeon during his waking hours—and perhaps during his drowsing ones as well—that there were moments when Estis forgot that another Simeon—*Scipio*—had existed at all.

At the used-clothing store, this new reality, their reality, held sway. Simeon had committed the New England portion of the national map above Estis's work desk to memory, down to the contours of Massachusetts's mountains and inlets. He could recite the peddler Carvalho's descriptions of country towns and terrain so completely that he no longer hesitated to describe his fictional birthplace or the invented story of his upbringing. He was *only* Simeon Walker, the son of the freedwoman Isobel, who had lived along the Housatonic, and a slave named John whose face he barely recalled. His mother had died of a blood-borne illness when he was in his teens, and his siblings had scattered, leaving him no family and no prospects, thus sending him down to the bustle of Manhattan's wharves and, for a period, the maritime life. A friend in the city, originally from Connecticut, had recommended him to Estis, and so now here he was. Other than Estis, no one else had heard any other account, which both agreed was best.

Although Estis was particularly leery of Simeon's interactions with whites, including the non–slave-holding masses of the Bay State, who nevertheless had no stake in maintaining his freedom. Neither he nor Simeon had forgotten that according to the law, Simeon was not only a fugitive, but still enslaved. Estis had cautioned him early on to remain vague about his Atlantic itinerary, because as a port city Boston drew visitors from across the Atlantic world, and talk of the sea especially drew men's interest. He thought the risk of someone spotting Simeon was small, but not inconceivable. Marylanders and even Englishmen from the Caribbean colonies did venture this far north. As great a danger was that someone might hear one of his accounts, place a name or be related to someone who knew someone else; a chain of associations might become a noose. Some of Estis's regular customers were, or worked with, men who traversed great swaths of territory as if they were crossing through the Common. At any rate, Estis had not come across an advertisement for his return in any of the gazettes or handbills that were so common in certain parts of town. How would it read, he sometimes wondered?

> *Likely Negro named Scipio*
> *short but powerfully built very dark*

> *late 20s X-shaped marking on his left shoulder*
> *skilled at building and marine trades*
> *speaks several languages ran away*
> *from the Maryland capital in May*
> *a sufficient reward to be given for news*
> *of him or his return contact Oscar Havergood*

So they were careful. Even among their fellow Boston blacks, although Estis saw no real perils for Simeon among them. As queer as they probably considered him, living alone and unmarried, staying studiously away from church, wearing his leather breeches and crimson coat at all times of the year, and cursing white politicians and real estate agents and constables at every opportunity, he had no real enemies among them. Most were friends or acquaintances, and he had led a number of the men his age in battle against the British. That esteem had not faded in two decades. Every day of his adult life, moreover, he'd put his profound belief in solidarity and charity into practice, which was one reason he'd help to found the Abyssinian Society. There wasn't a black Bostonian, he ventured, who didn't know this.

Yet he knew not to be complacent. Newcomers like Simeon, though with less to lose, were arriving every day, and one never could be fully sure when the the question of a reward loomed, or at the very least of knowledge that could, for a price, be useful to whites. So Estis and Simeon maintained their tale to everyone, no matter how much either thought about lowering his guard.

Simeon rolled over onto his back, flopping his arm onto Estis's stomach. The blow, though soft, made him wince, for Estis was already experiencing his usual stomachache, and he wondered whether this pain, like the ones that often struck his jaws and neck, was a harbinger of something more serious. He hadn't called upon Dr. Wiswell in a while; Martha's homemade tinctures and potions had sufficed. But he watched what he ate anyway, even at special events like the Society's dinners. He'd pared down his diet to a minimum: a daily morning sliced apple, unless he felt too dyspeptic or gassy; plums, berries, and roasted walnuts he also picked from his yard, as well as a piece of jerky, for midday; and stewed oats or potatoes. If he went out for cribbage or cards, he passed on food altogether. On those evenings once a week when his niece brought by jellies or cakes or her mother's own rich concoctions, he might indulge himself a little, though he gladly offered up the feast to Simeon. He knew his *Lightning* ought to be on his list of things to forgo, or at least enjoy sparingly, but he couldn't imagine doing so, especially now that Simeon also enjoyed sharing some with him every night. At the dinner, he now recalled, he'd sampled only a little of his tortoise soup, some yam-raisin pudding, and the Newport wine that George and Eliza Cherry always brought up for special occasions. Several cups of it had made the need for his regular nightcap unnecessary. Glancing over at Simeon, he conjectured that the wine, and the exquisite meal, which Simeon had devoured, also made his dreams more serene. That thought worked like an analgesic, and his stomach no longer ached. Then Estis sat up. He had to pee.

He levered Simeon's arm out of the way and rose. Because the two men shared the bed, Estis kept two chamber pots beneath it, his own zinc one on Simeon's side, and a battered but wide tin bowl on his. He'd had to teach Simeon how to use one—while Simeon no longer befouled his stairs or his cellar floor, he didn't want the younger man to clomp downstairs and head for the bushes every time he needed to relieve himself—but quickly realized that just one pot between them not only filled up quickly but increased the potential for a grand mess in the darkness, as well as a stench that not even burning tallow could dispel. He grabbed his chamber pot and glided into the shadows. The candlelight threw his elongated silhouette across the facing wall, so that it loomed above him, as tall and powerful as he had once felt. But now, he thought to himself, his body was gradually but surely deserting him. Yet he was succeeding in saving another man's life—was there any greater power than that?

He hitched up his nightshirt and guided the metal rim to his pelvis. He was trying to be as quiet as possible, though given how soundly Simeon was sleeping, it probably didn't matter. The snoring continued with mechanical consistency, even as Simeon turned again and now lay supine.

When Estis finished, he realized he was aroused. He wasn't surprised; this happened all the time. Often the sight or sound, or thought alone, of Simeon, his very presence—aroused him. For Estis, even glimpsing his muscular, downy shoulders or calves by candlelight was enough to provoke the most intense fantasies. When they were undressing or washing up, he had to harness every fiber of his will to control his desire. Simeon, who was hardly modest, at least in a physical sense, in public, was even less so in intimate quarters. He had, after all, spent years at sea, in addition to his time in bondage on land, and in both cases, just as in the military, maintaining one's dignity was almost always at base a mental act. Simeon made no effort to conceal himself, and evinced no shame in doing so.

He also evinced no shame, nor embarrassment, at Estis's nudity; when the older man stripped or relieved himself before him, Simeon was as affectless as a statue. Estis assumed his lean but silvery chest and thighs were still fit enough not to provoke disgust, but he perceived no arousal either. In fact, Estis had never noted him getting aroused at all, which confused him a bit, because Simeon, despite his earthiness, rarely talked about women, except in a rather general and pleasant manner. In this he was not especially different from most of the other black men Estis knew, who only spoke of the females they were closest to with a pronounced respect and protectiveness, and would not broach the subjects of their lust, such as the prostitutes prowling the the edges of the Common, except perhaps during a long evening of games and merrymaking in all-male company. In the sole specific mention of a woman that Estis could recall, Simeon had spoken over supper of one of his stays with a crew in the Virgin Islands. He was only seventeen, and because of the almost preternatural cruelty of the captain, he'd thought about escaping once the *Newcastle* had docked, living off the land, and eventually finding a wife there. One of his fellow crewmen, a freedman, had been reared in the north of the island in St. Lucy's Parish and had several eligible sisters living there. Simeon had then broken off his account to recount his year on the *Newcastle*, which had included a near-rebellion in which he was only a peripheral participant, and the subsequent punishment he'd endured upon returning to Annapolis. From that point onward, Estis tried to discern any conventional hints of desire—for women, for a female companion, for a whore, for marriage—but Simeon's words and actions yielded nothing. This aspect of his slate was unchanged from the day he arrived: blank.

Simeon withheld little else from Estis, however, and was liberal in his affection. As Estis sat at his worktable, carving a piece of wood or tightening his fiddle strings, he would feel the younger man's broad, calloused palms on his neck or ears. Simeon would leave them there as they spoke, as Estis worked, the warmth of the connection moving between their flesh. On some evenings, as they sat side by side in the parlor, singing or recounting the events of the day, Simeon would take Estis's hand in his and hold it tightly, occasionally going so far as to knot their fingers. Estis thought he ought not read too much in such expressions, given Simeon's nature and past and his own experiences. He had walked arm in arm with many a man, lain spooned with others, and such times had meant nothing more than the purest form of amity men could share. Still he cherished Simeon's touch, whenever it came, whatever it meant.

For his part, Estis had repeatedly mentioned his departed companion, Amedee, providing Simeon with the fragmented biography of a man that he hadn't spoken to in almost three years. He had described how they had secured the mortgage for and built this house on Pinckney Street together, from the foundation up, and how, when Amedee had abruptly decided to get married and close down his hairdressing shop, he'd decided, perhaps out of spite or revenge—but why, Estis wanted to know, what had he ever done to harm Amedee?—or, worst of all, Estis thought, indifference, to contract with a wealthy, white speculator from Beverly who'd tried to convince, cajole, and bully Estis into selling off his rights, before promptly and successfully suing to divide the building in two. It pained Estis even to recount it. He doubted that Simeon grasped the depth of the betrayal—not even his sister Martha, who'd witnessed the entire ordeal, fully appreciated it—though he'd made clear more than once that the dividing wall, which both delivered and restrained the noises of the renters next door, remained an underlying source of torment.

But he had left the specifics of his life with Amedee an unfinished sketch. Sometimes he felt he had no words at his disposal to describe it, or the words that came were simply inadequate, as if he were trying to carve wood with only one hand, or with dulled tools. At other times he wanted to draw upon a larger story he hoped might capture it, and impress Simeon with understanding, though the only one that came to mind was the story of Jonathan and David, and he wasn't sure which figure correlated to whom. Despite his reputation for bluntness, and the knowledge that Simeon had spent much time at sea, where male friendships predominated and the natural order often capsized, on this topic utter candor eluded him. What exactly should he say, and how? How much? His friendship with and support of Simeon hadn't trod upon that ground at all. He occasionally hoped it would, but at the same time, he had already resigned himself to the events of the past, particularly Amedee's departure, and after the first night that Simeon—Scipio—slept on the cot in his cellar, he'd resolved that his chief goal was the same as Simeon's: to get the younger man on his feet, free, and capable of living his life as he planned.

Estis opened the window. He immediately heard the mewling of a cat—was it in heat?—in a nearby thicket. Checking that no one was below or approaching from either direction, he emptied the full pot onto the brick sidewalk. A gust of wind, however, blew much of the yellow liquid out onto the cobblestoned street. It also blew in the mixed aromas of manure, and dry leaves, and the brackish bay, and garbage and oily rags burning in some distant pits: late autumn. The cold air made him shiver, so Estis shook the tin dry and shut the window. He walked slowly and carefully toward the bed, replacing the pot beneath his end of the footboard. Then he extinguished the wick between his moistened fingertips. The room surrendered to the blackness. Still aroused, he groped his way to the bed, crawled under the sheets, and, leaving a narrow gulf between himself and Simeon, turned his back and pulled the cover up to his throat.

Although he was tired, he still wasn't yet ready to sleep. Instead, his mind glided back to the Society dinner. He and Simeon, who wore the dove-gray wool Spencer coat, matching waistcoat, and white breeches that Estis had pulled from his recent acquisitions just for this purpose, had walked the six blocks to the Second Baptist Church, which sat at the base of Cambridge Street, not far from Estis's shop. As was his custom, he brought his fiddle; once upon a time, he and Amedee, who was blessed with a sterling voice, had performed as a duo to great acclaim at such events, but in recent years, Estis joined the Society's ensemble for only a tune or two that he knew by heart. The annual dinner, like the other social events the Society held, aimed to raise monies for a variety of causes, including an anti-slavery fund, a Samaritan orphanage, and a Common Pool, for widows, indigents, newly freed slaves, fugitives, and the infirm. Many of the Society's members also took part in the services the Reverend Frederick Prévost held at the church, whose primary congregation was white, and had been collecting funds for several years to build their own Meeting House, in the current, red-brick style, on one of Beacon Hill's unoccupied lots, so a small portion of the proceeds would be allocated for this purpose as well.

A number of those attending the dinner had already met Simeon at various points during the summer. Only after he and Estis had cemented their bond of trust and practiced the story of his past enough that it sounded convincing did Estis think it safe for him to leave the house and begin working in the shop. At no point had they encountered any probing or undue questions from any of their fellow black Bostonians. Some among them had sheltered fugitives, including relatives, before, or were escapees themselves. There was not a person, Estis knew, who did not have a story that might or ought never be revealed. Simeon's charm had fostered something close to quick fellowship with some of them. At Estis's shop, he had chatted with Robert Blackwell and Henry Cope, who both also dealt in clothes and had their own shops in Brattle Street; the laborer Primus Turner and his wife, May; young Tuck Gardiner, the metalsmith; Estis's nephew and assistant, Nathaniel, and his fiancée, Susannah; and young Crispus-Attucks Wilson, who hoped to read law but was working as a waiter. During the Negro Election Day festivities, he had conversed with the newspaper agent George Cornwell; his wife, Hannah; the Chappelles; and the Barbadoses, while the mariner Peter Rounsaville had talked him up at Faneuil Hall, believing wholly, it appeared, in Simeon's invented life story. And on one of his first ferry rides across the Charles to Cambridge, Simeon's conversational companion had been one of the most prominent blacks in the town, the doctor and landowner Alexander Warfield.

There were a few people present whom Simeon hadn't already met, like Mrs. Samuel Bullocks and Jupiter Livermore, whose habits of prying and volubility worried Estis even in the best circumstances, but during the conversational hour before the meal, Simeon had glided effortlessly among them, leading Livermore, who prided himself on his wit, to remark to Estis that his "new friend" was "fitting" quite well. Most fortuitously for Estis, Simeon also hadn't yet run into Charles Earls, who was rather infamous for his carousing with young laborers. At the dinner he was preoccupied with a new young mulatto Estis had spoken with outside the State House during one of his sales calls, and gave Simeon no more than a polite but perfunctory review.

During one midsummer trip to the market, Estis had introduced Simeon to the widow Elizabeth Lowe and her unmarried daughter, Ginevra. Both women immediately took to Simeon. To Estis, the reason was clearest in Ginevra's case. Her previous betrothals had all fallen through, and while it was unlikely that people with any standing would marry their daughter off to an unknown with an obscure past and no income or resources in general to speak of, the pool of single freemen, including widowers, always remained small. For a single woman advancing into her thirties like Ginevra, it was minuscule. Despite Mrs. Lowe's suggestion, neither Estis nor Simeon had attempted to call upon the women, and neither had run into them at all since. During a break between courses, however, Estis observed Ginevra hovering over Simeon. During another break, they fell into quick intimacy. Later, during the music period, they had danced together to several extemporized overtures. Watching them, Estis felt his jealousy starting to rise—as if Simeon were his, as if he had ever had full claim to another man, even Amedee!—and he'd restrained himself from cutting in, taking Ginevra off to a corner of the hall, and dressing her down. Instead, he left them alone, and reminded himself that Simeon was going to make his own choices, which very well might include a wife. He also acknowledged now as he lay in the dark that watching the pair had excited other passions, especially the sight of Simeon's large hand in the small of Ginevra's bodice, his thighs fast against her red lawn dress. . . .

To distract himself, he'd turned to his sister Martha and her husband Jeremy, who were sitting next to him in a circle of conversationalists, and listened to Joseph Barbados's account of a trip to see his brother and sister-in-law in Philadelphia. Barbados and his wife had hired a carriage, which had cost a small fortune—two months' wages!— and had stocked up on provisions for the journey, in case they could not find inns that would lodge them, and—then a hand grazed his jacket sleeve, and he looked up to see Simeon standing behind him, his face smiling and expectant, as if he expected Estis now to join him on the floor. Estis returned the smile, trying to suppress his relief. He gestured for Simeon to join them. Ginevra, he saw, was deep in conversation with another bachelor, the elderly widower Oliver Russell, and Simeon appeared not to care. For a few more hours they listened, expounded, and laughed, and then, when the church's grandfather clock struck eleven, they walked back up the Hill with Martha, Jeremy, and a band of other revelers. Once in the house, they went straight up to bed. Estis thought about broaching the subject of Ginevra, but Simeon was already asleep before he could do so.

Estis stretched out. He was starting to drowse, but the specific image of Simeon waist to waist with Ginevra Lowe lingered. Perhaps it was the wine, or the evening's cheer, or one aspect of his will giving way to another, but he felt more daring than he had in quite some time. He slipped his hand up under his nightshirt and began to stroke himself. He had never done this before—out of respect, out of discretion, since neither fear nor shame were in the equation— while Simeon slept beside him. Usually he crept down to the cellar or waited for those rare periods when Simeon went out on his own. But he was as aroused as he had ever been, and he could hear Simeon's snores, low and regular, which emboldened him. He was trying to be careful, making sure not to jerk his arm or rustle the sheets. He turned his mouth toward his pillow to stifle the coming cries. Slowly he moved his hand, feeling the foreskin glide back and forth, as he recalled Simeon and Ginevra deftly cutting the floor, weaving in and out of the other couples, the fabric of Simeon's coat straining against his shoulders, his buttocks pushing his tails out, and as one air gave way to another, the sweat was beading on Simeon's brow, rilling down his cheeks, collecting on the slope of his upper lip, and he turned, and spun, and thrust his hips forward—and Estis rose and cut in, taking Simeon's leading hand in his own, resting the other one in the small of his back, and he moved closer, until their chests, jaws, crotches came together—and he smelled Simeon's wine-flavored breath, felt it warming his ear, he could not make out what he was saying, the words moved up his neck, then came lips— and Simeon was behind him now, his calloused fingers between Estis's thighs, his heavy sex pushing, against Estis, into him—and for a second Estis clearly heard the moans that had been snores, and felt the hard arms clasping him, the teeth biting his shoulder, the hands that were so expertly drawing out his own moans, bringing him to the breaking point. . . .

Estis lay in bed, fast asleep. Wrapped around him, Simeon also slept, the covers swaddling them both. He emitted a soft but steady rasp, as if he were dragging a small, wooden spoon back and forth across a tin washboard, and its rhythm, like the conjoined fragrances of rosewater, sweat, and pomade that scented the bedding, slowly diffused throughout their dreams.

GAME (2004)

James Hannaham

W e're in carnivore country now," Inigo says, swinging open the car door to whiff the scent of burning pork. The street is packed with shiny, fat SUVs. Six brown girls stop double-dutching in the traffic circle to watch Gayle parallel-park in front of a necklace of mansions. Inigo would rather not have come to Verity Battle's barbecue, but Gayle has insisted. He does not like the upper reaches of Westchester; ostentatious places remind him that none of his successes— academic prizes, mostly—have brought him any money.

The day is ideal. Gayle wears a silk top with a plunging neckline, and Inigo has on a synthetic dress shirt. Embarrassed that they may have overdone their wardrobe in hopes of fitting in with the bourgie set, he makes a plan to explain that they are headed to a fancy night-club afterward. Sweat beads at his hairline as they walk to the house. Gayle checks herself everywhere—her pantyhose, the corners of her mouth, the undersides of her pumps. He doesn't like to see her this self-conscious.

Watching a fighter jet make a tail across the blue, Inigo thinks that Verity Battle couldn't have paid for a nicer afternoon to hold her birthday cookout. He is about to voice this comment when he and Gayle reach the driveway and face the steel-gray mansion. Stunned by its Scandinavian, minimalist opulence, its vaulted ceilings, and numerous skylights (implying exorbitant winter heating costs), he smiles. No, he corrects himself, if there was a way, she could have paid.

"Since when are you a vegetarian?" Gayle responds, so late that Inigo has forgotten his earlier comment.

"Since a week ago, when I read that article about the 'livestock holocaust' in *Mother Jones.*"

She stares upward. "Some place, huh?" Nodding in agreement, Inigo thinks of the studio apartment in Bed-Stuy he struggles to pay for, with its low water pressure and moderate bug problem, and of Gayle's shared railroad apartment—paint flaking from the ceiling, erratic gas service. They find the door ajar, and step onto a clear mat at the edge of a sea of white shag. The interior is plush and intimate, the sunken living room packed with thin-limbed wooden sculptures of giraffes and African figures. Instinctively, they remove their shoes. "Helloo?" Gayle calls. A small dog the same color as the rug accosts them, yipping aggressively, as if she were truly capable of protecting the occupants.

A singsong voice echoes Gayle's "Helloo?" from the kitchen area, and Inigo notices Verity, her back turned as she arranges a tray of water crackers. She is dressed casually, in an African-print shirt and a pair of tight jeans. The dog scuttles down a hallway when they approach the kitchen. Verity turns to greet them. She rolls gracefully toward them, arms outstretched, like the part-time dancer she used to be.

Verity and Gayle raise their voices and exclaim the thrill of seeing each other for the first time since last week. "Happy birthday, girl!" "You look great!" "You look thin!" Inigo follows Gayle, and like a ringbearer, removes their immaculately wrapped and bowed mutual present from the bag. He sets it on the free-standing counter. Inigo waits for the shrieking to die down, and eventually Verity notices him. She shrieks again, with less enthusiasm, wraps her arms around him and kisses him. Her handmade bracelets tinkle like a tambourine. Her lipstick makes a red butterfly on his cheek and he wipes it into rouge.

Because Verity produces a television show about makeup, Inigo had at first tried not to reduce her to a meringue of insincere gestures and snobbish anti-intellectualism. Gayle, who studied film at NYU, met her while working as a production assistant and introduced them at a bar. "There's this book-" he'd said, to illustrate some point, and she'd cut him off. "Who has time to read?" He pictured her calling boats useless while talking with a fisherman. Or hating on fish.

Still, he doesn't trust first impressions, because he knows he gives a false one himself. That a large, fit black man can be a homosexual and an English professor, he has noted, confuses even other gay black English professors. Regular folk vault him into a category with contortionists, apes that speak sign language, and extraterrestrials.

However, the stories he has heard about Verity from Gayle, who joined her Thursday lunch club, have yoked him to the conclusion that she fits her stereotype snugly, almost proudly. Gayle reported that she had objected to the use of the word "existential" and screwed up her face when everyone thought she ought to recognize the name Bayard Rustin. At this, Inigo's indifference toward Verity deflated into a mild distaste.

Still, she had never been malicious toward him; he knew she had merely rubbed his fur the wrong way, and though they would probably not be friends, they could certainly maintain a civil attitude, perhaps even erect a façade of camaraderie together. In the meantime, Gayle became close with her, in the nearly sincere way that the poor and ambitious befriend people who can get them work.

Verity, done with greetings, slides the glass doors open to the patio, careful to block the still-yipping lhasa apso—introduced as "Joie"—from bursting out into the yard and running freely among the guests.

"I'll be out shortly, after I change." Inigo remembers how tough it is to believe that her high, breathy voice isn't a put-on. Verity has left it to them to realize that they must go back for their shoes, carry them across the fluffy floor, and put them back on while standing on the deck. Outside, they don their footwear and arrive at the edge of the porch.

Gayle's face falls as she notices that the two of them are in fact, *under*dressed. Women wear rose-colored satin strapless gowns. Men have on tailored suits and ties, or loose-fitting solid-color silk. The two of them stand agog at the scene. Diamonds of light glance off the fluted champagne glasses. Good silver is held delicately, like a tuning fork. The wind puffs up the blinding white tablecloths, momentarily obscuring the geometrically arranged trays of chicken parts and spareribs charred with neat stripes, the arrangements of lilies and Queen Anne's lace, and the centerpiece, an ice sculpture in the shape of a bull, paying homage to Verity's astrological sign. Gayle and Inigo share a confused moment.

"She did say 'cookout,' didn't she?" Gayle says.

"If I recall correctly, she told you 'little cookout.' Should we drive the thirty miles back home and change?"

"Shoot. This is as good as it gets for me, baby."

"I guess this is a taste of what the wedding is going to be like."

"Good point. She wants these niggers to grovel for invites."

Inigo snorts at her use of the N-word in this context. It cuts the overstated elegance down to size, a talent he has always admired in her. The only Caucasian, he notes, is a bartender with cornsilk hair and an angular head. Anything can happen now that we've slid over this bridge, he thinks. Anything at all.

Inigo and Gayle announce themselves on the sunlit balcony and descend into the backyard. Inigo stomps hastily down, focused on his shoes. Gayle follows with care, panicked by a wobbling heel on step number five. Inigo waits for her at the landing. Padding in the soft, healthy grass, he surveys the attendees.

They are impeccably groomed and enjoying it. Inigo, who doesn't like the added challenge implicit in a straight crowd, withdraws a bit, and can't avoid adopting a look of frustration. After the few seconds this process takes, he notices that Gayle has arrived at the same assessment, but an anticipatory smile rises on her face. He pushes himself to be happy for her. She grunts her approval of the crowd.

"Down, girl," he says, touching her wrist.

"I'll fight you for him."

"Him? Which him?"

"I can't believe I have to point him out to *you*." Gayle gestures subtly with her head and eyes. Inigo clumsily whips his head around.

"Where?"

"Shush. There. On the thing."

Inigo spends a few moments deciphering Gayle's instructions. They have already dawdled conspicuously at the bottom of the stairs. He can feel stray eyes landing on them, brows rising with confused scorn, eager to exclude anyone unusual in their path. Then a vision materializes in front of him, of a man in a tailored suit, leaning back in a wrought-iron loveseat.

On first glance, he actually looks a little disheveled. He's removed his tie, or perhaps didn't care to wear one. His shirt collar is unbuttoned. He seems not to have combed his hair, though its gentle curls have a healthy sheen, and he hasn't shaved. But he has skin the color of a perfect pancake, noble bone structure, and a luxuriously elongated torso. His lips blush pink like veal and he smiles asymmetrically at everything, as if he is seducing it. Still, he seems unaware of his attractiveness, almost disdainful of it. He makes it seem as if he needs someone to inform him of it, as if hundreds of people do not do so regularly. He has the kind of beauty that drives people mad, Inigo decides, turning away from the inevitable drama of unrequited lust. But desire still revs up like a V8 engine in his chest, and he looks back almost immediately, this time more carefully.

"His eyebrow is sliced in two," Inigo notes.

"You're crazy. If he had fifteen eyebrows on his back and looked that good, I'd still fight you for him. The eyebrow thing is probably a scar, which only makes him that much sexier to me."

"You can have Scarface," says Inigo, although his heart has blown open like an airbag.

"You're so full of it. I know you want him."

Inigo lets a silent, bashful smile speak for him.

"See. You can't deny it. I have got to meet that one," Gayle mutters, almost to herself. She strides off toward the bar, away from him.

"Then where are you going?" Inigo says, still trying to extinguish the faint hope burning in his chest.

"I can't meet a guy without finding out who he is first. Don't you know anything about men?"

"I'm going to ignore that comment and see if there's any food here I can sublimate with." The two part ways and Inigo takes a side-long glance at the guy, who has crossed his legs and arms, body language that Inigo knows means "stay away." Inigo looks everywhere he sees the guy looking, searching for clues to his interior mono-logue. He seems most interested in tree bark, the roof of the house, his gold watch, and his shoe. Inconclusive.

Inigo turns to the buffet. The main dishes are ham hocks cut from the crispy pig still roasting in the pit, and a bleeding hunk of brisket. Big slabs of ham float in the mustard greens. Even the potato salad has bacon in it. Inigo finds his options limited to cru-dités, salsa, cheese, and crackers. He loads his plate and mentally prepares himself to sit in the empty place on the wrought iron loveseat, next to the guy. Best to be bold.

When he turns, he sees a radiant Verity sitting in that spot. Now clad in a gold-lamé gown, she has metamorphosed into Patti Labelle. Inigo can't decide whether the outfit is brave or tasteless.

The man caresses her bare shoulder with his knuckle, his head down, nose practically in her ear. Inigo flinches, as if a bullet has pierced his stomach. The unfairness and the sheer inevitability of the fact that he is her fiancé race each other through his mind. Gayle appears in a moment and gives voice to his anguish.

"Ain't it always the pretty, vapid people that get over?" she whispers into his ear. It feels as if she is inside his head.

Inigo lets out a breath. "Well, the more you appeal to the lowest common denominator, the wider your appeal, the more money you make. We see this in literature a lot."

Gayle rolls her eyes. "That is a mass-market romance if I've ever seen one. Ghostwritten, too. They've known each other about a month. I can see why she didn't bring it up much at brunch. The rest of us are single. We'd tear her apart from jealousy, then we'd make fryer parts out of him." For a minute or two, they watch the lovers surreptitiously, until an evil cloud of covetousness envelops them. "We're going to die alone, in cramped apartments," Gayle sighs.

"But first we're going to lose our minds and forget how to use toilet paper."

"Don't paint too rosy a picture, honey."

"We'll still have each other."

"No offense, but I hope not. I want children. I want a legacy. I want to be taken care of when I get old. I would be a great mother. I will be a great mother. Even at thirty-nine. Or ten—that's right, thirty-ten."

"I'd rather baby-sit your children. Or teach them freshman comp. I see it as part of my biological destiny. Besides, there's no guarantee your children are going to take care of you."

"Oh yeah? If they don't, I'll beat the living bejeezus out of them."

"So much for the perfect mom," he laughs.

As if she can see the green miasma surrounding them, Verity notices the two looking on from across the yard, and the beneficent smile of a princess—a real one—descends on her face. She rises, taking the man's hand in hers, and glides through the attendees toward them.

"Gayle. Inigo. Meet my fiancé, Creed Peoples."

Gayle squints at him during their handshake. "I knew you seemed really familiar to me. You're the new Eyewitness News weatherman, right?"

"Close—I do the travel report." Creed smiles. The sun cloud passes behind a cloud, as if the young man's glow has shamed it.

"Whoops. Oh, right, right, Bundy Peterson does weather. My bad."

"I am going to have to get a television," Inigo announces.

"So, have you gone anywhere interesting?"

"I just got back from Uganda."

"Uganda! Wow. My sister lives in Uganda. She's a doctor without borders."

A considerably long discussion ensues between Gayle and Creed, first about how bad the roads are in Kampala, the irregular electricity, the ludicrous exchange rate between U.S. dollars and Ugandan shillings, and how terrible Africans are at waiting tables and running hotels. It makes Inigo a little queasy to think how colonialist they sound. Still, Inigo suspects Gayle of using inside Uganda info to prolong her exclusive hold on Creed, and he wants to pull her away for pressing a point that to him seems moot. Naturally Verity recoils at any mention of unsanitary conditions.

She links her arm with Inigo's. "You need a drink," she burbles, already leading him toward the bar. He doesn't want to leave the two of them alone; despite the extinction of his ambitions, the urge to compete still gnaws at him. As Verity walks Inigo away, Gayle says something Creed finds very funny. Inigo turns, his face mildly sour from the betrayal. Something about the elegance of the turn, like a minuet, seems calculated.

Verity glances back at Creed in tandem with Inigo. "He's very handsome, isn't he? What do you think of him?" Verity muses. Inigo can practically hear the raised eyebrow in her voice, as if she is hoping for bad news, a negative opinion that will level her adoration.

"Well . . ." Inigo takes a pause, wondering why his opinion has suddenly gone public on Verity Battle's stock exchange. He feels that this question always requires one to ask oneself why it is being asked before answering. But his mind is clouded with fantasies that run counter to Verity's plans, so he hesitates, pretending to consider his response thoroughly. He certainly can't voice his real opinion.

"I know. You want to sleep with him. Everyone does. . . . Well, I need you to do me a favor." Blood rushes to Inigo's face, and he is glad that his buffalo-brown skin conceals the redness. They reach the bar, and Verity orders a Riesling. The bartender turns the bottle upright and cold, golden liquid gushes into the highball. "Try to."

"Try to what?"

"Sleep with him."

Inigo chuckles, overjoyed beneath his bafflement. The bartender uncaps a lite beer for him. "And how would that be doing you a favor?"

Verity cocks her head to the side, to reinforce the impression that she is thinking. Inigo almost admires the virtuoso performance of her naïveté. "I haven't known him that long, and I have some doubts. Not serious ones, but I'd like to know beforehand."

"Couldn't you just ask him?"

"It's a touchy subject; that's what makes me think something might be up. He says things. Mean, unnecessary things, things that seem out of character, out of place."

"The lady doth protest too much, eh?"

"Huh? I don't know what you mean."

"It's a line from a play."

"You are so sophisticated," Verity observes, as if a child has just shown her a fingerpainting. Gayle has described Verity as "smart" on several occasions, and Inigo wonders if one can still qualify for that title without recognizing *Hamlet*. Then he chides himself for his elitism. But on the other hand, he thinks, intelligence implies a curiosity about the world, an interest in human endeavor. If life is more or less a vacation on earth, wouldn't *Hamlet* be one of the main attractions? Perhaps in this context, "smart" means she has figured out how to make lots of money. Inigo has heard the word used that way. Yes, he concludes, the evasion of knowledge in the pursuit of profit does take a measure of cunning.

"What is it you want me to do?" he asks.

"I'll leave the how up to you. Obviously, I'd rather you only went so far. Which is why I'm offering you five hundred dollars."

"Oh, you don't have to do that."

"Yes, I do. You need an incentive to behave."

"If you don't trust me, then don't ask me to do it."

"Gayle thought you'd say something like that. So maybe not the money. But I'll bet you need some nice antique bookshelves." Gayle must also have mentioned the plywood piece of junk that collapsed under the weight of Thomas Hardy and Henry James last week. "A friend of mine deals in art deco. We'll discuss it later."

Years ago, she inspires him to remember, Inigo had dated a guy, Phil, who said his high school friends hung out in gay bars because they wouldn't get carded there. For kicks they would play a game where the guys chatted up a barfly and gave him a fake number. Only Phil would really give them his number, and go on dates with them. Inigo can't help admiring anyone who can so deftly con a con. Sometimes he suspects it is the only real way to be free in America. Bookshelves, money—loyalty to Verity will mean nothing if he can have Creed, even momentarily. The floodgates now open, he admits that he wants everything else she has, too—easy money, glamour, even Joie. He exhales a lacy "Okay."

Tingling with excitement now, he crosses the yard and strategically places himself among a group of men—including Creed—at a patio table under a spotless umbrella, at an angle from which he can volley charged glances with Creed. The men—Verity's uncles, it turns out—argue about politics and racial tensions, and Inigo defends Creed's opinions, or agrees and embellishes, with frequent conspiratorial grins. By the end, they have become a unit. The older men tire of the discussion and find excuses to rejoin their wives or use the facilities. Inigo takes the opportunity to fill an empty seat at Creed's side. As if this were not prize enough, Creed pats his shoulder, squeezes it lightly in solidarity, and grins in brotherhood. Inigo's blood feels effervescent at the warm onrush of acceptance.

"You been watching the playoffs?" he asks. Inigo suspects he means basketball, but there is no room to express doubt.

"Oh yeah," he says. "That was a rough one last night, huh?"

"You mean the night before last."

"Was it? No wonder, it took me so long to recover."

"Iverson was something else, eh?"

"You know that brother can move."

"He's not so good on the three-pointers, though."

"Got that right." Inigo wondered how long he would have to bluff. In his mind he compared the nape of Creed's neck to a high Sahara sand dune in the evening light.

"You think the Sixers are gonna make it to the finals?"

"Hell yeah, it's no competition against Alverson." Or whatever his name is. Inigo knows to maintain a confident attitude, especially when he screws up. But Creed seems not to notice.

"Miller's had a good run though, could be an upset in the works."

Inigo gets a little drunk on his dissembling, and how easily it loosens Creed. "Naw, man, Miller's got game, but not like Iverson." It all seems to be working.

"Fleet Center? Oh man, that brother had to be on some serious crack at the Fleet Center. Like he could see the net, but it was five feet away from where he was looking."

"You know he was not happy about that."

Creed stops and looks at his watch. He rewinds it further than it turns and polishes the face with a napkin. "Tonight's game is supposed to start in about fifteen," he says, conspiratorially. "Matter of fact, the pre-game show is probably under way right now. I'd look antisocial going up to the TV room alone. But if I had company . . . safety in numbers. . . ." He raises his eyebrows and directs the full force of his pleading face at Inigo. Inigo tries to imagine a request that would make him say no to that face. *Do you mind if I set off this twenty-megaton bomb? May I kill and eat your immediate family?*

Creed enlists Inigo to gather a few beers while he piles a plate with dishes from the buffet. He leads Inigo upstairs to a room that houses a widescreen television, a puffy leather couch, and two matching chairs. Boxes for video games and movies are piled up on a coffee table in front of the couch. Creed moves the boxes to the windowsill and sets down the food. He has collected only barbecued ribs and chicken parts. Inigo carefully puts four coldly sweating beer bottles in a row beside the plate and takes one for himself.

They sit on either side of the couch and the playoffs begin. As the Sixers' aggressive offense makes its opening statement with a three-pointer, Creed gets up and closes the door, while still taking his first bite of a sparerib. Inigo, his heart racing, wonders for the first time if *he* is being seduced, then hopes that he is. Creed sits back down a couple of inches closer to Inigo than previously. He leans forward over the food and takes another rib. He licks his fingers free of barbecue sauce and Inigo momentarily forgets to breathe. A foul is called, Iverson stands at the free-throw line. Steeling himself, Inigo reaches across Creed's personal space to grab a beer in a deliberately clumsy way, so that his bicep will brush Creed's forearm. Creed does not appear to register the new sensation, though Inigo feels weak, almost hungry. Iverson makes both shots.

At a commercial break, Inigo mutes the sound. Creed turns a blank face toward him, as if waiting for him to speak. The party downstairs has shifted to a more intimate mood, the music lower and more sensuous. Sunlight burns orange against the beige walls. Guilt rushes up Inigo's spine, as if initiating the silence has somehow exposed his intentions, as if there is now no way back from them. Creed licks his lips without breaking the glance, and Inigo's guilt suddenly switches to an enflamed excitement. He opens his mouth slightly and almost imperceptibly moves his head forward into Creed's personal space. Inigo prepares himself to savor what he believes will be a turning point in both their lives. He lowers his eyelids.

Creed turns back to the silent television screen and adjusts his position on the sofa, accidentally making an almost obscene squeak against the leather. Inigo's whole body retracts like a pedestrian in a rainstorm who has jumped back to avoid getting splashed with mud by a car. He lets a minute or two parade by. He turns toward the window next to the couch, through which he can see Gayle downstairs in the throes of the party, writing her number on a scrap of paper and handing it to a man. Good for her, he thinks, whatever the situation.

"So you must be really excited about getting married."

"Excited, yeah, and a little freaked out."

"Why freaked out?"

"Tee's kinda changed up on me recently. Ever since I came back from this trip I took to the Adirondacks with a couple of my Kappa buddies, she been giving me the cold shoulder, if you catch my drift. I think there might be someone else. Did you catch a vibe from her?"

"Not at all."

"I'm thinking of hiring a detective," Creed says, without irony.

"Seriously?" Inigo raises the beer bottle to his lips to mask his disapproval.

The game returns. Creed reaches across Inigo's lap to grab the remote and unmutes the television. Just below the sportscaster's nasal voice, the chirping of sneakers against polished wood rises into the room.

The unbearable longing in Inigo has built to its climax; Creed's comment makes it burst somewhere above him, showering him in gory bits of shame. With sudden disgust, he spits a mouthful of beer back into the bottle. It doesn't all go but he conceals the dribble with a napkin. A burning sensation wells up in his esophagus and the beer's bitterness envelops his tongue. Slowly, the sensation passes over like a thundercloud.

"I can do without those bookshelves," he says to himself after a while.

Creed frowns and assesses the credenza to his right. "Huh? I like them okay. They're pretty simple, actually. What's not to like?" Inigo turns his head to the side to read the spine of one of the larger books. *The Complete Works of William Shakespeare*, it reads.

"They're not as simple as they look."

Creed leans over and tears the flesh off another rib with his teeth. As he sets the clean smooth bone aside, he grunts at Inigo with his mouth still full as if to ask, "Don't you want any?" Inigo returns an unenthusiastic "No." Creed, not comprehending, holds out a rib to him anyway, and Inigo takes it, grudgingly at first. The Sixers skid toward the opposing basket, and Creed slides to the edge of his seat. Having lost interest in the competition, Inigo holds the rib between his fingers at an angle and turns it over, considering whether or not to bite. Slowly he sinks his teeth into the sweet meat and scrapes them across the bone, promising himself it will be the last time.

FROM WALT LOVES THE BEARCAT (2004)

Randy Boyd

Marcus and Walt are strangers who discover that, thanks to a cosmic phenomenon, they are living as a famous football couple in another dimension of time and space. However, in their real lives, they must confront the fact that Walt, a white man, is not attracted to Marcus, a black man, even though both of them are in their forties, attractive by most standards, and both are lovers of men. The following scene takes place in their real life (as opposed to their football fantasy life).

The deck was warmed by the morning sunlight filtering through the tall oak trees. Birds and squirrels chirped in the adjacent woods, their low-grade ambience blending with the occasional rustling of the winds in the forest. Marcus stared into a void of swaying leaves beyond the cabin. Even the sound of breakfast plates hitting the table didn't budge him.

Walt had finished half his orange juice and most of his bacon by the time Marcus took his first bite of scrambled eggs. They'd only known each other for a few days, but Marcus realized the silence was natural. He himself wasn't much of a talker upon waking, and Walt never uttered a word until his blood sugar came alive. Marcus lost focus in the pale yellow of the eggs on his plate. In his periphery, Walt downed more orange juice, then grabbed another slice of bacon.

"You know—" Walt took a bite of the slice.

For the first time today, their eyes met. They were strangers, in this, their *real* lives anyway, and already they each knew the morning routine of the other man.

"—one thing about all this," Walt said after swallowing, "and life in general sometimes: Ask a question and you definitely get an answer. Often."

Marcus stuffed half a piece of toast in his mouth, using it as an excuse to mumble something he hoped would pass for agreement. Meanwhile, his eyes retreated to the swaying leaves beyond the deck.

"Talk about questions," Walt continued. "In the fantasies we win Super Bowls, right? Where? Did I ever play for my Bears? Was Evil Announcer Guy on our trail trying to seduce or out my butt then?"

Marcus went for his glass of milk and drank as much as he could to avoid the inevitable: dialogue.

"You can't blame me for wanting to know," Walt said casually. A little too casually.

"Cardio. Be back." Marcus rose abruptly from the table, causing their breakfast to rattle like a small earthquake. Not caring, he began a demonstrative jog away from the deck, the cabin, and Walt Yeager, ignoring the half-hearted pleas growing fainter behind him.

"What'd I say? Where? . . . Marcus . . . talk to me."

"Need a break," he said without looking back. "Cool? Cool."

"Come on, tell me what's happening now."

Marcus couldn't take another word from that deep, self-assured, *white-man-in-charge* voice. The fake jog became a real jog. He disappeared down the dirt trail that led to the woods. The half-hearted pleas faded. Marcus saw it as a small victory, but his stomach was still churning. He began power-walking, his preferred workout. The pathway went for miles around the mountainside. He decided to see how much he could cover before he ran out of anger, at least for the time being.

"Hold it," came wafting through the trees, followed by: "Don't . . . attitude."

Fuck him.

He ran.

What will they think if they see a nigga tearing through the woods in the middle of nowhere?

Fuck them.

Once he hit the woods, the trees formed a tunnel that blurred by him. Speed was never his thing, but determination was. He stayed on the pathway—*not getting my ass lost on account of him*—but he sprinted as fast as he ever had, over hilly terrain, fallen branches, all while keeping an eye out for signs of life wilder than him.

". . . not helping . . ." came from the white man chasing him. ". . . alone . . ." was all he managed to shout back. ". . . show up . . ." was all he heard in return. He shot a peripheral glance backward but didn't see Walt. They were too far apart. In oh, so many ways. Marcus hurdled a tree trunk blocking the trail, knowing Walt would be leaping over that same slab of deadwood before long. They exchanged more salvoes that echoed in the forest as the white man pursued and the nigga made his escape. Through the trees, Marcus saw the river on the left side of the forest, letting him know they were racing parallel to the only landmark he knew. At least he wouldn't get lost, but Walt's *white-man-in-charge* voice grew even closer.

Okay, so maybe the ex-quarterback is faster.

Marcus ditched the trail, ignoring the pleas from his own body to stop. He darted into the woods and scampered toward the river, ducking tree branches while juking his way through the natural disorder of the unspoiled forest. By the time he reached the riverbank, he could hear Walt's footsteps crunching the foliage behind him.

The clearing was long, wide, and grassy and presented three options: go long to the right; go long to the left; go deep across the river. Out of breath, out of shape, and running on empty, Marcus chose a fourth alternative: collapsing on his back in the tall grass like a tired, soon-to-be recaptured slave.

The things my mind will let me think.

Seconds later, Walt emerged from the forest, heaving and wheezing, and fell to the ground on all fours, his lungs just as spent.

"This . . . one . . . white guy," Walt huffed and puffed, "who . . . outrun your . . . arrogant black behind anytime."

"Said . . . needed a time out." Marcus raised himself up by the elbows, then regarded the breathless ex-jock. "Feel free to go back to your gay, bi—whatever you are—white, all-American, D-and-D-Free, UB2, whites-and-Latins-only, *Queer-As-Folk* world for a while and leave me be."

"You're still—" And then it finally penetrated the sometimes thick helmet that was Walt Yeager's skull. "You really do think I'm a racist."

Suddenly Walt overcame his exhaustion and stood up straight, still gasping but nonetheless determined. His smooth blond face was so damned serious as he lifted his arms like a conductor.

"Uh, listen, Walter," Marcus rolled his eyes, knowing Walt was about to show off his little time-travel trick, "unless you're about to transport us back to a *booth*store in your past so I can witness you fucking around with somebody at least one-eighth nigga, you can skip the cosmic tour on my behalf."

"I can't concentrate if you use the N-word," Walt inhaled as if to suck in the river, the forest, *and* the sky.

"Nigga, nigger, or both?" baited Marcus. "You never did say."

"Fine." Walt exhaled, all exasperated. "Let's get this out now. Forever. You think I'm a racist."

"I don't think."

Walt's shoulders sank in relief.

"I know."

Then tightened up again.

Walt eyed him. Marcus imagined the pinkish asshole between those big blond ass cheeks constricting in equal measure.

"Based. On. What?" said Walt. "You knowing so much about the gay world because you've been doing *the gay thing* longer than me?"

"Answer me this." Marcus sat up. "Have you ever been with a black guy?"

Walt shrugged. "I haven't been with many guys period."

"It just takes one man for that man to be a nigga."

"You're wrong about me being attracted to whites and Latins only," said Walt.

"Am I now?" asked Marcus, part skeptical, part hopeful.

"No Rico Suaves for me." He sank his thumbs into his armpits to simulate wearing overalls. "I'm only into one-hundred-percent Boy-Next-Door crackers."

Marcus shook his head in the direction of the river.

"You gotta laugh about it," said Walt. "The irony, come on. Can't you lighten up at all?"

Marcus forced himself to stand, then walked along the riverbank toward the general direction of the cabin. For an instant he felt vertigo. *Lighten up?* He reached for a tree but realized he was still in the clearing. It was go long or go deep. He headed for the cabin.

"Okay, so I admit it." Walt came bounding along as if invited. "I'm only attracted to white guys. That does *not* make me a racist. I thought we settled this."

"What world was this in?" Marcus walked on. "I must have been in the wrong dimension that week."

"Why bring this up now?" Walt kept walking.

"Maybe my ass is tired of caring about you in a fantasy life knowing what I know about you in this life." Marcus stopped. "We're going through all kinds of crazy, parallel-universe shit neither one of us understands, but *this* Marcus knows *this* to be true: *my poz black skin is repulsive to you.*"

"You make it out—"

"The two things about me that ain't gonna change: my skin color and the virus beneath. They're like one of those terrorist dirty bombs to your libido."

Walt declared, all slow and drawn out: "It has nothing to do with you."

"And the thing is," said Marcus, "they could announce a cure *and* vaccine for HIV on *World News Tonight*, and you *still* wouldn't want me because of the one thing that'll *never* change: I'm a nigger."

Walt fumbled around his mind for a response, but they were interrupted by the sound, then sight of a speedboat coming up the river. Two white men wearing sunglasses and brown jackets eyed them for a moment before waving with approval as they sped on. The Man on patrol.

"*Who* I choose to sleep with," Walt said, retaking command of his thoughts, "is my erotic preference. Nothing more, absolutely nothing less."

"Right," Marcus guffawed. "And what do you call it when white folks try to stop black folks from voting on Election Day? Political preference? How 'bout when white families send their kids to white schools? What is that? Educational preference?"

"Be real now."

"No, you be real, Walter." Marcus shook his head in astonishment, turned toward the river, then turned back. "What do you call the white flight to places like Idaho and Montana? Geographic preference? What pretty little name do you have for white neighbors burning crosses in their black neighbors' yards? Location preference? And I don't wanna hear *one word* about shit like that being in the past. They still burn down black churches."

"Don't put—"

"What's that? Theological preference? Talk about word games."

"I am not the same as any of that crap and you know it."

"Personally, for me, it's worse. I don't want your religion, your education, or your real estate. I want you. Or at least the opportunity not to be shot down before you even know what the fuck I'm all about just because I happen to originate from the Dark Continent."

"I cannot help what I like. What? What? So if a guy doesn't like women, that makes him a sexist? If I don't date men over sixty-five, what, am I an ageist? What am I if I don't date midgets?"

"I don't know; why don't you go ask a midget. Better make it a white one; you don't want to confuse things."

"And, and," Walt began, all excited, "what about *black* guys who only date *black* guys? You see that online all the time." He went into his Black Imitation. "Brutha for another brutha only. On the down low 'cause I'm a brutha."

"Whoa," Marcus laughed. "Don't throw all your best justifications at me all at once. In fact, keep 'em to yourself. I've heard 'em all before and you won't change your mind. The racist never sees himself or his actions as racist. Sorry I brought you into my world—worlds. Literally. I can't tell you how much I wish I could take it all back. Really, I can't."

"I'm sorry you feel this way."

"What way?" asked Marcus. "Rejected? Or just not okay with it?"

"You play your own kind of word games, you know."

"Are we done here?" Marcus looked toward the river, then started walking again, knowing he wouldn't be traveling alone.

"If you ever make this Walt/Bearcat movie about all this someday, you're gonna omit all this racial stuff, right?"

"So you'll look better?" asked Marcus.

"So people won't start screaming and demanding their money back. You've got this pretty good story so far, me and you in this life, finding about you and me in the football life. People want to hear about football, not a *Crossfire* debate on race relations."

"New idea for better movie—"

"You'll start a race riot with all this. Rodney King Part 212. People yelling 'don't stop the movie. We're ready for some football.'" Walt cupped his mouth with his hands and made the sound of a stadium full of fans booing. Crowd noises. A guy thing Marcus himself used to do and something that would have endeared him to Walt under different circumstances. Like a fantasy world where they were racially compatible.

"New movie," said Marcus. "Stupid young nigga falls for a picture of a young white jock dude who turns up twenty years later as a member of the Gay Nazi Party."

"Do I get *any* slack from you?" asked Walt. "*Ever?*"

"Better idea," Marcus stopped again, as did Walt. "Let's just cut to the part where we come to the conclusion that you'll never see my life my way, vice versa, et cetera, ad nauseam. Sounds like the ending to me. Unless you have a better idea."

"Discussing this without anger comes to mind."

"So you can see things from my point of view?"

Walt scoffed. "Of course not."

Marcus started walking again, as did Walt.

"Lighten up, for heaven's sake," cried Walt. "Who doesn't joke?"

Marcus stopped for what they both knew was the last time.

"About something that is killing me, there is no humor."

He didn't wait for a response. Nor did Walt expect one. Or follow.

* * *

Since summer was days away, the fireplace in the cabin was empty. There was no bearskin on the hardwood floor either, just a maroon beanbag on which Marcus sat.

"Ready to talk?" came from the doorway to the living room. They had been apart ten whole minutes since the riverbank.

"So you can convince me you're not a racist," Marcus said without looking up.

"Because I need to."

"To quantum leap back into the other life and start throwing TD passes," said Marcus.

"Explain to me how racism is killing you."

The request seemed honest enough, certainly honest enough for Marcus to try.

"I've had HIV for decades," he said calmly, still focused on the fireplace. "Ever since testing poz meant *git yo' shit together 'cause yo' ass is checking outta dis mutha fucka soon.* I've been through the gamut emotionally, been in the hospital sick, fighting for my life before the 'miracle' meds. I've taken drugs that have sent me on psychedelic trips that make ours seem like a kiddie ride at the state fair."

"Look at you," said Walt. "You look great, handsome, healthy, athletic."

Marcus couldn't even begin to put his finger on that bit of irony. The man who won't fuck around with him because of his skin color complimenting him on his looks.

"Inside this body," he said, "is a disease more toxic and potent than AIDS ever dreamed—no, hear me out. You asked. Remember the rules of the game. Ask, get answers. Honesty advances you."

He paused for an objection that never came.

"You, your daddy, the whole Straight White Man's world created *this* disease, and I've been a host, sometimes willing, sometimes unwilling. Either way, it's chopping up my gut, drowning my senses, swirling around my brain so much I can barely separate the brain cells infected with racism from the rest of my brain."

"I'm not getting the analogy."

"I'm living with AIDS, Walter, but I'm dying from racism, racism from the gay community, the place I sought refuge, belonging, love."

What do I have left but the truth? No one else to be anymore.

"You date all colors," said a more tender Walt. "Why not find a black guy into black guys? Or someone else?"

"This disease resides in all of us. Based on my twenty-five years of ho'ing around, I believe eighty-five percent of all gay men, regardless of *their* race, won't date a black man."

"That just cannot be true."

"Because *you* know this type of shit," said Marcus.

"You've heard of the phrase 'there's no accounting for taste.' You'll go batty trying to get inside that part of the head. Taste has zero to do with racism. Let it go."

"And lighten up, right?"

"If it helps."

"Doesn't at this moment." Marcus fell silent.

Both men retreated to their own corners of the one-bedroom cabin for the rest of the day, steering clear of the other while lounging, napping, and channel-surfing. Around dusk, they exchanged enough words to agree to the cookout as previously planned. After all, the fridge was full of thawed burger meat and lunch had been a casualty of the race war.

"God, I hate myself right now," was the first thing uttered that wasn't small talk. It came from Marcus near the end of the night as they sat at the wooden dinning table on the deck, digesting their meals.

"Is that your final answer?" asked Walt. "Why would you say something like that?"

"I spent my whole life in love with guys like you, and not one of them has loved me back, either because I'm black, gay, or I got HIV. Or, of course, the combo platter. And this isn't about self-pity. I don't want you if you don't want me back and I certainly don't need any man's approval. This is about wasted time. I hate myself for wasting my time. Not always. Just this very moment."

"How do you think I feel, not being able to give you what you want?"

"You don't care what I want, Walter. And that's why it hurts so much."

"That's not true."

"You don't care enough to open up your mind and your heart."

"My dreams didn't come true, either," said Walt. "Look at my life. *Three* divorces?"

"Pardon me if I don't attend the pity party for the rich, white, straight-appearing Neg man who can get all the Neg ass he wants in the gay world, and all the greenbacks he can in the straight."

"All about you, huh?" Walt rose up and cleared the dishes as if he were angry with them for being dirty. "Do I get equal billing, or is it just you and your crap?"

"My crap is your crap and vice versa."

Walt disappeared into the kitchen. When he reappeared, Marcus fired without warning.

"Quick: name a famous black person in history who has nothing to do with sports, entertainment, or a crime."

Walt picked up the cucumber tomato salad, said "M. L. King," and disappeared again. Upon his return, Marcus said, "Name another."

Walt thought for a few seconds, gathered their empty beer bottles, then disappeared into the kitchen again. A beat later, he reemerged and uttered, "X. Malcolm." After a nod filled with conceit, he disappeared again.

This time Marcus followed him into the kitchen with the remaining dishes. ""Name another," he said immediately. "Remember no bats, balls, cameras, or recording contracts."

"I can't, okay?" Walt set the beer bottles in the sink in exasperation. "Not right now, off the top of my head like this."

"Because your world isn't populated with niggers. The only ones you know about are the ones the Image Keepers show you."

"The *who?*" Walt asked, running the plates under the faucet before their turn in the dishwasher.

"No, not the Who. The Image Keepers. The ones who control all the images you see in all the places you see them. Movies, TV, whatever. Billboards. There's a quote in that Michael Moore film, *Bowling for Columbine,* the movie about guns and shit."

"Sorry, missed that one." Using the dishrag as his football, Walt hunched over as if he were about to hike the ball from an imaginary center. "Forty-four . . . eighty-two . . . red, white . . . blue fourteen, blue fourteen . . . hut!" He handed off the dishrag to Marcus, the running back, and said, "I cook, you pre-wash. I'm too busy raising kids. Haven't seen a movie that was meant for anyone over age twelve in eons."

"Michael Moore goes to South Central LA," Marcus said as they switched positions at the sink, "and he's wondering why he's not getting shot by random bullets flying all over the place because that's all he's heard about South Central. This other white sociologist guy who's walking with Moore through the uneventful ghetto streets says something like, 'What do you see all over TV? Dangerous, unnamed black guys doing bad things. And we've seen this our whole lives.' Do you honestly, think, Walt Yeager, that those images have *nothing* to do with your preferences?"

"I don't like Asians either and I haven't seen them as criminals on TV."

"Have you ever seen them portrayed as sex symbols? Asian males, I'm talking about. This would be excluding the guy from *American Idol* we all turned into a fifteen-minute freak show. She-Bang, She-Bang."

"I was exposed to black guys through sports," said Walt, "not the local news."

"Then what you got against getting busy with a brutha? You must have seen some *phyne* chocolate in your day in the shower. You scared of getting turned out?"

"Were you this ornery in our fantasy life? Because I was never one who found ornery sexy in women or men."

"In that life, you empathized. I didn't have to be this ornery."

"I might empathize now if you didn't attack me so much. The race problems of the world are not this white man's burden."

"Okay." Marcus closed the loaded dishwasher. "No more attacks. Just a little show and tell." He stepped away from the kitchen counter, his demeanor as serious as ever as he lifted his arms like a conductor. "Allow me to take you on a non-fantasy, time-travel visitation to my real life, just like you did with me the other day. Just one sec." He did a series of moves with his arms, encircling his body as if to harness enough energy to do whatever it was that Walt did the one and only time he was successful at this.

"Doing your Madonna vogue impersonation?" asked Walt.

"I can manage this if you can," Marcus said, his voice straining as his body contorted in the name of tapping into some cosmic frequency. "You know what Sanchez says. More alike than we know."

"Need some help?" Walt said, clearly amused.

"Not from Whitey," said Marcus. He attempted a few more physical incantations but nothing worked. "Fuck it," he finally decided. "Verbal tour instead of a visual one, Sophia Petrillo–style—the old lady on *Golden Girls* for the uninitiated, late-blooming gay man in da house."

"I know who you mean."

"Picture it. Summer before my freshman year in college. I'm working three jobs for what's essentially disposable income when I get to school, because I got scholarships and financial aid, and *I* am going to live the college high life, cheerleading, frats, keggers, homecoming floats, hopefully a closeted boy like me on the side—I wanted the whole University of Big Time College experience. Hell, I picked my schools for sports traditions, not academics.

"But I digress. Anyway, school doesn't start until September, but I'm more psyched than a Klansman ironing his robe for a lynchin'. August rolls around and I get this thick magazine in the mail from USC—remember, I went there before UCLA. The magazine is all about the fraternities and filled with pictures of hot young guys having the time of their lives. There was a separate page for each frat, and many of them showed their house pictures, you know, the one where they dress up and strike a brotherly pose for the annual photo?

"I spend that day poring over that book, trying to figure out which frat I was gonna be a rat at. Oh, and, uh, did I mention the magazine was in black and white? Or should I just say white? Because there wasn't one picture of a nigger in that whole goddamned book. Maybe they had the black frats in the back or something, I don't remember. But I do remember being confused. I didn't know shit about fraternities except that they were the next logical step for all the hottest, most popular boys in high school and I was ready to sell my soul to play in their reindeer games. But there wasn't one guy in that book who had a small Afro like me or Negroid skin like mine.

"My main job that summer was for a phone bank. One of my co-workers, Kelvin, went to school in Pennsylvania and was in a good frat. I took the book to work, showed it to him and asked him what gives? He explained to me the circa 1980 laws of de facto fraternity segregation. Maybe one or two niggers might make it on the row, but the blacks had their frats, the whites had theirs, and the two never mixed. Literally.

"Now I'd grown up in an integrated neighborhood, had gone to an integrated high school, and didn't want to be segregated. I wanted homecoming floats and toga parties. I wanted *Animal House* but with hotter guys than John Belushi. The black frats didn't TP the trees in somebody's yard, then get drunk and celebrate it. They didn't steal sacred alumni statues from the front lawns of sacred alumni head-quarters. I wanted *college* as seen on TV. I wanted my fucking drunk-ass frat bros and me running through the sprinklers in our underwear.

"But, as Kelvin explained in the most gentle, loving way he could, I had to make a choice: get branded by Omega Brutha Brutha, kiss ass, and hope for a miracle with Kappa Klan Klan, or go it alone as a GDI, a goddamned independent, which everyone made sound like exile to some soulless island. They didn't make many movies featuring the college hijinks of wallflowers, niggas, and science geeks—and this was before *Revenge of the Nerds*—so my choice was obvious. I had none. I got to school and had no place to go.

"I made one trip to Greek Row during rush week The jock frat had a nigger and everyone knew about it and knew his name. Beau, I think it was. The only people I've ever known by that name are on soap operas, but this nigga Beau somehow got plugged into the jock frat at USC. Late in the game during rush week, I visited that frat to see for myself and to see if there was hope for me anywhere on the Row. But I never even got past the stares they gave me on the front porch. I was bold, but not that bold.

"Plus, a few days earlier—this is all my first week in college, mind you—I'd been called nigger while passing the Sigma Chi house late one night. A bunch of us black students were heading home after a black dance, probably sponsored by a black frat—I check 'em out, the black frats. Their dances took place in school facilities because they didn't have frat houses like the white boys. Anyway, we're escorting one another home after this party and we pass the Sigma Chi house. It's quiet on the street, but just inside a front window, laughter abounds. A group of frat boys are hanging out, doing whatever frat boys do behind closed doors. They hear the passing of people outside. Somebody peeks through the curtain in anticipation of sorority girls or more beer.

"'Oh . . . niggers,' one of them says, disappointed, disgusted, I don't know. They laugh some more, then go back to being frat boys behind closed doors.

"That was my first week at the University of Southern California in the fall of 1980. The Village People had a song called "Ready for the Eighties." I had it on eight-track. I sure wasn't ready for that."

"We don't have to do this," Walt said, producing a Kleenex out of nowhere.

"I'm not crying for me." Marcus pressed the tissue against his face, using it to catch but not stop the cascade of tears. "I'm crying for that determined eighteen-year-old boy with all those headstrong dreams. He wanted so bad to fit in, to find one other guy at college to live the college life with and make it all worthwhile."

"And there's nothing wrong with that."

"Of course not. And nothing wrong with me crying for that boy's pain now. I love that boy. I just wish I could have spared him all that. I wish he didn't have to see the things he saw. Fucking Los Angeles. Eighteen years old in 1980. One disease is rearing its ugly head in nearby West Hollywood, and another is being injected into me at my institution of higher learning in the ghetto. What a great fucking place to be, huh?"

They both got a chuckle out of that one.

"I'm crying for every black kid who ever had his dreams squeezed to death like that. I know how it feels. I have no clue what it's like being rejected for being a midget or a person in a wheelchair—I can like and open my heart up to them—but I know how it feels to be called nigger by the guys you wanted to spend the rest of of your life with. Is it any wonder a couple of weeks into the semester I knew I was gonna get the fuck outta Trojan Territory? I wasn't rich, I wasn't white, and I wasn't Beau, the one lucky nigger at USC, or so I felt at the time."

"How did you know UCLA would be any different?"

"I didn't." Marcus laughed as he began drying his tears. "I took a chance. Couldn't get any worse. Eventually I met some of the cheer-leaders over there, got to know their campus, and figured things *had* to be somewhat better over there. After all, we're talking a private school with rich white scions versus a state school that mocked all that wealth by waving credit cards and car keys at all the sporting events between them. That was all my young black ass had to go on. That's all I need to know."

"Your first college dream didn't work out, just like mine," said Walt.
"I guess in that way we are alike."

"Four-thirty-one," Walt said, looking at the clock over the sink, only now realizing they had been standing the whole time, their backsides resting against the kitchen counter.

"Enough with diseases for one day, huh?" Marcus said agreeably. "I'm gonna master your cute time-travel trick. I've got more I want you to see. But not tonight, and only if you wanna see."

"Show me anything you want, Marcus. I think we both realize neither one of us has veto power over these mind trips the universe is taking us on right now."

INFIDELITY (2004)

Bruce Morrow

W̶e met on the subway—which in my many years of experience is never a good beginning. We met again the next day
by my apartment—which like all coincidences should have drawn a
bright red flag. We had brunch together the day after that, fucked,
fucked again a few times more, and then I never saw him again. I've
been sitting around waiting on his call ever since, waiting for a voice
mail or e-mail, a text message or simple smiley face. Waiting and
wanting. Even as I wait to be seen for my appointment, I feel consumed, possessed, like a spell's been cast on me and only he can set
me free.

Let me start from the beginning again. We met on the subway. He
stood only a few feet away from me on the crowded rush-hour platform. We waited side by side for the train door to open, then
entered the air conditioned car at the same time. Was that fate, a
coincidence, or totally random? I'm not sure. We held the same pole,
our hands only inches apart as the train rumbled into our future.
Was he reading a gay novel? *Before Night Falls*. I remembered only the
movie and not the book. He closed his eyes for more than a
moment, and I finally had the freedom to stare at the slope of his
nose and folds of his ears and the red fire in his brown skin.
Attached earlobes are sexy as hell. Did he turn away first, or did I
try to ignore him, not let him see me looking at him or me see him
looking at me? I put away my newspaper and pretended to read a
book I'd been carrying around for months, *Rabbit at Rest*, which was

part of my investigation into flawed American characters. What do Nick Carraway, Holden Caulfield, and a used car salesman have in common with our president?

We got off at the same stop and then transferred to the same train. I studied the back of his head, looking for a flaw. A bald spot. A mole. A bishop fold at the base of his sculpted skull. But even the back of his head was attractive. Slim but muscular, leggy but not tall, his feet looked too big for the rest of his body. He didn't really seem trendy, even though he had all the trappings. Gray-flecked goatee. Close fade. Flat-front khakis. Silver earrings, hanging like commas from both ears.

When this guy—who didn't seem to be cruising me, but didn't seem to be ignoring me, and had now followed me all the way from Harlem to Union Square—got off at the same stop as me, I sort of let him see me smile. He smiled back, bashfully, then put his book away and quickly exited the train.

We reached the top of the stairs at the same time.

Was I trying to catch up to him, or was he really following me? Was it synchronicity or coincidence or plain old random luck? They all make me nervous. They make me feel like somebody's pulling my strings, forcing things to happen before they have to.

Spooked into action, I cleared my throat and said, "Hey, wassup? I see we have the same commute."

He looked startled but not alarmed. "Oh," he said, then paused. "I just moved uptown. It's not bad. The commute, I mean. I mean the neighborhood." He started all over again. "I love it uptown." He seemed to have a hard time putting his thoughts together, which is always a bad sign. Which is probably why I felt like being a little more provocative.

I laughed. "Well, for a minute there I thought you were following me."

"What?"

"Just joking," I said and shook his hand. "The thought just crossed my mind." We both imagined that for a while and then I said, "See you later," and quickly walked away. I lost my courage. I thought I heard him say something, but I didn't want to get something started that I couldn't finish, especially with a neighbor whom I'd run into all of the time.

I had to keep reminding myself: I'm married. I'm in a long-term relationship. I've got a good man. Mitch, I love you.

So there he was the next morning, Saturday morning, in *my* neighborhood, walking out of *my* deli as I'm running in to get coffee and milk for me and my man. A vision in blue sweatpants. What a coincidence! If only I could've turned around or snuck by. But he stood in my way, waiting for the secret password.

"Hey. What's up?" he said, smiling, not letting me by. "We met on the train yesterday. On the way to work. Downtown. You called me a stalker." He chuckled but looked me right in the eye. When it was clear that I wouldn't stop staring, he gave up. "I'm Okolo, by the way."

Okolo? What kind of name was that? It reminded me of okapi, and I couldn't help but imagine him eating mangos in a lush Congo forest. It was eight-thirty on a Saturday morning and I felt so guilty for having an active imagination. No one should be put on the spot during a quick trip to the deli. One should only nod at neighbors and quietly continue one's errands. One doesn't start a conversation. One just shouldn't do that.

It took me awhile to get my name out. "Jimmy. Nice to meet you. Again." You hunk, I wanted to add. Me? I'm a mess. Me need to comb my nappy head. I couldn't decide if I felt more like Tarzan or Jane. Possessed. Not myself. I tried to recover. "I'm just running in and getting a few things. This place gets all of my money. I'll probably be back later to pick up more things. I really should just go to a real supermarket." With no caffeine in my blood, I babbled.

"I like it. It's so neighborhood-ie," he said, shifting his weight to his other foot and shifting my world upside down. I'm married—or as married as gay folks can get. Fifteen years in a relationship is a lifetime in gay relationships.

He smiled. "I love the name of this store, Mee Happy Deli. And," his disarming smile miraculously widened, "I ran into you. So what's up?"

I told him I lived right in this building and I needed to buy some milk and coffee. I've said this enough but I repeat: I really, really don't like coincidences. Or someone sweeping my feet. Or a hat on a bed. Or anonymous sex. I didn't add: and my boyfriend's waiting upstairs for me to fix breakfast. Okolo's smile made it easier for me to forget. He had this way of smiling, not only his mouth but his whole face seemed to be smiling at me. Even his ears. When we shook hands I noticed how nicely his hand fit inside of mine. Like the binding of a book glued to its pages. I didn't want to let go.

What spilled out of my mouth next, I couldn't believe:

"You know there's a concert at Grant's Tomb tomorrow. Jazz, I think. Roy Hargrove. Wanna check it out?" It was as if someone had made me say that, as if a spell had been cast, a mojo worked.

"Oh, yeah. My roommate told me about that. We were thinking about going. You want to join us? Maybe take a bottle of wine."

I definitely didn't want to make a commitment. Not this early in the morning. Not before a cup of coffee. I pulled my hand away from his. Finally. The pages took to the wind. Leaf by leaf. I noticed his was trembling, his fingers shaking. Was he as nervous as me?

"Sounds great, Okolo. We'll see. You know, I've just got to get some caffeine inside of me," I said. But what I really wanted to say was, I'll worry about fitting you in later. I gave him my business card and rushed to the back of the store to pick up a can of Café Bustelo and some 100% Lactaid milk. It's so much easier on my stomach.

• • •

When I got home I closed the door and leaned against it to ensure that Okolo hadn't followed me and wasn't going to knock the door down even though I wished he would and was—*knock, knock, knocking on my back door.* I wanted to know everything about him. What he did for a living. Where he got his name. Did it mean anything. Did he like to kiss. Just the basics.

"Did you get some bananas?" my boyfriend Mitch yelled, and I jumped almost to the ceiling. He was sitting on the toilet with the bathroom door open. He must have been watching me the whole time. "Did you get some bananas?" he asked again. "I need some fruit for breakfast. Some fiber. I'm trying to keep up with this five servings of fruits and vegetables a day. It really works."

For a graduate of Georgetown Law, Mitch can be a little wacky at times. He's what you'd call a little hyper. But it comes with the territory. He represents teenage multimillionaire hip-hop entrepreneurs and haggles over half-million-dollar kill bonuses—to start their own labels so they won't guest star on a music video with an artist from another label. He's done well for himself—for the both of us. We own this cute condo and we're thinking about buying the building on the corner to develop some rental income. Real cute.

But it's getting to the point when I want to smack anyone who ohhhs and ahhhs when I tell them Mitch and I have been together for fifteen years. "Bless your hearts," they say. "Let me rub some of that on me," and they take my hand in theirs and squeeze so tight that I have to look to see if there's any juice coming out. Even though I think it is a big deal—a true long-term gay relationship's a rarity—it's now weighing me down. Our history together isn't holding me up anymore, keeping my head above water, lifting me up over that traffic jam of sexy men walking the runways of Christopher Street and Eighth Avenue. I'm stuck in a gridlock and I don't care if I get a ticket. I've become a compulsive looker. It's hard for me to concentrate in public places. Like the subway. Mitch, of course, always points out how rude I'm being.

"What are you doing?" he asks. "You look so dramatic standing there, like you're holding the door against some big hurricane or tornado or something."

"What?" How'd he know? Hurricane Okolo is expected to reach land at any moment now. "Oh. Nothing. Aren't there bananas here? I could have sworn there were some," I said, trying to change the subject of the conversation that was going on in my mind. So loud and clear. "I just need a cup of coffee."

"You seem so flustered," he said, washing his hands. "You all right?"

"Sure, I'm fine. Don't test me until I've gotten some caffeine in me. A'right? I need an IV. You want a cup?"

"Naw, that's all right. Can you make banana pancakes? And bring me the phone. Please, sweetie, can you make us a little breakfast? Pretty please?" He kissed my cheek and turned away.

"We'll see," I said, knowing full well that I was going to make a big breakfast because I felt so guilty. Big pancakes, the size of Frisbees, with lots of cinnamon and creamy chunks of bananas.

All while I was cooking, I thought about running into Okolo and my good fortune at seeing him yesterday, today, and perhaps again the next day. What wonderful coincidences! Would he call me tonight? Tomorrow? Not giving him my home number might have tipped him off. When I closed my eyes I saw his face, smiling—even his ears—as he floated closer and closer to me. I burned two pancakes that way.

With two cups of extra strong coffee in me, I finally started getting on with my Saturday routine. After breakfast I made a few calls, cleaned the kitchen and bathroom, and then went over to my friend Paul's house to do some more of the same. I've been making weekend visits to Paul's for about two years now. He has full-blown

AIDS. Until a couple of months ago, Paul was nothing but bones held together by scotch-tape skin, hallucinating and sinking deeper into dementia. Another new protease inhibitor combination drug helped him bounce back. His T-cell counts had gone up and his viral load had zeroed but he was going completely bonkers, hallucinating at night, having bouts of nausea and aching neuropathy in his feet and hands. It's like he's on both sides of the net, playing tennis against himself. He has to worry about eating so he can get better, so he can seize this moment of being relatively healthy and just live for a little while. He got his libido back too— or maybe he's gotten a prescription for Viagra—because now he's not satisfied with telling nasty stories and watching porn all day. He's actively seeking. He can now walk up to that nasty part of the park twice a day and get a great workout. And does he tell that guy he's kneeling in front of, "I'm almost undetectable now?" Paul's crazy. I can tell him things I would never ever tell Mitch and he doesn't flinch.

My Saturday routine ends with Paul giving me a quick haircut before I sweep and mop the kitchen. He's an amazing hair stylist, even though there's not much to trimming and fading my hair. He's always talking about when he used to do hair at this fabulous Upper East Side salon, and how those high-society party girls would send a car to pick him up and take him home so they could have their hair done right before stepping into the limo.

"Paul, I think I'm ready to have an affair," I tossed in the air like a tennis ball. Serve! He was putting the finishing touches on my cut, snipping away at those little hairs that never act right. All of a sudden his scissors stopped in mid snip. Ace!

"Miss Thang," he said dryly, "I'm so glad you've finally come to your senses. You've been in a daze for years."

"But I've only known you for two."

"Well, I could tell the first time you walked in that door that you hadn't had a passionate moment in years. I could smell it. Just joking." He thumped me on the back of the neck. "Seriously, he must be something if he got your attention." I told him all about the coincidences and the stalking joke and the thick feet and the funny name. "Okolo," he repeated, exaggerating the vowel sounds, "like Ricola, 'Nature's way of soothing a sore throat.' I'm having a hard time fitting that one into my mouth." Like schoolgirls, we couldn't stop giggling.

When I asked his opinion on what I should do, how I should proceed, he said just let it happen. "You make the choices. Don't let fate do it," he said. "That's what my psychic keeps saying. You should get a consultation. The first one's free because you're a friend of mine."

I could tell he was excited about the prospects of my having an extramarital affair, because he helped me finish cleaning up the kitchen after my haircut. As if he were born in a manor and accustomed to being served. Paul usually doesn't lift a finger to help me. But that day he said, in a very dry soprano voice, "Let me give you a hand now that I can. I might not need you for much longer. But why get rid of cheap help?"

Before I left he gave me a big hug, and I could feel that he'd put on a few pounds and was working on a little potbelly. The excesses of life when heaven is resting on your shoulders.

The next morning, right after I checked the refrigerator and found nothing in it, I checked my voice mail. There was a message from Okolo inviting me to brunch. I didn't hesitate. Didn't have second thoughts. Mitch had left early in the morning to go to a hip-hop networking breakfast, to which I, being his homo DL lover, was never invited. I called Okolo back and set a time and place. His place.

Okolo made a wonderful breakfast of omelets, toast, homefries, coffee, and fresh squeezed orange juice. With no ulterior motives at all, I brought over a cheap bottle of champagne that had been sitting in my refrigerator for months. We made mimosas. There's something about drinking with breakfast; it makes your head go snap, crackle, pop just like Rice Krispies. With each drink it became easier to talk to him. I asked if he'd finished *Before Night Falls* and he said yes, he liked to read fast. He was reading *The God of Small Things* now and loved all the flights of fancy. I asked about his name and he said his parents met in the Peace Corps in Africa and—get this!—his name means "one who is loved by all in the village."

After we finished eating and freshening our drinks, we moved to the living room. I plopped down on the couch. Before he put in a CD, he asked if I liked Mary J. Blige and I said sure. For some reason she'd always rubbed me the wrong way, too much sampling with too much ghetto girl posturing.

"I don't think I could stomach reading *all* of Updike's books," I shouted over the music, "but I'm almost finished with his Rabbit series."

"You're a better man than me." He touched my shoulder as he continued. "Just because he wrote that *Witches of Eastwick*, in my opinion, he should never be allowed to publish another novel or win an award. The Nobel Prize is out of the question. I'd rather reread *Beloved*. Or *Autumn of the Patriarch*. Or *Herzog*, for that matter."

"Really. Are you sure you're not a literature professor?"

"Nope. I'm a dancer. Mostly modern. And you? What do you do?"

"I'm an architect, but I work for a firm that doesn't build buildings. We design interiors more than anything else. Theme restaurants and casinos. Cruise ships and museum collections. I specialize in all things African American. I'm the black face of The Spencer Group. Besides heading the team that designs the narrative flow of museum collections, I do a lot of writing of proposals and, in the end, writing the information on the panels in the exhibits."

"Cool. So you're a real architect. When I was little I always wanted to be an architect. Then my teacher told me architects had to be good in math."

"That's not really true," I started but got distracted by the music swelling, filling my head with more snap, crackle, and pop. Or was it the champagne or the taint in the room? "Who is this?" I asked even though I'd seen him put in the CD. Her voice was seeping into my blood, grinding into my hips.

"Mary J."

"Really. She's changed or something. This is like real music. She can really sing." He told me he thought that Mary J. Blige was our modern day urban juke-joint singer with a touch of church and I had to agree. It's a wonder what perseverance and life experience can do to a voice.

By this time, I was leaning on him or he was leaning on me as we sat on his couch, pressing against each other, balancing against each other's weight. We kissed. I kept thinking that it should feel strange to be kissing someone other than Mitch, we'd been doing it for so long. Fifteen years. But that thought lasted as long as the moment before I pulled Okolo into my arms. I surrounded him and he enveloped me. We stitched and glued ourselves together like pages in a book. Bound. Sex hadn't been like that for a while. I read him. He read me. We didn't skip a word. He pressed my head against his chest, covered with a soft downy of hair. I'd never been attracted to a man with a hairy chest before. When would it start getting in my way? I asked myself, already leaping ahead to the future. A future? There wasn't going to be one. Really!

After he'd gotten up and gone to the bathroom, I thought, Now what am I supposed to do?

Lost in thoughts of what if and if only, Okolo appeared with a bowl of plums. Large. Purple black. The size of tennis balls.

"How'd you know?" I asked, taking a wet plum and rolling it in my hands. "I'm hungry again."

"What's that?" he asked, getting back into bed. He tugged on my anklet and fingered the little silver charms. I noticed that his hands always trembled. As if he were nervous or standing on a fault line. "What are these? Initials?"

Caught. Testing the ripeness of my plum, I gathered my thoughts. I told him he didn't want to know, but he kept asking while playing with the little silver letters dangling from my anklet. It was a silly gift Mitch gave me when we were in the Bahamas. He went to one of those tourist trap junk shops and bought two silver charm bracelets with our initials on them. MTM and JSJ. It was very sweet. We laughed at the symmetry of our initials and where the "charm" in charm bracelet came from. Miss Manners's protocols or voodoo rituals? But I had no intention of ever wearing a bracelet until one day, on a whim, I put it on my ankle. It felt nice, looked nice. Like I practiced some cultish religion. I liked the way the anklet felt in my socks and how it looked when I wore sandals or took a shower. Like a charmed snake. At first I thought about lying to Okolo, brushing it off, telling him it was to remind me of my mantra or something, but I couldn't.

"You don't really want to know," I said.

"Come on." The ball kept bouncing back to me.

"You don't want to know."

He tried to laugh it off but he had a serious look on his face.

"Well, I have to tell you this. And I hope you're going to understand. I never thought this was going to happen, even though I wished it to." I took a deep breath. "I've been in a relationship for fifteen years. I have a boyfriend." He raised his eyebrows. "But I don't know where we are right now. He's all into his business. Right now he's at some meeting negotiating some million-dollar deal for some ignorant rapper who's not even old enough to vote and is too stupid to do so even though he's always talking about rights and the wrongs done to his people. I want to tell you this because I want to be as honest as possible. I don't think it would be fair to not tell you. I could've just said something stupid, but I want you to know, Mitch gave me this. I don't even know why I'm wearing it. I hate jewelry." I turned so I could look directly at him. He held his small trembling hands in front of his mouth. "So what do you think?"

Even though he looked away, I felt him still eyeing me. "I wasn't expecting that. I mean, I like the way you're talking about this. You sound honest. And to be honest with you, I don't want to be a mistress. I don't think I'm made of mistress material." He must've been thinking about a future too.

"That's not fair. You're right." I didn't know what else to say, even though I wanted to tell him that one sex act doesn't necessarily make this an affair or him a mistress. We were both leaping ahead to the future, some future we were going to share together. Without Mitch. Without the home I've built for fifteen years. How could I have done so wrong? With all lost, all gone, would I suddenly have a heart attack and die? I tried to think of a better literary reference as quickly as possible. "Have you ever read *Madame Bovary?*" No, she poisoned herself. "*Anna Karenina?*" No, she threw herself on the train tracks. "Someone like Colette? I guess she's the writer I think of when I think of affairs. Always the mistress. Never content, really. She never seemed to get the love she wanted the way she wanted it." This wasn't turning out to be a good choice either.

He said flatly, "I've never read Colette."

"Oh, she's great. I guess she completely covers the position of the mistress and their stake in love affairs." I bit into the dark purple skin of my plum. Bitter tart quickly changed to honey sweet. Okolo ate a plum too. We put our pits back in the bowl and I hugged him, I put my head on his furry chest and tried to match my heartbeat with his. We stayed like that for a while. I fell asleep. We dozed. Darkness stretched across the room and somehow we ended up reading chapter one again, unsticking the pages, leaf by leaf, only to get them stuck together again.

It was a short walk from Okolo's apartment to mine. How convenient, I thought. With each step I became more determined to tell my boyfriend everything. Finding Okolo wasn't just a coincidence. He'd understand. Mitch would get that and give me time to figure things out.

Instead of stopping at the store and picking up something for dinner, I found myself on the train, headed uptown to Paul's. I should have called Mitch, but I didn't feel like facing reality or making any excuses yet. Perhaps I could spend the night at Paul's, maybe even move in, become the live-in maid and cook and clean in exchange for my rent. I should've called Paul, too, because he wasn't home. I rang several times, but he didn't answer. So I let myself in with my own key. His apartment smelled of lavender and sage and burnt toast. What a great old apartment. Beautiful moldings and painted wood paneling in the living room. Too bad it was all painted over, cracked and chipped. If this were my place, I'd lay it out, strip all the woodwork and, because the apartment's in the back, paint the walls a light yellow to give the appearance of sunshine. With grand visions of a complete renovation, I fixed myself a cup of peppermint ginger tea and sat at the kitchen table. I rummaged through Paul's old mail. Bills. Donation letter from the Lesbian and Gay Community Center, GMAD, and Teaching Tolerance. Calendar of events from the Asia Society. Catalogues from Abercrombie & Fitch and TLA, which by the looks of it, were both gay soft porn distributors. Paul's a collector. He has newspapers stacked almost to the ceiling, books stacked in chairs, magazines stacked on top of the toilet tank, and CDs and videos stacked four feet high in the middle of the floor. Didn't I just straighten up in here yesterday?

"It's me," I yelled when I heard the keys jiggling in the door. I didn't want to startle Paul or scare away one of his little Latino johns from the park. Paul's weakness is Dominican *plantainos*.

He stood in the kitchen doorway, taking off his jacket and cap. "Let me guess, it happened."

"How'd you know?"

"I can tell by that ecstatic look on your face. You're blushing just at the thought of him. I hope you're not feeling guilty. I told you: monogamy is not only boring, it's a fallacy. You think Mitch has been faithful the whole time?"

"Yes. But that's not the point. It's more about truthfulness."

"Yeah. Yeah. Yeah. Chil', I just had Truth and he was so quick to whip his dick out, it almost poked me in the eye. All that meat and no potatoes. I've been having a streak. Can't stop. Can't stop. Just let me hang this stuff up. Fix me a cup of tea, would you please? We need to talk." He disappeared down the hall but he kept talking, raising his voice while hanging up his jacket in the closet. "I've got something to tell you. I didn't say anything yesterday. But I'm dying to tell somebody." He giggled at his inappropriate exaggeration. He sat down at the table and wrapped his hands around his cup of tea. His face went blank. Then he blurted it out. "I stopped taking my medicine. Two days. I didn't tell you yesterday because it was too soon."

I didn't understand. He looked really good now. All those drugs had really worked. He looked great. Thin, but in that "I work hard to be thin" sort of way. His hair wasn't so baby fine anymore and it had a cute reddish tinge to it. I'm sure he'd tinted it to accentuate his eyes, which have a thin sky-blue ring around his golden-brown irises. They sort of looked otherworldly. Mysterious. And Paul knows how to work it. "I don't get it, Paul."

"See, nobody's going to understand." He didn't act angry or upset. "I've just had it. I can't take it anymore. Everybody thinks I look great, but I feel like shit. All the time. I'm tired of being saturated with drugs. It's like taking poison every day. At first it was only at night. I'd sweat all night and become coated with this thick mucous-like stuff. And I'd vomit. And I have what can't even be described as diarrhea anymore. It's like every pore in my body is vomiting, shitting. I'm so tired."

But not too tired to walk up to that park, I wanted to say but didn't. "Can't you switch drugs? Can't you decrease your dose?"

"Oh, I've tried it all. They all make you sick, one way or another. It's like voluntarily giving yourself poison every day, every single day of your life. Might as well go to a witch doctor. And I'd rather just get it over with and die."

That wasn't a threat. Was it? It was just a statement about his present condition. I wanted to cry, but I also wanted to help Paul hold everything together, keep everything in place, be logical. I can't even take Claritin for more than four days without getting sick of the medicine. And now that he had stopped the drugs it was prob-ably better that he not start again or decrease the dose himself or take only part of it. Everything causes cross-resistance.

"So enjoy your affair," Paul whispered, and across the top of his table covered with bills and junk mail, our hands, warmed by our teacups, touched. "It sounds nasty." A sly smile spread across his face. Like a jack-o'-lantern, his smile was missing a front tooth, which made him look even more mischievous. "Enough about me. I'm sick and tired of me and my HIV. Let's not say another word about it for a while. You should keep your little tryst a secret too. Keep it safe. And keep it a secret."

"But I've got to tell Mitch."

"Well, it's not an affair if you tell your husband."

I couldn't believe that I was already contemplating having sex with Okolo again. Already. It had taken over my life, this clandestine operation. This affair. I was struck by the idea that this affair was really happening to me. Correction: I was having him. An affair. They really happen. Like in books and magazines, they take over your body and your mind, possess you, and make you do things you'd never imagine.

I bought a six-pack after I left Paul's and started drinking in the subway station. I took a piss at the end of the platform, in the shadow of the tunnel, but I had to cut it short because the train pulled in to the station. The wind almost blew me over and I panicked. What would it feel like after I'd gone under the train? The front of my pants was stained, and I had to hold the bag of beer in front of my crotch. Having finished the first six-pack on the train, I bought another one when I got off. Just a little something to wash down the bad news I was going to tell Mitch.

Nothing was simple now. When I got to the front of my building, I saw a parked ambulance and my heart started racing. I don't know why, but it must have been the beer. I'm such a lightweight. I can drink whiskey or wine or champagne and I'm fine, but beer goes right to my head. The ambulance looked like a shining omen; it was parked, not running; there were no flashing lights or EMTs, no stretcher with ailing patient attached to IVs and respiratory devices. As innocuous as an ice cream truck, the ambulance just sat there. And yet I panicked. I couldn't get in the building fast enough, couldn't wait for the elevator, so I ran up the stairs. I dropped the beer while trying to wrestle the door open.

I found Mitch sitting in the living room, listening to the radio with the lights off. He never listens to the radio; the commercials drive him crazy with their constant jabbering, which competes against his constant jabbering. But when I finally realized the ambulance out front had nothing to do with Mitch's life, I started worrying about why Mitch was sitting in the dark, listening to the radio. Sunday night slow jams. Old Dinah Washington. New Jill Scott.

He asked how my brunch was and why I hadn't called. He'd been worried. "If anything," he said, "you should have just called and let me know you were all right and when you were coming home."

"You were too busy with your case. I didn't want to interrupt you."

"Bullshit. That's bullshit, Jimmy." I wasn't expecting anger, even though I should have.

"Well, I have something to tell you. You want a beer?" I asked and, without waiting for an answer, I handed him a bottle. He looked at it as if a genie might fly out of the cold green glass and grant him three wishes. I didn't want to take a guess as to what he would wish for first.

When I opened my beer, it sprayed my face. A cold wet slap. "Just let me clean this up," I said, wiping my face with my sleeve.

"No, Jimmy. It can wait. I've been waiting all day for a call, the floor can wait to be wiped up."

For a person sitting in the dark, Mitch looked illuminated, as if light, a bright white blanket, had gathered around him, ready to protect him from the cold truth I was about to tell him.

"I had sex with someone."

"I knew it. I knew it the minute you walked in the door."

"Well you had your brunch and you can't bring your wifey to those kinds of functions, can you, Mitch. Let me finish," I said, even though he wasn't trying to interrupt me. "I feel trapped in our relationship. I can't move. If I want to talk with you, I should call your cell phone. Or send an e-mail. Or send a FedEx package. But it's not really that. I just want to make sure we're together because we love each other, not because we're on some marathon to see how long this will last, not because we're setting an example for the rest of the gay community. For GMAD or something. For our friends to gush over. I'm losing myself. I don't want to be an architect that doesn't build buildings forever."

He rushed to me. Just in time for my head to rest on his shoulders. So my tears could be absorbed by his blanket of light. He took the beer out of my hand and whispered that it was all right, everything was going to be all right. "It's going to be all right now. I've seen this coming. It's been like watching a storm gather force out at sea. It's all right, Jimmy. Just let it go. Let it out. It's time. We can"—he quickly corrected himself—"I can help you get help, if that's what *you* want. Therapy. It's time."

I didn't know where it came from. All this emotion. It must have been the beer. Was Okolo already not everything I thought he was? Was the sex really good, or was it just new and different? Or did I just need someone who didn't see me as a "we"?

Okolo and I have gotten together three times since then, and now—now that Mitch has moved out and rented a loft space big enough for him to live and work in—now he says he only wants to be friends and we'll both have time to think about it because he's going on tour with a dance company. California. Three weeks. I send him e-mail almost every day, but he hasn't replied. He hasn't returned my calls either. I'll call him again after this appointment and fill him in.

I never thought I would be here in this psychic's office asking for help. The lamps are covered with black lace. A yin–yang sign hangs over the door. The whole waiting room smells of frankincense and burnt orange. Paul talked me into trying his psychic before getting a shrink. He said all those signs, the coincidences, the charmed anklet, the blanket of light surrounding Mitch really added up to something that therapy wouldn't be able to handle. Maybe Jungian therapy, but not psychoanalytical. Therapy wasn't right. Yet. I keep remembering that Mitch might not come back. I keep going over how I'm going to tell this story to some woman dressed in a satin turban sitting in front of a crystal ball. I don't want to come out looking like the selfish one. The asshole. Like that asshole Rabbit, who deserved to die all alone, without his sister, without his son or grandchildren or his "nut brown" wife who drowned his baby daughter in the first book and stayed with him through three more volumes of tragedies. Infidelities. What an awful man! I finally finished that book on the way to this appointment and Rabbit is dead.

WHAT I DID FOR LOVE (2004)

E. Lynn Harris

S ometimes things that stare you right in the face can feel like they've hit you from out of the blue.

I was in the middle of my shower; the warm water had started to chill, when it dawned on me: I was in a slump. Maybe even seriously depressed. Now, that would be quite ironic, wouldn't it? A doctor who makes his living helping other people deal with depression, finding himself suddenly in his patients' shoes?

I stepped out of the shower and reached for a neatly folded beach-size white towel, wrapping it around my body. I heard a female voice in my head. It sounded like one of my favorite "when did you get that old" celebrities, dance diva Debbie Allen, commanding me to *get on out there and live, child. What you waitin on?*

As I brushed my teeth, I stopped for a moment and moved my face close to the mirror for inspection. I searched for wrinkle lines and wondered, had I grown too old for true love or something close to it? The few strands of gray could be dealt with, but was Botox in my future?

It had been almost a year since dawg-ass Jeff, my lover of fifteen years, had left me for Jesus. Or was it God? Whoever He was, He better truly love cheating mutherfuckers, which was what Jeff had been for at least thirteen years of our alleged relationship. For all I know it could have been the entire fifteen, since for the first two years I had been so blissfully in love that I most likely didn't notice the warning signs. I guess that's what you get when you break your own rules.

One of my first rules was never to look for love in all the wrong places. Example: the clubs.

I remember the first time I walked into a packed gay bar in midtown Atlanta and saw a roomful of beautiful black men. I was feeling awfully proud of myself because I had graduated from medical school before age twenty-five. I was a smart mofo and that applied to knowing how to deal with men, too. I told myself don't ever look for love in a club. All my prior experience showed that the clubs were there for a good fuck and a "so glad to meet you." And for about two or three months, that's what I used them for. I never went on more than two dates, maybe three if he really knew how to lay pipe. I thought I was happy the whole time, but deep down I knew I needed more.

It was while I was on my way out of the club one night that I bumped into Jeffery Donnell Palmer. I've since asked myself a million times why I didn't just respond to his cocky, "Wassup, slim," with my standard, "It's all about you," and head to my car. Only hours before, I had told my latest fuck buddy that he had reached his limit. I was moving on and looking forward to crawling into my bed alone. But there was something about Jeff other than his six-foot-four, two-hundred-plus-a-quarter-pound body. His smile could melt frozen ice cream back into milk.

After fifteen minutes of small talk and batting my eyes like a sorority pledge, I broke my rule: I commanded Jeff to follow me home in his car. Despite his size, he seemed to follow rules well, and I loved being the boss.

Once we'd consumed a couple glasses of wine, a half beer, and a blunt, Jeff and I were off to the sex rodeo—and boy did I enjoy the ride! Rule number two was broken about an hour later when Jeff told me between condom-changing that he had a lover. Of course he wasn't in love with his lover, he assured me. He had been searching for someone like me, he swore. I guess Jeff was a quick study, since he knew all this before the night was over. Or maybe he just liked the way I "saddled up."

As I picked out a comfortable pair of underwear for the night, I recalled that I was less than a month away from turning forty. The thought saddened me, because I remember as a child how old my mother and father looked to me when they turned forty. I know too how the media has convinced the general public that forty is the new thirty. That's cool, but it still makes me stutter when I think of saying, "I'm forty years old."

I walked into the bedroom that I had shared with Jeff and thought for a moment about sleeping in the downstairs guest room. So many unhappy memories in our bedroom haunted me. I didn't know if I was going to let Toni Braxton or Paul Winfield on *City Confidential* lull me to sleep. Still, I knew I'd need more than Toni or Paul, so I went to the kitchen for a glass of Merlot then to the bathroom for an Excedrin P.M. to hurry sleep along.

Right before I popped my magic potion, I made a decision. A major one: the first thing I was going to do in the morning was to put this former love nest on the market and start over in a brand-new home.

"What's good?" Christian asked, looking at the menu and then around La Madeleine, a French bistro/bakery that I loved and Jeff hated because he thought it was "too frilly."

One of my few gay friends, Christian bonded with me immediately when he turned up at a Morehouse Alumni mentoring meeting. He was twenty-five, good-looking, ambitious, and loved the dating game. Like me, he had been born and raised in Mississippi, where he spent his childhood longing for Atlanta: the gay capital of the South. More than just the computer whiz who helped set up the computer system in my office, Christian had become a treasured friend.

"Everything is good," I said.

"Yo, Doctor C, this is a real nice little spot. Really classy, like you," he smiled, a tad flirtatiously.

I smiled back at him as the waitress brought us glasses of water. I instructed her to bring a bottle of sparkling water instead.

"Sure, I can do that. You gentlemen know what you want?" she asked. A busboy was summoned wordlessly to remove the unwanted glasses of water.

"Give us a few moments," I said. I could tell that Christian hadn't decided, since he was still studying the menu. A few minutes later, our attentive waitress returned and Christian ordered a Wild Field salad and the rotisserie chicken. I ordered tomato basil soup and the chicken mushroom pasta.

When the waitress left, Christian leaned back in the booth and asked, "So, what do you want to talk to me about, Dr. C?"

I nervously twirled my sparkling water as if I were on the first date with my dream boy. Why was I having cold feet at the last minute? In spite of his youth, Christian surely would be able to relate to my predicament. I grinned and said finally, "How do I go about getting back into hanging with the kids?" I added slowly, "I'm thinking about dating again."

Christian laughed sympathetically and replied, "First of all, we don't call it dating. I guess it has been awhile for you."

"Then what do you call it?" I asked, realizing I had a lot to learn.

"Hooking up. Hanging. You know, terms like that."

"Damn, I feel old."

"Naw, Doc, you're not old, but I can help get you up to speed with a little refresher course in no time."

Over soup and salad, Christian told me how nobody really went to the clubs to meet people for hook-ups any more. They went to clubs to dance. He said a lot of people now met instead over the Internet for quick sex, which I surmised had replaced the cruising of parks that once ruled the black gay populations of Washington, D.C., New York, and Atlanta when I was coming up. Although meeting a mate over a computer screen seemed a bit cold, I was feeling lost enough that I was willing to see if it would work. Plus, it wasn't as dangerous or disgusting as cruising the parks.

"The best site is called WhenTyronemetLeroy.com, because it's mostly brotha's who are on the DL," Christian said.

"I don't mean to sound stupid, but what is DL?" I asked.

"It's nothing new. Just brotha's who can't admit they love men's asses and a little dick every now and then. Most of them have baby's mama drama, a pretty girlfriend or a wife. When they meet another dude they want to fuck out of his draws, they always say something like, 'let's keep this between me and you,' or on the down low," Christian said.

"We called it *trade* in my day," I said.

"Oh, they still call guys trade and thug love," Christian added.

"So I go on to the site and then what?"

"That site has pictures of guys along with lists of what they like, don't like, their dick sizes, ages, and other information that everyone lies about," Christian laughed.

"But are any of these guys worth looking at?"

"Yeah, but please don't pick somebody who looks perfect, because it most likely ain't them. Same thing for those fools who just put up pictures of their hard dicks and bubble butts. Nine times out of ten the person who shows up at your door is something that looks like a gold tooth goblin, 'Yo, playa, I'm your date.'"

"Then why do people go online to meet each other?"

"'Cause every now and again a real diamond likes myself shows up," Christian smiled.

• • •

When I got home after dinner with Christian, I decided to take a shower before turning on my computer to check some of the sites he had written down for me. I looked at the piece of paper with names like Bigdickblackboyz.com and ThugsRus.com, and I shook my head. I couldn't believe that my life had come to this. As depressing as the bars had always been, at least there you ran into friends and had some laughs. Welcome to mid-life.

While I was in my relationship with Jeff, I guess I had become oblivious to what was going on with the world of black gay men. Bit by bit I found myself withdrawing from the gay scene, which felt like it was getting younger and younger by the minute. My only ongoing connection was information I gathered from some of my gay patients during therapy. But even much of what they talked about sounded foreign to me. For all practical purposes, it felt as if Jeff and I were married. And like most marriages, we were hopelessly unhappy much of the time. Worse still, Jeff didn't want us to associate with other gay couples, saying it would only cause problems for our relationship. I agreed with him, never realizing that this was Jeff's way of keeping all of his flings from seeping out into the open. I even gave up the few gay friendships I had maintained through college and medical school.

Before I headed to the shower, I glanced through the information the real estate agent had left advertising my home. The perky Emily had already created a two-page glossy with four color photos of my house that announced "A steal in Buckhead: Act fast." She made my house seem so fabulous that I almost wanted to buy it again, despite the many bad memories that clung to it. I had forgotten about the lap pool and Jacuzzi, because I never used them after finding out Jeff had skinny-dipped with one of his tricks while I was visiting my parents. The bitch had left me a gift of a pink jock strap that I knew Jeff would not be caught dead in and was certainly not his size.

One of the really sad things about my breakup was that after spending so many years trying to deny that their only son was gay, my parents had accepted and loved Jeff. Although I had told my two sisters about my breakup, I didn't have the heart to tell my parents. I don't know if it was because I was ashamed of my choice of a mate, or thinking maybe my parents were just playacting and would rejoice over the breakup. Maybe they still held out hope that I would give them grandchildren and keep the family name going.

After spending three hours at two different Web sites where I was supposed to meet the love of my life, I was deeply depressed. The men were not only horny but seemed to be pissed off at the world and very discriminatory. Each profile featured a handsome man with perfect body parts. From reading their profiles, it seemed that I had to be perfect as well if I ever wanted to meet one of these handsome Adonises.

You couldn't be too fat, gay, or old. Some ads were in search of DL guys, while others begged them to stay away. Instead of pictures showing faces, the majority of the profiles had pictures of hard dicks and plump asses. I hadn't seen this much dick and ass since I had ventured into a bathhouse on my first trip to New York some twenty years before.

I thought it was sad that while so many black gay men struggled to be accepted, many treated each other with the same outlandish disdain that they felt everyone else inflicted on them.

As I tried to sign off, I found myself at a Join Now screen and began wondering how many men I could attract with my photo and a few details about myself. Surely there had to be a handful of sincere, successful guys out there like me. Besides, playing it safe with Jeff had gotten me nowhere. I took the plunge. What did I have to lose except my dignity?

For the first time in my life, I was being asked the size of my johnson by a colorful computer screen. There I was, sitting in front of the computer, filling out information about my body for the entire world to see. Or maybe just the gay world. My first task was to pick a screen name. This was going to be hard, since the ones I had already viewed were almost pornographic, like *9thick-blackinches4U, hardblackcock,* and *dickreceptionist.* I wanted something catchy that would attract potential suitors or at the very least a couple of hot dates. I decided on *sexydoc.* I wanted to be honest with the survey, just in case my new soul mate was out there reading my profile. How would I explain that everything I had said about myself wasn't true?

My first test was putting down my real age. Sure I was almost forty, but everyone told me I didn't look a day over thirty. Was there a difference between thirty-nine and forty?

Answering questions like whether I was out, a smoker or non-smoker, if I did drinks or drugs, and to name my zodiac sign were easy. HIV status, on the other hand, was tricky since I hadn't been tested in four years. After all, I was in a monogamous relationship, even though I was the only faithful one.

Then came the physical component. Five-eight or could I fake five-ten? One hundred and sixty-five pounds or one seventy? Was I a top? No. A bottom? No. So I plugged in "versatile." Was I looking for friendship? Hell, no! One-night stands? Maybe. Was I into group sex or three-ways? I didn't know since I had never been asked. Then came the Miss America portion, where I was asked to talk about myself in one hundred words or less.

Handsome doctor trying to mend a broken heart. I still believe in love but will settle for hot sex in the meantime. Love to travel and prepare romantic dinners. What should I serve?

Finally I went back to the beginning, where I was asked about my dick size. I put 8.5 thick, cut. I didn't know if that was true, but I felt like I was bigger than average. If I was wrong, sue me. When I clicked the enter button, I felt the same tingle I had years ago when I dialed the number of the first boy I had a crush on. Now all I had to do was wait for the magic to happen. My new love would reach out and connect with me via the mystical Internet.

In spite of my skepticism about the whole venture, I woke up the next day with the excitement of a little boy on Christmas morning. I went straight to my computer before even brushing my teeth.

I had twenty-six messages. Wow! This was a breeze. Where do I start? I wondered, as I looked at some of the screen names of the men who had respond to my profile. Names like *Nopunksallowed, cutenicca4U, Hothungandhorny,* and *cuteapplebumnatl.* Trying to figure out what some of the names meant was like trying to read Latin for the first time, but I had to admit that my spirits were suddenly the highest they had been in months.

I opened the first profile from *ricannicca4u.* He was a black Puerto Rican looking for love in Atlanta. The guy was attractive but seemed self-absorbed, so I wrote him back saying thanks for getting in touch. *Nopunksallowed* greeted me with the picture of a huge erect dick, and I quickly deleted it. Too early in the day for porn.

I was half way through my messages when I opened a reply from *blacksoutherngent.* There wasn't a picture of a dick or ass, but instead of a handsome man dressed in a button-down oxford shirt that made him appear as if he'd stepped out of a college yearbook. His note read:

Sexydoc:
Do you still believe in romance? Do you like long walks down a beautiful beach with pink sand? Do you like nice glasses of wine and lingering kisses? Do you like a man who will treat you like a man and

make love to you like only a man can? Do you like intelligent conver-
sation about something other than dick size? Then I am your man and
I can't wait to meet you and start our romantic journey.

The Gent

I felt my heart beating faster than my fingers typing on the keyboard as I wrote:

Gent:
Thanks for responding to my profile. In answer to your questions there
is only one way to respond. YEAH!
What do we do next?

I went into the bathroom to shave. Returning to my computer
some fifteen minutes later, I found three new messages from Gent.
The last one included his phone number and name, asking me to
call him on his cell. I scribbled down the information and then went
to my closet to pick out a pair of slacks and a light knit sweater to
wear to the office.

As I dressed, the romantic fantasies began unfolding in my head. I
imagined what it might be like to walk down the beach hand in hand
with this handsome man, who with just one e-mail message had made
me consider that maybe romance really was possible. With the patience
of a five-year-old, I wanted to call him right away, cancel all of my
appointments, and suggest that we jump in a car and head for Amelia
Island on the coast where Georgia and Florida meet. Instead, I played it
safe and went to the office, waiting until after lunch to call my new love.

After a few rings a rich and authoritative voice answered. I was in
trouble.

"What's good?" it said.

"Can I speak with Wade?"

"This is he?"

E . L y n n H a r r i s

"Wade, this is Coe Hathaway. You sent me your number and asked me to call," I said nervously.

"Yeah . . . yeah, sexydoc. What you got goin', doc?"

"Just taking a little break from my day," I said.

"So you like my profile?"

"Yeah, and I love the way you responded."

"I knew after I read your profile I was going to have come for you big-time. A lot of those dudes on there are full of shit. Just looking for sex with those fake-ass pictures," Wade said.

"I just got on there," I said. I wanted to ask him if that was really him in his picture and if he really was six-five and 235 pounds. I wanted to know how a man that big and handsome didn't have a lover and would he walk down the beach with me hand in hand.

"I know that," he said quickly.

"How so?" I asked.

"There is a section on the site that has new members, and your handsome face and profile was the first one that appeared. I was like, 'Yo, that's what I am talking about.' I said to myself, 'I bet this brother is crunk.'"

I didn't know what "crunk" meant, but assumed by the way he used it that it meant something good, like the way we used to say "fly."

"So what do you do?"

"Don't you remember? It's in my profile," Wade said.

"I'm sorry, I forgot."

"I'm a personal trainer and I attend Georgia State."

"What's your major?"

"Business, with an emphasis in sports management."

"So, would you like to meet me?" I asked.

"But of course. I can't wait to have a few drinks and chill with you," Wade said.

"When?"

"What's good for you?"

"Whenever."

"How about this evening?"

My heart pace went to pedal-to-the-metal mode.

"That would be wonderful. What don't you come by my place," I said. I wanted to show off my house before Emily sold it from under me. I was already dreaming about me and Wade in the pool followed by the bed—and I hadn't even been in the same room with him yet!

I gave Wade, a total stranger, my address and invited him to meet me at eight o'clock sharp. My romantic longings were halted briefly when I realized that I might have been inviting a black Andrew Cunanan into my life. I needed a backup plan, I thought, just in case Wade needed a therapist more than a boyfriend.

I quickly called Christian and told him about Wade, then asked if I had done the right thing.

"It's too late now, but you should have met him at a public place. Then if you liked him, you could take him back to your house."

"Should I call him back and suggest that?" I asked.

"Naw, he might think you're flakey and this might be the one."

"Yeah, maybe you're right," I said.

"I'll tell you what I'll do. I'll come by right after you let him in. Act like you're not expecting me or that I'm dropping off something from your office. If I feel like you got something to worry about, then I'll stay. If not, then I'll bounce with a wink and nod," Christian said.

"That's a great idea. Thanks, Christian."

I stopped at Eatzi's, a hip eatery in Buckhead, to pick up a few items for my romantic evening. I got fresh strawberries, grapes, kiwi, cheeses, French bread and olive oil. I also got four different types of wines and champagne, just in case there was reason to celebrate.

When I got home, I prepared the fruit and cheese on a colorful serving plate and then took a glass of wine upstairs and took a soothing bubble bath. Afterward I walked into my closet and decided against going with nice slacks and sweater, going instead with white linen pants and a peach linen shirt. I wore a black Speedo under my pants, which were so thin you could see the black trunks. I put on a simple silver chain around my neck with a matching band. I sprayed my favorite cologne in the air and then walked into it. I was ready for my close-up.

At eight sharp the phone rang. I looked at the caller ID and saw that it was the phone from the gate. I knew it had to be my date, because Christian had the code.

"Hello," I said.

"Yo, it's Wade. I'm at your gate."

"I'll buzz you in. I'm in the house at the end of the cul-de-sac," I said.

"That's what's up," Wade replied.

A few moments later the doorbell buzzed. I took a deep breath and opened the door.

"You must be Wade," I said with a big smile.

"That would be me," he answered as he walked in. Wade was gorgeous. Skin the color of toasted wheat, he was tall and well built with a wide mouth, with pillowy lips and perfect teeth. He had thick eyebrows and penetrating dark brown eyes. He wore tight jeans and an untucked pink cotton shirt that didn't look the slightest bit feminine stretched across his massive chest. I suddenly felt warm moisture settling around my neck and felt like fireworks were exploding inside my body the way they did on wet, sticky summer nights.

"Come on in," I said.

"Nice place," Wade remarked as he followed me downstairs to the den. He was so close behind me that I could feel his fresh-smelling breath on the back of my neck.

When we got downstairs, I put on my Heather Headley CD and uncorked bottles of red and white wine.

"Would you like some wine?"

"Sure, some red would be nice. But remember I'm driving," Wade said, with an easy sexual assurance that matched the cocky grin that hung on his face.

"Can I say something really honest?" I asked.

"Sure."

"I hope you don't take offense to this, but I can't believe how handsome you are. I mean, I heard that a lot of guys use fake pictures on that site. Why would a man who looks like you need to meet men through the net?"

Before Wade could answer, the doorbell rang.

"Excuse me," I said, setting the bottle of wine on the counter.

I raced upstairs to open the door, gave Christian a *boy am I happy smile,* and snatched the envelope out of his hands.

"Thank you. See you tomorrow," I said, quickly slamming the door in his face. I placed the thin envelope on the entry table and headed back downstairs to Wade.

"Now, you were saying," Wade said as he patted the empty spot on the sofa next to him. I deliberately ignored his gesture, moving instead to the bar to pour him a glass of wine.

"You were telling me why you use the net to meet guys," I reminded him.

"I could say the same thing about you."

I heaved a sigh of relief at his words. He thought I was hot. Together we'd make a smoking couple and Jeff would be pissed.

"I went on there because somebody whom I trust told me this was the best place to meet people," I said.

"Yeah, ain't nothing but a bunch of club queens at the club. Worried about fashions and trying to take one another's pieces. I never went for that shit."

Two glasses of wine and a little fruit later, Wade and I were outside looking at our reflections in the pool. Twilight was gathering and there was an exquisite sexual tension over the wet area behind my neck. I wanted to jump in the pool fully clothed to cool my body.

"So do we get in?" Wade asked.

"Sure," I said as I set my glass of wine on the wrought-iron table.

I watched Wade fumble with the pockets of his tight jeans as if he were looking for keys or something. Then he took off his shirt and revealed a perfect chest. When he took off his jeans, he had on white Lycra underwear that had seemingly memorized the size of his cock. I stood dazzled by Wade's sexual confidence and his partially nude figure. My entire body felt moist with lust.

As I moved through the water, I could feel Wade's body heat on my trail. Then when I stopped suddenly, his dick pressed against my ass; I felt that I was just moments short of ecstasy. I didn't want to move, but my body shook when Wade cupped his hands and poured water over my shoulders. He kissed the back of my neck. I turned around quickly and kissed him. Wade responded with a flurry of soft kisses on my lips followed by deep, hungry kisses.

"Let's go to my bedroom," I said, grabbing Wade's hands.

"Lead the way."

We left our clothes and wine glasses on the patio and raced through the house to the bedroom like we were Olympic sprinters. I was in my Speedos and Wade in his wet, now transparent underwear.

He dived onto my neatly made bed. Suddenly Wade threw the bedspread and pillows onto the floor and laid on his back with his erect dick standing at attention.

"Come here, you," he ordered.

"What do you want with me?" I teased, lighting the candles next to the bed.

"Come here and let me show you."

I moved to the edge of the bed and Wade grabbed me in a wrestling position. We rolled on the bed until his large, hard body was on top of me. He was dry-grinding against my body, kissing me while whipping our bodies into an erotic frenzy.

"Are you ready for all this dick, baby?" Wade asked.

"Yes, I'm ready," I said, as I rolled over on my stomach. I couldn't believe I was ready to submit myself to him. This would be the first man I had been with since I had met Jeff. Damn, was I ready.

Wade pulled down my trunks, and when he leaned over me, I could feel his naked penis against the crack of my ass. "Do you have any condoms?" he whispered

Condoms, I thought. *I don't have any fucking condoms!* Jeff had taken the last box when he moved, and I hadn't bothered to replace them.

"No, I don't," I answered. In my head I wanted to scream into the pillow like a baby. How could I have overlooked something so essential? What if Wade walked out and never called me again?

"What are we going to do?" he asked.

"Damn, I can't believe this."

"Just let me stick it in. I promise not to cum," Wade said.

"Is that safe?" I asked, knowing full well that what he was suggesting wasn't safe. But, fuck, I wanted him inside me.

"Come on, I promise," Wade said.

I didn't want to think about the consequences, so I just turned back over on my stomach and spread my legs. I suddenly felt Wade pushing inside of me and a shudder ran through my body. In no time a pool of warm liquid spread beneath my stomach and upper thighs, sticking to me and the sheets. Wade kept his promise, and soon after I felt a sudden spray of cum across my ass.

The next day I walked into the office with some pep to my step. Although I tried to listen to my patients as best as I could, I was thinking only of Wade. I couldn't wait to get home to call him and tell him I now had condoms.

Lunch came and I finally had the chance to phone him. There was no answer, so I left a message. Then later I left another message, and yet another that evening.

I went to bed that night alone, with the condoms staring at me from the nightstand.

A week passed and still no call back from Wade. I wondered if something tragic had occurred. Maybe a bad car accident, or could be that he met the wrong person online. I left message after message, pleading for him to return my calls to let me know he was okay. He didn't call.

Two weeks later and still no word. I knew he was alive, because he had found time to change his number, while the new one went unlisted. Finally I got his message loud and clear: it was time to go back to the site and find my next Mr. Right.

I guess it shouldn't have come as a big surprise to me that my last patient of the day was going to be the most challenging. I had been seeing Tamara Hudson for over three months, and for every step she took forward, she would somehow manage to take two steps backward.

"So you don't seem too surprised that I ended up sleeping with Koy again," Tamara said.

I guess my face showed more than my silence.

"Well, Mrs. Hudson, this is like an addiction, which might take a little longer to resolve than you'd like. But if you still want to save your marriage, this affair will have to end. We both know that," I said as I took the pen away from my mouth, a habit I had picked up when I was a boy and bored with my teacher.

"I know, but it's like he has some kind of hold on me. I told you he was from New Orleans, didn't I? Maybe he has put some kind of voodoo on me. I mean that huge cock of his seems to be like some magic stick," Tamara said. How refreshing that gay men weren't the only size queens.

"But is that enough to maintain a long-term relationship? Is it enough for you to give up your marriage?"

"I would have to say no. Besides, my parents would just go fucking crazy. I mean, my mother and father think I have the most perfect marriage, one just like theirs. Thomas is a wonderful man, always has been. He works hard to give me the life my parents always dreamed I would have, but he doesn't bring any passion to our bedroom."

"Has he ever?"

"No," Tamara said quickly. "The sex has always been lame."

Tamara was a black Buckhead wife who was living life dangerously. She was married to Thomas Hudson, who was the only black partner in one of Atlanta's largest white law firms. She had a household staff of three, a personal assistant, maid, chef, and was on the board of directors for several local Atlanta charities, including AIDS Atlanta and the Atlanta African Dance Company.

She had started an affair with someone who was not only fifteen years her junior but who also sold drugs for a living out of his midtown apartment. Tamara herself had described Koy as a thug, but a chance meeting in the post office had led her to the best sex of her life.

"Have you thought about doing couples counseling?" I asked.

"No amount of therapy is going to change our sex life. With Koy I feel like I am discovering sex as a teenage girl again. This brotha knows how to touch a girl's spot. It's taking over every aspect of my life. Just the other day I was heading to a board meeting near Colony Square. My board had even sent a car service for me. But when we drove down Peachtree, I realized that his apartment was about five minutes away. The next thing I know, I'm telling the driver to take me there instead of the board meeting. I ended up at the meeting halfway through, minus my underwear," Tamara laughed.

"It looks like our time is almost up. Would you like to see me next week at the same time?"

"I might as well. I don't know if this is doing any good, but at least I have someone to talk to about Koy. If I trusted any of my so called 'good-good girlfriends,' I'm afraid the word would get out, or one of them bitches might try to get him for themselves. Did I tell you he asked me for a loan for twenty-five thousand dollars?"

"No, you didn't," I said.

"I haven't given it to him, but I sure am thinking about it. I just need to make sure I can do it without Thomas finding out about it. I might just take it out of my vacation kitty, but I guess we can talk about that next week."

"We can. Mrs. Hudson, please don't do anything drastic before we talk. If you need to see me sooner than next week, please call my office and I will see if I can rearrange my schedule."

"Thank you, Dr. Hathaway," Tamara said as she picked her leather clutch bag from the floor and stood up.

"Take care of yourself, Mrs. Hudson."

The phone rang just as I was getting ready to put on my jacket and head to the parking garage. I started to let the answering machine pick up, but figured if it was an emergency call from one of my patients, I might as well get the problem solved sooner than later. But

I was eager to get back to my home computer to see if I had any messages from potential new boyfriends. It had taken a great deal of discipline not to check on my office computer or even go home for lunch. I didn't want my assistant coming into my office and seeing some man's dick or ass glaring at her from the computer screen.

"This is Dr. Hathaway," I answered.

"Hey, Coe. Glad I got you. This is Gerald Miller."

"Gerald, great hearing from you. It's been awhile."

"Yes, it has. Sorry, but I've been so busy," he said.

"Then that means the practice must be doing well."

"Yes, it is, which is one of the reasons why I'm calling."

"What can I do for you?"

"Can you see a new client tomorrow?" Gerald asked.

"I don't know. Let me look at my book," I said as I moved behind my desk to open my appointment book. The scheduling of clients was one of the few things Dee Dee hadn't transferred to computer or Palm. I could see from her excellent penmanship that the day was full, but I saw two appointments had been marked through.

"Hey, Gerald, looks like I got an opening. Can your patient come in around three-thirty?"

"It's not one of my patients," he said. "It's a call I got from the concierge at the Ritz-Carlton. I used to do a lot of business with them, but now I just don't have the time. They said it's some highly confidential patient. I won't even have a name to give to you until I tell them that I've found someone who can handle this."

"So it's top-secret," I joked.

"Actually, it is. When I get these kind of referrals from the hotels, it's usually someone who is either rich, famous, or both. If I told you some of the people I have treated, it would leave your mouth hanging open. You know, they get away from home, have a meltdown, then need to see somebody before they end up going home in a wooden box," Gerald said.

"Oh, I understand. Will I have to go through some kind of security check?"

"No, my recommendation will be enough."

"Cool."

"How long will you be in your office?" he asked.

"I was on my way home. Can you leave the information with my service?"

"Sure, I can do that. It will most likely be some name like Bob Smith or Joe Blow. They always have an alias."

"I understand."

"Thanks, Coe. I owe you dinner for this."

"No problem. Thanks for the referral," I said. I hung up the phone and left my office wondering who would be knocking on my door the following afternoon.

When I opened the door that evening to greet my "next new boyfriend," I wanted to slam it shut. Another FPer (fake picture). Not only had he lied about his height and weight, he looked about three inches shorter than six feet and about thirty more pounds than the one eighty-five his profile had promised. This was my third date from the site since Wade, and none of these guys had gotten even a kiss. I was tempted to go to the clubs or find a park.

"Are you Coe?" he asked, waddling through my door as if he smelled a gourmet meal cooking inside.

"Yes, and you must be Alan." I moved slightly to allow him a little extra room.

"Looks like I hit the jackpot," he said. "Most of those mutherfuckers use other people s' photos like models and shit, but you look like your photograph."

"Thanks."

"I know what you're thinking; I don't look like my photo. But I put on a few LB's in the last couple of months. You know, I eat when I get depressed," Alan said.

I wanted to ask him what had happened that had changed the color of his eyes and skin. His photograph had showed a light-skinned brother with avocado green eyes. Alan was mud-brown, with even darker eyes.

"Why don't we go down to the den," I said. I hoped my pager was somewhere close by where I could page Christian and then have him page me back with a fake emergency. I wanted this date over now.

"Nice house. What did you say you do?" Alan asked.

"I'm a doctor," I said.

"Are you a gyno?"

"No, why do you ask?"

"I don't know, I just know a couple of gay guys who are doctors for bitches. How they can stand to look at pussy and titties all day is beyond me. If I was going to be a doctor, I'd be a dick doctor," he laughed, taking up half of the love seat facing the entertainment system.

"Would you like something to drink?" I asked, looking around the room for my pager.

"Yeah, a beer would be nice," Alan said.

I wanted to say, "That's the last thing your fat ass needs." But I told him I would be right back.

I took a couple flights of stairs to my kitchen and spotted my pager on the marble counter. I paged Christian with a 9-1-1. If our system worked, he would call before Alan had his first sip. I pulled out a beer and a Diet Coke for myself and headed back downstairs. Just as I heard the fizz of Alan popping the top, the phone rang. I picked it up on the second ring.

"Dr. Hathaway," I said.

"I guess it's not going well," Christian remarked, almost smiling through the phone.

"Yes, he is my patient," I answered back.

"What, a fake picture or body odor?" Christian laughed.

"Yes."

"'Yes' what?"

"Which hospital?"

"Okay, I will play along. The Hospital of the Broken Hearts," he said.

"Thank you. I will be there in fifteen minutes," I said.

I located my keys on the desk, then Alan stood up with his beer in hand and asked if everything was okay.

"I have a patient who's been admitted to the emergency room," I said.

"Would you like for me to go with you?"

"What?" I asked. Just what did this fool think he could do if it was an actual emergency?

"You want me to tag along with you, or would you like me to wait?"

"No, Alan, I think we should just try and get together later," I lied.

"Do you know when? I'm free all next week."

"No, why don't I give you a call when my schedule lightens up," I said.

"Damn, I hope it's soon, 'cause ole boy is horny as hell," Alan said as he licked beer suds from his lips.

"Yeah, right. Listen, I don't want to be rude, but I need to change shirts before I get to the hospital," I said as I started to walk out of the den and upstairs toward the front door.

Then Alan asked if he could get a little kiss. I wanted to use that famous movie line about having "just washed my hair." I turned toward him and said, "I don't do anything little. Wait until the next time. It will be worth the wait."

"I heard that," Alan smiled as he opened up the door.

I breathed a sigh of relief as I heard the door click closed.

BIBLIOGRAPHY

Als, Hilton. *The Women* (Farrar, 1996).

Baldwin, James. *Just Above My Head* (Dial, 1979).

_____. *The Price of the Ticket: Collected Nonfiction 1948-1985* (St. Martin's 1985).

Beam, Joseph, ed. *In the Life: A Black Gay Anthology* (Alyson, 1986).

Belasco. *Brothers of New Essex: Afro-Erotic Adventures* (Cleis, 2000).

Belton, Don, ed. *Speak My Name: Black Men on Masculinity and the American Dream* (Beacon, 1995).

Boyd, Randy. *Bridge Across the Ocean* (West Beach, 2000).

Boykin, Keith. *One More River to Cross: Black and Gay America* (Doubleday, 1996).

_____. *Beyond the Down Low: Sex and Denial in Black America* (Carroll & Graf, 2005).

Brandt, Eric, ed. *Dangerous Liaisons: Blacks, Gays, and the Struggle for Equality* (New Press, 1999).

Carbado, Devon W., ed. *Black Men on Race, Gender, and Sexuality* (New York UP, 1999).

Carbado, Devon W., Dwight A. McBride, and Donald Weise, eds. *Black Like Us: A Century of Lesbian, Gay, and Bisexual African American Fiction* (Cleis, 2002).

Carbado, Devon W., and Donald Weise, eds. *Time on Two Crosses: The Collected Writings of Bayard Rustin* (Cleis, 2003).

Cassells, Cyrus. *Soul Make a Path through Shouting* (Copper Canyon, 1995).

Clay, Stanley Bennett. *In Search of Pretty Young Black Men* (SBC, 2001).

Corbin, Steven. *Fragments That Remain* (Alyson, 1993).

Constantine-Simms, Delroy, ed. *The Greatest Taboo: Homosexuality in Black Communities* (Alyson, 2000).

Datcher, Michael, ed. *My Brother's Keeper: Black Men's Poetry Anthology* (Datcher, 1992).

David, Christopher. *I'm On My Way* (1st Books, 2003)

Delany, Samuel R. *Tales of Nevèrÿon* (Bantam, 1979).

———. *Flight from Nevèrÿon* (Bantam, 1985).

———. *The Mad Man* (Kasak, 1994).

———. *Times Square Red, Times Square Blue* (New York UP, 1999).

D'Emilio, John. *Lost Prophet: The Life and Times of Bayard Rustin* (Free Press, 2003).

Dixon, Melvin. *Vanishing Rooms* (Dutton, 1991).

———. *Love's Instrument* (Tia Chucha 1995).

Douglas, Debbi, Courtnay McFarlane, Makeda Silvera, and Douglas Stewart, eds. *Ma-ka: Diasporic Juks: Contemporary Writing by Queers of African Descent* (Sister Vision, 1997).

Duplechan, Larry. *Captain Swing* (Alyson, 1993).

Gay Men's Press. *Tongues Untied: Poems* (Gay Men's Press, 1987).

Glave, Thomas. *Whose Song? And Other Stories* (City Lights, 2000).

Gomes, Peter J. *The Good Book: Reading the Bible with Mind and Heart* (Morrow, 1996).

Hadju, David. *Lush Life: A Biography of Billy Strayhorn* (Farrar, 1996).

Hamer, Forrest. *Call and Response* (Alice James, 1995).

Hardy, James Earl. *B-Boy Blues* (Alyson, 1994).

———. *2nd Time Around* (Alyson, 1996).

Harris, E. Lynn. *Invisible Life* (Consortium, 1991).

———. *Just As I Am* (Doubleday, 1994).

———. *What Becomes of the Brokenhearted: A Memoir* (Doubleday, 2003).

Heath, Gordon. *Deep Are the Roots: Memoirs of a Black Expatriate* (U of Massachusetts P, 1992).

Hemphill, Essex, ed. *Brother to Brother: Collected Writings by Black Gay Men* (Alyson, 1991).

———. *Ceremonies: Prose and Poetry* (Plume, 1992).

Hunter, Michael, ed. *Sojourner: Black Gay Voices in the Age of AIDS* (Other Countries, 1993).

Jackson, Brian Keith. *The View from Here* (Pocket, 1998).

———. *Walking Through Mirrors* (Pocket, 1998).

_____. *The Queen of Harlem* (Pocket, 2002).

James, G. Winston. *Lyric: Poems along a Broken Road* (Grape Vine, 1999).

Jones, Cy K. *Sweep* (Bloody Someday, 1996).

Kenan, Randall. *A Visitation of Spirits* (Grove, 1989).

_____. *Let the Dead Bury Their Dead* (Harper, 1992).

Mann, G.B. *Low-Hanging Fruit* (Grape Vine, 1996).

Morrow, Bruce, and Charles H. Rowell, eds. *Shade: An Anthology by Gay Men of African Descent* (Avon, 1996).

Other Countries, eds. *Other Countries: Black Gay Voices* (Other Countries, 1988).

Parker, Canaan. *The Color of Trees* (Alyson, 1992).

Phillips, Carl. *Rock Harbor: Poems* (Farrar, 2002).

Reid-Pharr, Robert F. *Black Gay Man: Essays* (New York UP, 2001).

Ross, L.M. *The Long Blue Moan* (Alyson, 2002).

Ruff, Shawn Stewart, ed. *Go the Way Your Blood Beats: An Anthology of Lesbian and Gay Fiction by African Americans* (Holt, 1996).

Saint, Assotto, ed. *The Road Before Us: 100 Black Gay Poets* (Galiens, 1991).

_____. *Here to Dare: 10 Black Gay Poets* (Galiens, 1992).

_____. *Spells of a Voodoo Doll: The Poems, Fiction, Essays, and Plays of Assotto Saint* (Kasak, 1996).

Scott, Darieck. *Traitor to the Race* (Dutton, 1995).

_____. *Best Black Gay Men's Erotica* (Cleis 2004).

Sedgwick, Eve Kosofsky, ed. *Gary in Your Pocket: Stories and Notebooks of Gary Fisher* (Duke UP, 1996).

Shepherd, Reginald. *Some Are Drowning* (U of Pittsburgh P, 1993).

Smith, Charles Michael, ed. *Fighting Words: Personal Essays by Black Gay Men* (Avon, 1999).

Smith, Michael J., ed. *Black Men/White Men: A Gay Anthology* (Gay Sunshine, 1983).

Vega Press, ed. *Milking Black Bull: 11 Black Gay Poets* (Vega, 1995).

Vega Studios. *Men of Color: An Essay on the Black Male Couple in Prose, Illustrations, and Photographs* (Vega, 1989).

West, Tim'm. *Red Dirt Revival* (Poz'Trophy, 2002).

White, Marvin K. *Last Rights* (Alyson, 1999).

Wright, Bil. *Sunday You Learn How to Box* (Scribner, 2000).

About the Contributors

JAMES BALDWIN is the author of more than a dozen novels, essay collections, books of poetry, and plays. His novels such as *Giovanni's Room* and *Another Country* are hallmarks in the African American, gay, and black gay and lesbian literary canons.

JOSEPH BEAM was the editor of *In the Life: A Black Gay Anthology*, as well as the creator of the follow-up book, *Brother to Brother: Collected Writings by Black Gay Men*. He was a board member of the National Coalition of Black Lesbians and Gays and founded that organization's magazine, *Black/Out*. He died of AIDS in 1988.

Journalist **DON BELTON** wrote the novel *Almost Midnight* and edited *Speak My Name: Black Men on Masculinity and the American Dream*.

Writer and publisher **RANDY BOYD** is the author of *Uprising, Bridge Across the Ocean,* and *The Devil Inside Me*.

KEITH BOYKIN is one of America's leading commentators on race and sexual orientation. He is the author of *One More River to Cross: Black and Gay in America, Respecting the Soul: Daily Reflections for Black Lesbians and Gay,* and *Beyond the Down Low: Sex and Denial in Black America*.

Journalist **SIDNEY BRINKLEY** is the founder of *Blacklight*, Washington D.C.'s first black gay and lesbian newspaper (http://www.black lightonline.com).

CYRUS CASSELLS is the author of three books of poetry, including *Mud Actor, Soul Make a Path Through Shouting,* and *Beautiful Signor.*

Poet DON CHARLES has been featured in publications such as *Here to Dare.*

Novelist STEVEN CORBIN is the author of *No Easy Place to Be, Fragments That Remain,* and *A Hundred Days from Now.* He died from AIDS in 1994.

SAMUEL R. DELANY is the highly innovative, award-winning author of more than thirty books, publishing in a wide variety of areas that include most prominently science fiction/fantasy (*Dhalgren, Tales of Nevèrÿon*), gay pornography (*The Mad Man*), and cultural studies (*Times Square Red/Times Square Blue*).

MELVIN DIXON is the author of the novels *Trouble the Water* and *Vanishing Rooms,* as well as a collection of poetry, *Change of Territory.* His work has appeared in *Men on Men, In the Life,* and *Brother to Brother,* among others. He died of AIDS in 1992.

LARRY DUPLECHAN, whose first work of fiction appeared in *Black Men/White Men,* has published four novels, including *Eight Days a Week, Blackbird, Tangled Up in Blue,* and *Captain Swing.*

GARY FISHER was an unpublished author up until his death from AIDS in 1993, when scholar Eve Kosofky Sedgwick collected his stories, diaries, and poems in the posthumous volume *Gary in Your Pocket.*

SALIH MICHAEL FISHER has been published in *Yemonja* and the anthology *Black Men/White Men.*

DAVID FRECHETTE, a journalist, was published in *Here to Dare: 10 Black Gay Poets*. He was a member of Gay Men of African Descent, Other Countries, and Men of All Colors Together/New York. He died of AIDS-related complications in 1991.

DANIEL GARRETT is the author of the novel *Heroes and Friends* as well as the play *An Enemy of the President*. His writing is also featured in *In the Life*.

Activist GIL GERALD was executive director of the National Coalition of Black Lesbians and Gays. His essay, "The Trouble I've Seen," was published in *Black/Out*.

THOMAS GLAVE is the author of *Whose Song? And Other Stories*. "The Death and Light of Brian Williamson" was published in *The Jamaica Sunday Gleaner*.

Poet FORREST HAMER is the author of *Call & Response* and *Middle Ear*.

JAMES HANNAHAM has had fiction published in *Fresh Men: New Voices in Gay Fiction, The Ex-Files* and at Nerve.com, and his non-fiction in *The Village Voice, Spin, New York* magazine, and other publications.

Credited with launching the Afrocentric gay hip-hop romance genre, JAMES EARL HARDY is a journalist and novelist, whose books include *B-Boy Blues, 2nd Time Around, If Only for One Nite, The Day Eazy-E Died,* and *Love the One You're With*.

First published in the gay press, including *Blackheart* and *The New York Native*, CRAIG G. HARRIS broke out as a writer with *In the Life, Brother to Brother, The Road Before Us, Tongues Untied,* and *Sojourner*. He died from AIDS in 1991.

At the time of his death from AIDS-related complications in 1995, poet and writer ESSEX HEMPHILL was widely regarded as the premier black gay poet in America. He is the author of *Ceremonies: Prose and Poetry*. His work also appears in *In the Life, Brother to Brother,* and the anthology *Tongues Untied*. Essex can be seen in the films *Black Is . . . Black Ain't* and *Tongues Untied*.

BRIAN KEITH JACKSON is the author of *The View from Here,* winner of the First Fiction Award from the Black Caucus of the American Library Association, *Walking Through Mirrors,* and *The Queen of Harlem*.

United States Marine Corps veteran DONALD KEITH JACKSON has been published in *Fighting Words: Personal Essays by Black Gay Men*.

ISAAC JACKSON is a founding member of Other Countries and served as editor of *Blackheart: A Journal of Writings and Graphics by Gay Black Men*. His work is featured in the poetry collection *Tongues Untied*.

Poet G. WINSTON JAMES has been included in the books *The Road Before Us, Milking Black Bull,* and *Shade,* to name a few. He is also author of the collection *Lyric: Poems along a Broken Road*.

GARY ALAN JOHNSON is a writer, scholar of African history and culture, and world traveler. His work appears in *Shade, Sojourner: Black Voices in the Age of AIDS* and *Brother to Brother*.

CY K. JONES, whose work has been published in *The Journal of New Jersey Poets, Gay Sunshine,* and *Fag Rag,* among others, is the author of *Sweep*.

JOHN KEENE is the author of *Annotations* and the forthcoming art-text dialogue *Seismosis.* His work has been awarded the John Cheever Short Fiction Prize and the Solo Press Poetry Prize.

RANDALL KENAN has published books in a variety of areas, including a novel (*A Visitation of Spirits*), a book of stories (*Let the Dead Bury Their Dead*), an ethnographic travel book (*Walking on Water*), and a young adult biography of James Baldwin.

BRUCE MORROW is an associate director at Teacher's & Writers Collaborative in New York. He edited *Shade: An Anthology of Fiction by Gay Men of African Descent,* and his writing has been published in *Speak My Name* and the *Men on Men* series.

ROBERT E. PENN is an AIDS activist whose work has appeared in *Sojourner: Black Gay Voices in the Age of AIDS.*

ROBERT REID-PHARR, professor of English at The Graduate Center of City College of New York (CUNY), is author of the nonfiction works *Conjugal Union* and *Black Gay Man.*

CARL PHILLIPS is the acclaimed author of *The Rest of Love; Pastoral; From the Devotions,* which was a finalist for the National Book Award; *Cortege;* and *In the Blood.*

The Emmy award-winning filmmaker MARLON RIGGS directed ground-breaking documentaries about black gay life, including the powerful *Tongues Untied* and *Non, Je Ne Regrette Rien,* as well as films about the larger African American experience such as *Ethnic Notions* and *Black Is . . . Black Ain't.* He died of AIDS complications in 1994.

L.M. ROSS, author of the novel *The Long Blue Moan,* has had his gay erotic short fiction published in numerous magazines and anthologies.

Assotto Saint, a Haitian poet and performer whose work is collected in *Spells of a Voodoo Doll*, was also editor of a handful of the most prominent black gay literary anthologies of the early 1990s, including *The Road Before Us: 100 Gay Black Poets* and *Here to Dare: 10 Black Gay Poets*. He died of AIDS complications in 1994.

Darieck Scott is the author of the novel *Traitor to the Race*, and his short fiction appears in *Shade*, *Giant Steps*, and the *Flesh and the Word* series, among others.

Reginald Shepherd is a widely published writer whose books of poetry include *Some Are Drowning, Angel, Interrupted,* and *Wrong*. His work has also appeared in *Grand Street, The Iowa Review,* and *The Kenyon Review,* as well as *In the Life*.

Jerry Thompson, a bookseller and writer whose work was first published in *In the Life*, is more recently the author of a poetry collection, *What Happens!*

Tim'm West is a poet, rapper, and author of *Red Dirt Revival: A Poetic Memoir in 6 Breaths*.

Vega is the author and publisher of *Men of Color: An Essay on the Black Male Couple in Prose, Illustrations, and Photographs* and *In Our Own Image: The Art of Black Male Photography*.

Marvin K. White, author of *Last Rights*, is a poet, performer, and community arts organizer. He is co-founder of B/GLAM (Black Gay Letters and Arts Movement), an arts organization dedicated to black gay artistic expressions.

Poet **Donald W. Woods** has been published in *In the Life* and *Brother* to *Brother,* as well as other publications. He appears in Marlon Riggs's film *Non, Je Ne Regrette Rien.*

Playwright and novelist **BIL WRIGHT** is the author of the novels *Sunday You Learn How to Box* and *One Foot in Love.*

PERMISSIONS

We gratefully acknowledge all those who gave permission for written material to appear in this book. We have made every effort to trace and contact copyright holders. If an error or omission is brought to our notice we will be pleased to remedy the situation in future editions of this book. For further information, please contact the publisher.

About the Editor

E. LYNN HARRIS is the author of eight novels: *A Love of My Own, Any Way the Wind Blows, Not a Day Goes By, Abide with Me, If This World Were Mine, This Too Shall Pass, Just As I Am,* and *Invisible Life.* More recently, Harris published his memoir, *What Becomes of the Broken-Hearted?,* which chronicles the author's childhood and coming of age as a black gay man. In 1996, *Just As I Am* was awarded Blackboard's Novel of the Year prize. In 1997, *If This World Were Mine* was nominated for a NAACP Image Award and won the James Baldwin Award for Literary Excellence. In 2002, *Any Way the Wind Blows* won Harris his second Blackboard Novel of the Year prize, and *A Love of My Own* was recently named Blackboard Novel of the Year, making Harris the first author to receive back-to-back honors and to receive the prize a record three times. In 2004, he was awarded the Bridgebuilder Award by the Lambda Literary Foundation. He has also been named in the ranks of *Out* magazine's "Out 100" and *New York* magazine's "Gay Power 101." Currently a visiting professor and writer in residence at the University of Arkansas–Fayetteville (where he is cheer coach for the Razorback Cheerleaders), Harris divides his time between Atlanta and Fayetteville, AR.